The Art of Survival

Gender and History in Europe,
1450–2000

Essays in Honour of Olwen Hufton

OXFORD JOURNALS

OXFORD UNIVERSITY PRESS

OXFORD
UNIVERSITY PRESS

1 Great Clarendon Street, Oxford OX2 6DP

Oxford University Press is a department of the University of Oxford.
It furthers the University's objective of excellence in research, scholarship,
and education by publishing worldwide in

Oxford New York

Athens Auckland Bangkok Bogotá Buenos Aires Cape Town
Chennai Dar es Salaam Delhi Florence Hong Kong Istanbul Karachi
Kolkata Kuala Lumpur Madrid Melbourne Mexico City Mumbai Nairobi
Paris São Paulo Shanghai Singapore Taipei Tokyo Toronto Warsaw

with associated companies in Berlin Ibadan

Oxford is a registered trade mark of Oxford University Press
in the UK and in certain other countries

Published in the United Kingdom
by Oxford University Press Inc., New York

A catalogue for this book is available from the British Library

Library of Congress Cataloguing in Publication Data
(data available)

ISBN 0-19-920802-6
ISBN 978-0-19-920802-9

Subscription information for Past & Present is available
from:jnls.cust.serv@oxfordjournals.org

Typeset by Integra, Pondicherry, India
Printed by Latimer Trend, Plymouth, UK

Past and Present Supplements, New Series

Volume 1, 2006

The Art of Survival: Gender and History in Europe, 1450–2000
Essays in Honour of Olwen Hufton
Edited by Ruth Harris and Lyndal Roper

The Art of Survival
Gender and History in Europe, 1450–2000

CONTENTS

Contributions and Communications (two copies), editorial correspondence, etc., should be addressed to The Editors, *Past and Present*, 175 Banbury Road, Oxford OX2 7AW, UK. Tel: +44 (0)1865 512318; Fax: +44 (0)1865 310080; E-mail: editors@pastandpresent. demon.co.uk. Intending contributors should write for a copy of 'Notes for Contributors'.

Typeset by Integra, Pondicherry, India, and printed by Latimer Trend, Plymouth,UK

Acknowledgements

Many people have helped to make this volume, which grew out of a confer-
ence entitled 'Gender, Religion, Poverty and Revolution', held at Oxford on
July 9, 2004 to honour Olwen Hufton. We would like to thank Clare Morton
of Oxford Journals whose idea it was that we should found the Past and
Present Supplement Series, and Gill Mitchell, Chris Payne, Claire Painter,
Jeff New and Catherine Macduff of the Press, for their help in production.
We would also like to thank the Past and Present Society for their support,
and the staff of New College Oxford, who did so much to make the original
conference a success. The chapter by Ruth Harris in this collection first
appeared as 'Letters to Lucie: Spirituality, Friendship and Politics during the
Dreyfus Affair' in *French Historical Studies* 28 (2005) and we thank the
Editors for permission to republish a shortened version here.

We are greatly indebted to Caroline Ford, Robert Gildea, Ludmilla Jordanova,
Tessa Storey and Lotte van de Pol for their contributions to the conference;
Simone Laqua for her magnificent conference organization, and to Alice
Kelikian, Simone Laqua, Natalie Zemon Davis, Carol Dyhouse, Sarah Grieco
Mattthews, Clare Murphy, John Styles, Tom O'Reilly and all the members of
the audience at the event. The Editors would also like to thank Alex Shephard,
Paul Slack and Joanna Innes who acted as readers for the volume, and
Charles Philpin and Chris Wickham, for their help and advice throughout
the project. Iain Pears found the cover image. Finally, we thank Iain Pears
and Nick Stargardt as always for support and careful reading.

Introduction

This volume celebrates the achievements of Dame Olwen Hufton, who has done more to shape how the history of ordinary people is written than any individual now living in Britain. She had no smooth trajectory from Oxbridge College to Oxbridge Fellowship. As she was the first to acknowledge, her career reflected the extraordinary opportunities opened up to women of relatively modest origins by the National Education Act of 1944. Born in the north of England in 1938, she studied history at Royal Holloway College, London, and graduated from the University of London with a Ph.D in 1962. She spent twenty years at the University of Reading, where she wrote her pioneering work on poverty in eighteenth-century France. Her 'international' career began relatively late, first at Harvard, where she taught comparative European History and built up the Women's Studies Programme, and then at the European University Institute at Florence in Italy, where she met scholars and graduate students from across Western Europe. It was only after these experiences that she made her way back to Britain to a Leverhulme Research Professorship at Merton College, Oxford, where she stayed until retirement.

This brief curriculum vitae, however, gives little sense of the intellectual odyssey that accompanied her professional ascent. Olwen was remarkable for the way her own experiences inspired her historical questioning. She often recalled how, when she was a small child, her mother bartered tea for butter during the days of rationing; this encounter with the constraints and choices of household management in a period of scarcity left an indelible mark. As a student in the early 1960s she studied under Alfred Cobban, the historian of the French Revoution, and was attracted by both the Annales School and British 'History from Below', which helped her conceptualize her interest in material realities and how they related to social, political, and cultural history. Her approach, however, was rarely conventional: against a backdrop of radical feminism and student revolt in 1968, for example, she lectured on women in the French Revolution but, instead of concluding that bread riots were emancipatory, showed how the Revolution's approach to religion disrupted networks of sociability and undermined traditional welfare provision.

From the earliest work on the poor in eighteenth-century Bayeux, through her current work on how the Counter-Reformation was financed (by women as well as by men), to the exploration of time in the lives of women in the late twentieth century, Olwen has always been concerned with lived experience and immediate dilemmas. All her writings are perhaps inspired by a distinctive quality that is encapsulated under the banner of the 'art of survival', a theme that also engages the contributors of this volume. They seek, too, to emulate her chronological and comparative sweep by offering topics which extend from the sixteenth to the twentieth centuries.

If it is no longer possible to refer to 'the people' without remembering that the term includes both women as well as men, or to consider social change without pausing to ask whether it affected women in the same ways as men, this fundamental shift in orientation is largely due to Olwen and a generation of women historians who fought hard to make women's experience part of history. The history of women and the conceptual tool of 'gender' are some of the most significant historiographical innovations of the last quarter of the twentieth century, transforming forever how historians conceptualize class and politics. Few would now dissent from the proposition that early modern Europe was a patriarchal society, or deny that nineteenth- and twentieth-century European Christianity had become feminized. It is hard now to remember how large such claims seemed when they were first made; or how revolutionary it was to argue that relations between people in earlier times were governed by issues of power between the sexes. Patriarchy, after all, was a term too politically charged even for many feminists of the 1970s and 1980s.

At the same time that women's history was developing, social historians revealed a more various and complex vision of the 'people'. They investigated the lives of prostitutes, smugglers, poachers, and thieves, people whose 'class consciousness'—and gender—did not fit easily into a heroic vision of the working class. Olwen was central to this movement and key in illuminating the sometimes violent world of working men and women whose illegal activities were essential to their survival. Her work demonstrated a historical passion for understanding the precariousness of daily life. Her portrait of poverty in eighteenth-century France was strikingly humane precisely because it neither sentimentalized nor idealized the poor. For the first time, readers felt they were privy to the 'real-life' choices of people in the past and, like Olwen, refrained from judging them.

Despite the richness of this approach, social history became increasingly eclipsed by an interest in language and discourse, a trend which Olwen quietly, but resolutely, resisted, even though she was always alive to the importance of language. Now as the enthusiasm for the 'linguistic turn' ebbs away, younger historians have begun to look anew at her scholarship and to think about the developing sophistication of her approach. This volume is therefore dedicated to commemorating Olwen's achievement by both taking stock of the current state of social and gender history and examining how to stretch its conceptual horizons.

One of the distinguishing aspects of Olwen's work was its time-span, for, although she is revered as a pioneering early-modernist, her work traverses almost five centuries. This desire to encompass the *longue durée* emerged from a lifelong scholarly respect for Fernand Braudel and is the source of the contrast with the miniaturist approach associated with the 'textual' and 'microhistorical' that has dominated history in the last twenty years. But what distinguished Olwen from Braudel was the way she applied this vision of time to women. Despite the many caesuras of political history—and especially that of the French Revolution, which remained a field of study of particular interest—Olwen believed that the real change in women's lives only occurred in the 1950s. Although she acknowledged the rise of literacy among women, and the opening of a new sectors of female employment in the nineteenth century, she nonetheless maintained that the pre-First World War world was still a 'foreign country', in which the majority of people's lives remained constrained by shortages and limited opportunities. The 'modernity' of the inter-war period was overshadowed by the incomplete nature of post-war recovery and the Depression, which imposed strong constraints on incipient consumer culture.

As important as the *longue durée* was the commitment to a comparative approach. Inspite of the lip-service paid to the importance of looking across national, linguistic, and chronological boundaries, late twentieth-century historians became ever more specialized in their work. Olwen's ability to compare Northern Europe with Southern Europe, Protestant with Catholic Europe, as well as the sixteenth with the twentieth century, gave her a unique historical range. This permitted her to ask different questions, and to see unities where other, less knowledgeable historians saw only an unpatterned diversity.

What drives her work is the fascination with discovering exactly how life was possible, how women and men lived in the past, what limits shaped their lives, and how these affected their families and communities. Above all, her historical vision is always bounded by a sense of limits. While the neo-Marxists of the 1960s and 1970s saw the French Revolution as a moment of political possibility and broadening social horizons, Olwen presented it as part tragedy, uncovering the attack on female spiritual life and its ruinous impact on poor families struggling to survive the whirlwind of violence, hunger, and war. Her examination of elite women was also preoccupied with constraints, as she investigated how they and their daughters sought to defend their interests against powerful male networks of patronage and political power by trying to influence marital candidates or using their incomes to support their own charitable and educational projects.

Her concern with these gritty realities has a new significance now that the entire project of feminist history is threatened as the initial excitement fostered by the 'linguistic' turn is fading. The many intellectual trends encompassed by this term sought to counter the tired verities of neo-Marxism with a new radicalism. This critique argued that material realities could only be perceived through language. Following Derrida, exponents emphasized the limits of human understanding and promoted a programme of 'decoding' texts, rituals, and images. Of equal significance was Michel Foucault, who studied the development of the human and medical sciences, and the emergence of new institutions such as the hospital and prison. He revealed a world of repressive 'discourses' and practices of 'micro-power' embedded in the language of reformism and scientific expertise. Although much of the work that was inspired by these two thinkers was remarkable, it nonetheless had the effect of abstracting individuals and social groups out of the discussion. Also, repressive discourses seemed to proliferate without distinction, so that the repressive power of the state was seen as equal to that embodied in the healing gestures and language of a physician. This refusal to assess the power and impact—in concrete historical terms—of various 'discourses' meant that an important intermediate level of historical explanation was entirely neglected.

A new wave of microhistorical studies seemed, at first glance, to remedy the elusive quality of such analyses by focusing on individuals. This work sought to unsettle the soothingly anonymous quality of the abstractions of class and overturn the grand old narratives of historical development. The triumphal account of the Counter-Reformation, for example, looked decidedly different from the perspective of individual victims, such as Carlo Ginzburg's idiosyncratic miller, Mennochio, whose peasant pantheism showed the limits of Catholic reconversion. However, critics argued that individual cases of this kind were by their nature atypical, with one historian noting with dismay that his students wondered if his interest in microhistory resulted from the fact that the really good subjects had already been done by the previous generation, leaving only the unknowns and weirdos for him to explore. Even if such critics underestimated microhistorians' heartfelt desire to escape the deadening, often anodyne, pronouncements on 'the working class response' to 'x' or 'y', they aired a dissatisfaction with microhistory's incapacity to foster historical generalization.

The imperatives that had first driven feminist history also seemed to disintegrate at the same time that disillusionment with microhistory set in. For example, the revolutionary need to find a historical voice for gay men and lesbians seems much less radical, even puzzling, to a generation for whom homosexuality is more familiar and less disturbing. Similarly, the study of working mothers took on a heroic dimension, with early feminists finding models in the medieval women who ran household workshops, did accounts, and held positions of honour in their communities. For such historians, these women were refreshingly different from their own mothers, locked into the domesticity of the 1950s and early 1960s. But heroines like these had less interest for those feminists' children, who are only too aware of the contrary pulls on the loyalties of their own working mothers, and find little to idealize in that experience.

Moreover, within women's history, disenchantment set in among practitioners frustrated by the way their work was marginalized by the profession. They sought increasingly to separate themselves from what they condescendingly labelled as 'herstories', and to show the centrality of their concerns through 'gender analysis'. With this new linguistic perspective, they argued, feminism could enter political, constitutional, or even military history. Who could not be intrigued by the possibility of a 'gendered' interpretation of the French Revolution or Nazism, cardinal events in modern European history? But the undeniable success of 'gender analysis' shows how quickly such concepts could be contained within conventional topics and chronologies. There is no doubt that a feminist interpretation of citizenship during the French Revolution was illuminating, but it remained conceptually straitened by an idea borrowed from political theory. The project of toppling 'masculinist' models of historical change and periodization remained decidedly incomplete. Feminist history ran out of steam because the retreat into language, much as it seemed to offer, also made it less path-breaking. The fact that it is now regularly included in undergraduate history syllabi suggests that it has become only one among many standard approaches.

Moreover, the emphasis on language to the exclusion of all other interpretive concepts meant that large realms of human experience got lost. In her pioneering work on women in Western Europe between 1500 and 1800, Olwen offered an alternative vision. She was sceptical about the categories of political and intellectual history that many historians of the linguistic turn and of gender had unwittingly endorsed. Whereas the likes of Foucault remained wedded to the view that the Enlightenment was the moment of epistemological break in the birth of the human sciences, and American historians traced the rise of disciplines like sexology to the same period, Olwen resisted this vision of the eighteenth century as the birth of 'modernity'. In a field that was close to her own research speciality, she argued that the French Revolution did not feature as *the* moment that altered gender relations; despite massive upheaval, the map of power between the sexes was hardly redrawn, and in some ways inequality was even extended. And, while deeply knowledgeable about the spiritual aspirations of the sixteenth and seventeenth centuries, she was keen to point out that the Reformation and Counter-Reformation did not bring about radically new visions of womanhood either, though Joseph, she interestingly remarks, made a comeback as a model of elderly fatherhood. Rather than releasing women from previous stereotypes of subordination, religious authorities sought their increasing confinement and control. Indeed, what interests her is the way Protestant *and* Catholic women sought to undermine the strictures propounded from on high by exploiting the very stereotypes of their special spiritual vocation to further new religious enterprises.

In *The Prospect Before Her (1500–1800)*, published at the zenith of the theoretical and linguistic turn in gender history in 1995, Olwen chose to emphasize the hard realities of material culture, kinship, and reproduction from the poorest and most humble to the richest and most elevated. Readers responded so enthusiastically precisely because they hungered after an account of women's history that was both wide-ranging and based on a concept of generation and the life-cycle that resonates with the life-dilemmas of women today. Postmodernism may tell us that we fashion our own identities, but few women feel so unfettered. They continue the delicate, and often draining, juggling act between the demands of child-rearing, caring for ageing parents, and earning a living that Olwen elucidates in her historical work.

The Prospect thus explores in detail how a young woman's life was dominated by the hope of marriage as she scrimped and saved to put aside the money needed for a dowry; how the mature woman sought to manage a household 'economy of makeshifts' by whatever means available; and how some widows, for the first time, might dispose of money on their own account—though even then, Olwen has a lively sense of the competing loyalties such women faced. This focus on the 'three stages' of womanhood embodies a sophisticated methodology. First, Olwen recognizes that the realities of child-bearing and rearing, as well as ageing, must all have a central role in our historical account. Economics cannot be understood without reproduction; and social roles cannot be understood without thinking about the biological life-cycle and the transmission of social values and skills from one generation to another. This is why Olwen analyzes the economics of survival so powerfully: she is aware that we experience life as part of a household, with competing needs and skills, dependent on each other at different points in the life-cycle. Just how unusual this is can be gauged by the rarity of historical studies of motherhood, let alone of grandparenthood.

Within this broader vision Olwen always emphasizes the importance of hard material constraints, as she does in all her work. Even if she never fails to show parents' capacity for self-sacrifice, her view of life is decidedly unsentimental, at times even harsh. Indeed, she believes that the scope for choice was small, because often women were primarily concerned to secure a future for descendants. Olwen sees people in terms of their social bonds, rather than as individual agents, an apprehension that no doubt has to do with her knowledge of early modern culture in which values of family and kinship outweighed individual desires and aspirations. But this identification with people in the past no doubt springs from her own experience of motherhood, and her observation too that today parents continue to provide for the education and security of the young even in an era of apparent rampant individualism.

This might seem anti-theoretical, and in a sense, it is. Olwen's vision of the past exemplifies a peculiarly English, empiricist character, which avoids abstractions in favour of concrete situations, strategies, and stories. But the conceptual undergirding is always there, built on a foundation of class, gender, and time and their manifold interrelations. Her focus on survival allows us to consider the issues of relations between the generations within households, of respective power and of duty between mothers and daughters and grandparents and children. As Olwen points out, the obligations that a society owes are often conflicting, and the duty to care for the aged who no longer work has often competed directly with the responsibility for children.

She has a remarkable gift for spotting the detail of the unglamorous realities of life: who else would deliver a lecture on the importance of the pig to the trans-European early modern household economy? Or would pick up on the need for cleanliness, quiet, and an uncluttered space if you are trying to make lace? Or find time in a historical work to consider the physical labour involved in hauling water from a well several times a day? Long before it became fashionable as the history of material culture, Olwen was always aware of the importance of objects in people's lives, and the key links between objects and emotions. Economic history is about people, as much about the meagre trousseau of a Lyonnese silkworker as the wedding gift of fabulous jewels of a French aristocrat. Such objects denoted not only status, but also embodied aspirations and hopes.

In line with the debt we owe to Olwen, we therefore use 'survival' in this volume to embrace not only 'material reality' but also the cultural legacies that one generation passes on to the next. For Olwen, the image of St Anne teaching the Vigin Mary to read is iconic. No literate mother, she likes to remind us, ever produced daughters who could not read. Mothers confide their wisdom and knowledge to their daughters, leaving the younger generation to battle anew against the odds. The skills and values that were transmitted opened up new possibilities. Her work on religious communities and charity shows the practical incarnation of spiritual aspirations, while her study of women writers in the early modern period shows her vivid attention to the grievances and hopes of the most articulate.

This notion of 'survival' is very different from a Weberian vision of residues doomed to extinction in the march towards modernity. On the contrary, 'survival' suggests the active re-engagement with the past and its constant re-creation, even if that re-engagement entails rebellion or resistance. The emphasis on generational transmission reflects the shift among historians who now question the power of microhistory or the global application of a concept like gender. Because microhistory was so concerned with the unusual and the quixotic, it was less well equipped to explore questions of legacies or to examine the bonds of feeling across time.

The *Art of Survival* seeks to put such questions at the forefront of historical discussion, and, like Olwen, to use a comparative perspective based on a wide time-frame as our starting point. With this in mind, we have devised four sections, the first entitled 'Gender and Material Culture', which focuses on issues surrounding household budgets and the burdens of care within the family. In her analysis of the spending of eighteenth-century gentry families, Amanda Vickery shows how patterns of consumption are profoundly gendered, so much so that feminist historiography has tended to replicate the idea that shopping is women's business. While women might then, as now, be typecast as spendthrifts, Vickery demonstrates how often a majority of the household budget went on items of male consumption—horses, dogs, and carriages as well as bespoke tailoring and bootmaking. The dry account books demonstrate the reproductive itineraries of the life course, with massive apothecary bills testifying to the ills of infancy, and other expenditures demonstrating women's primary concern for the care of the young. Rather than being spendthrifts, women spent more money on their children and husbands than on themselves. Although their role as household managers gave them considerable influence, the inequalities of gender underscored the limited scope even comfortably-off women had for independence.

Just how powerfully such unequal access to resources continues to structure gender relations today is evident in Jane Lewis's sobering analysis of the distribution of the costs of 'caring' between men and women in contemporary Britain and Europe. Her comparative study shows governments seeking to grapple with the end of the 'male breadwinner family model', which designated men as having primary responsibility for earning money and women as caring for the young and old. She shows how women can no longer rely on a male breadwinner, but must continue to shoulder the unremunerated care for family members. Lewis challenges us to re-examine women's continuing lack of economic power, despite their massive participation in the workforce, and to acknowledge that, for many, the burdens of work and family have intensified rather than diminished in recent years.

The second section, on 'Objects and the Culture of Emotions', moves away from the dynamics of household management and gender relations to probe more fully the links between material survival and subjectivity. Nuns, one might think, represent women who have renounced the world and material possessions altogether; yet, as Silvia Evangelisti argues in a startling investigation of nuns' cells in seventeenth-century Italy, these rooms became intensely important to them, expressing their individual and familial status. Evangelisti shows how, even in reformed convents, nuns bought and sold cells and took care in bequeathing them. However, they often set up situations that would lead to years of litigation between favoured friends and relations. The resulting court cases tested the rival obligations of family and friendship to the limit, and the outcome was not predictable: even male judges acknowledged that convent women relied on fellow sisters in old age, and sometimes rewarded that loyalty. Evangelisti thus deduces the character of love and power from the disputes surrounding objects.

In the first serious study of the lives of clerical concubines after the Council of Trent, Simone Laqua also draws on struggles over money and goods to understand the relationship between priest and housekeeper. Her study of Münster in the Counter-Reformation shows just how difficult it was for the Church hierarchy to get priests to relinquish their concubines, relationships that often went back decades and where service, mutual dependence, love, and exploitation might be inextricably interwoven. Forced to defend their claims to a Church hierarchy, which did not think such concubines should exist, women had to find a way to insist on their rights to a share of the house and an income to support their children. Their pleas often succeeded in getting compensation by demonstrating past loyalty and service. Despite the harsh moral strictures of the Reformation—and the shamed status of such women—their plight nonetheless aroused the pity of clerical authorities.

The third section focuses on 'Religious Legacies, Friendship, and Politics', and the way that relationships and spirituality enabled women to build institutions and shape political sensibilities. Ruth Manning's work gives a sense of the psychological energy that underpinned Counter-Reformation spirituality by examining the spiritual 'love affair' of Jeanne de Chantal and St François de Sales and their joint foundation of the order of Sisters of

Charity. She shows how this laywoman and her confessor built upon a post-Tridentine legacy of spiritual exchange and cooperation. With its distinctive brand of Counter-Reformation social catholicism, or *le catholicisme au féminin*, they devoted themselves to the education of girls and the care of the sick. Without de Sales's political power, their mutual vision that placed women at its centre might never have been realized. But without the passionate spiritual love affair between the two, the plan for the new order—in direct contradiction to the ideals of chaste womanhood imposed by the Council of Trent—could never have been achieved.

Ruth Harris extends this discussion by analysing, for the first time, the hundreds of letters written to Lucie Dreyfus, the wife of the Jewish captain wrongly condemned for treason in 1894 and transported to Devil's Island. The majority of Lucie's correspondents were women who, rather than evincing the rabid anticlericalism of many leading Dreyfusards, instead identified with Dreyfus and Lucie as Christ and Mary martyred in the cause of Truth and Justice. They offered prayer and ecumenical solidarity, and saw the Dreyfusard movement as a religious crusade struggling against the evil machinations of the military. Harris continues by investigating the passionate friendships of prominent Dreyfusards, showing how these leading anticlericals were unable to divest themselves of the religious models and impulses they despised. Their missionizing zeal and secular absolutism reflected the intolerance of their religious opponents, hence heightening the passion invested in the cause. Assessing the impact of these various religious legacies, Harris argues, is central to understanding this key episode in 'modern' politics.

The final section of this volume deals with 'Trauma, Loss, and Survival' by looking at the repercussions of witchcraft, revolution, and war. Lyndal Roper examines the dialect poetry and plays of the monk Sebastian Sailer, showing how this Catholic Enlightenment cleric used Swabian dialect to construct a sentimental version of eighteenth-century village life which removed its deadly enmities in a fug of homespun folksiness. There are no women characters in Sailer's plays about rural life. Yet Sailer had worked in a village which witnessed a peculiarly vicious witch craze, in which six women were burnt while a seventh died of injuries sustained during brutal interrogation. That it could be possible for a witch craze to take place so late alters our picture of the Enlightenment and its discovery of 'popular culture'. Roper argues that the plays, which seem to be survivals of a rural idyll, are in fact creations of a nostalgia for a lost 'community' that denies the violent past and its smouldering hatreds and envies.

Alex Owen analyses the paradox of the decline of organized religion in conjuction with the growth of a 'religious sense' among British intellectuals in the 1920s. Rather than the stereotype of the 'jazz age' and 'flapper', she shows the widespread search for a 'mystic religion' in a period of overwhelming bereavement in the wake of the First World War. Through unorthodox spirituality and psychoanalysis, this generation sought to give new meaning to the 'self', transforming nineteenth-century traditions of theosophy, spiritualism, and Christianity.

It is fitting that this volume should end with Colin Jones's critical account of the differences between the history of Richard Cobb and Olwen Hufton. By setting their respective work in the context of the 1960s and 1970s, he gives a vivid sense of the impact of their divergent historical sensibilities on his own generation of historians. Rarely can we find a greater testimony to the impact of legacies in intellectual terms. Here were two titanic figures within the British world of French historical writing, with Cobb, the elder of the pair, providing an anarchic and individualistic vision of the activities of the French poor during the revolutionary crisis, and Olwen beginning her deeper investigation of the role of women during the same period. Both were concerned with the 'poor', but while Olwen's work increasingly developed into a broader structural explanation of material culture and generational survival across early modern Europe, Cobb turned more and more to anecdotalism and a rejection of broad-based historical interpretation. Cobb sought to rescue the 'people' from the past by accentuating their individuality and avoiding generalization, while Olwen sought to use stories about individuals to illustrate the plight of broad groupings—especially women—within society. This volume is dedicated to her enduring legacy, and to the way an even younger generation of historians have found inspiration in the questions she asked.

His and Hers: Gender, Consumption and Household Accounting in Eighteenth-Century England*

Amanda Vickery

The connotations of 'shopping' are deeply feminine. When a leading anthropologist of modern consumer behaviour, Daniel Miller, went into North London homes in the 1990s to ask about shopping, a high proportion of men got up to leave with the words, 'you need to speak to my wife, she's the expert'. Yet the masculine rejection of consumption is more rhetorical than real. On closer examination, the men were found to be skilled consumer researchers, bargain hunters, and collectors of certain kinds of goods. Nevertheless they still disavowed the verb shopping, admitting only to 'an interest in music', or 'a love of books'. Shopping for do-it-yourself, car parts, and alcohol was dominated by males, yet a 'tendency to distance themselves from identification with the act and concept of shopping' was still pronounced.[1]

In the eighteenth century it was no different. It was women who were *principally* identified with spending in the eighteenth-century imagination.

* For their questions and comments, I am indebted to the participants of the Conference in Honour of Olwen Hufton, New College Oxford, 9 July 2004, and above all to the organizers Lyndal Roper and Ruth Harris for their astute critical engagement. Versions of this paper were given at the Eighteenth-Century Seminar at the Institute of Historical Research, the Cultural History Seminar, Caius College, Cambridge, and the History department at MIT. I benefited from criticisms at all events. For references, suggestions, and critical readings, I thank Michele Cohen, Penelope Corfield, Hannah Greig, Charles Foster, Frances Harris, Tim Hitchcock, Mark Overton, Giorgio Riello, Naomi Tadmor, Pat Thane, and all the fellows of the AHRC Centre for the Study of the Domestic Interior. I am especially grateful to the archivists of the British Library, the Wiltshire Record Office, the Cheshire Record Office, and the Cambridgeshire County Record Office for their assistance and for permission to quote from their manuscripts. I would like to thank Andrea Wulf for bringing the Grimes account book to my attention. For copious criticisms, as well as quality childcare, my debt to John Styles is large.

[1] Interviewed by Amanda Vickery on 'Just Looking: A History of Shopping', BBC Radio 4; D. Miller, *A Theory of Shopping* (Cambridge, 1998), 39–40.

While the luxury debate raged, many were the critics who claimed that women were lost to sober housewifery and home production, in a rush for ready-made goods and the shops.

> Time was, when tradesmen laid up what they gain'd
> And frugally a family maintained.
> When they took stirring housewives for their spouses,
> To keep up prudent order in their house;
> Who thought no scorn, at night to sit them down
> And make their children's clothes and mend their own
> Would Polly's coat to younger Bess transfer,
> And make their caps without a milliner.
> But now a shopping half the day they're gone,
> To buy 500 things and pay for none . . .[2]

The gulf between the producing man and the consuming female is well entrenched, and seems to survive as a trope in the face of all evidence to the contrary. Why is female materialism criticized, while male consumerism often seems invisible? Men historically have disassociated themselves from shopping, but nevertheless they were open and enthusiastic consumers of certain categories of goods (horses, carriages, watches, alcohol, weapons, tools, books, and so on in the eighteenth century) and furtive consumers of much else. Major questions about the relationship of men, women, and goods remain unanswered despite the recent boom in consumption studies.

The skills, knowledge, and practical power which women gained as consumers have been noted for eighteenth-, nineteenth-, and early twentieth-century Britain and North America. Claire Walsh has recently emphasized the wife's ideological inscription as guardian of the purse-strings in eighteenth-century England, and her practical role in shopping for food and household basics: haggling, testing food for quality, spotting adulteration, deciding when to send servants or shop herself, and so on.[3] It was precisely because women were seen to manage the business of everyday shopping that American patriots made such efforts to ensure female cooperation in the

---

[2] Charles Jenner, *Town Eclogues* (2nd edn., 1773).

[3] C. Walsh, 'Shopping in Early-Modern London, *c.*1660–1800' (European University Institute, Florence, Ph.D. thesis, 2001), ch. 5; C. Walsh, 'Shops, Shopping and the Art of Decision-Making in Eighteenth-Century England', in J. Styles and A. Vickery, *Gender, Taste and Material Culture in Britain and North America, 1700–1830* (Yale University Press, New Haven, forthcoming, 2006).

colonial boycott of British imports, particularly tea, in the 1760s and 1770s.[4] Similarly, early nineteenth-century anti-slavery activists expressly targeted women because, 'in the domestic department they are the chief controllers; they for the most part, provide the articles of family consumption'.[5] An emerging consensus agrees that women enjoyed some recognized independence as routine consumers.

The deep psychic investment some women made in the world of goods has been established by recent research. Lancashire merchant's wife Elizabeth Shackleton, Massachusetts pioneer Hannah Barnard, Shropshire spinster Katharine Plymley, aristocratic tourist Elizabeth Berkeley Somerset, fourth duchess of Beaufort, among many others can be seen using possessions as props in self-fashioning, some creating an assemblage that came close to a self-portrait—a picture which could be shown-off, rearranged, or hidden as circumstances demanded. In fact, Joanna Dahn argues that the connoisseur and courtier Mary Delany, the twice-widowed niece of a nobleman, self-consciously crafted an 'objectscape' in china to testify to the cultured female community she did so much to nurture.[6] Women could use objects to convey a multitude of meanings, from fashion, taste, and style, to wealth and status, history, and lineage, from political and religious allegiance, to personality, relationships, memory, and mortality.[7] Material culture has thus

---

[4] M. B. Norton, *Liberty's Daughters: The Revolutionary Experience of American Women, 1750–1800* (Toronto, 1980), 157–63.

[5] Elizabeth Heyrick, *An Appeal to the Hearts and Consciences of British Women* (Leicester, 1828), 4, 6. C. Midgley, 'Women Anti-Slavery Campaigners in Britain' (Univ. of Kent Ph.D. thesis, 1989), ch. 2. Perhaps most famously, the early nineteenth-century women's anti-slavery societies forwent slave-grown sugar. The tactic lived on in the Chartist women's exclusive dealing campaign and the female boycott of feathers from endangered birds in late Victorian department stores.

[6] Johanna Dahn, 'Mrs Delany and Ceramics in the Objectscape', in *Interpreting Ceramics*, 1 (2000), http://www.uwic.ac.uk/ICRC/issue001/, 30 Sept. 2005.

[7] For a micro-study of the practices and attitudes of one consumer based on diaries, letters, account books, and ledgers, see A. Vickery 'Women and the World of Goods: A Lancashire Consumer and Her Possessions, 1751–81', in J. Brewer and R. Porter (eds.), *Consumption and the World of Goods: Consumption and Society in the Seventeenth and Eighteenth Centuries* (London, 1993), 274–301. A compelling reconstruction of the connotations of one piece of furniture is L. Thatcher Ulrich, 'Hannah Barnard's Cupboard: Female Property and Identity in Eighteenth Century New England', in R. Hoffman, M. Sobel, and F. Teute (eds.), *Through a Glass Darkly: Reflections on Personal Identity in Early America* (Chapel Hill, NG, 1997), 238–73. On the intertwining of gender, politics, religion, consumption, and aesthetics, see J. Dahn, 'Women and Taste: A Case Study of Katharine Plymley (1758–1829)' (Univ. of Aberystwyth Ph.D. thesis, 2001) and

emerged as an arena for the expression of considerable female eloquence and creativity.

However, it could be fairly argued that our fascination with women and the world of goods has overshadowed the role of men. Looking at the diaries of Thomas Turner, a Sussex shopkeeper, Reverends Woodforde and Holland of Norfolk and Somerset, and Robert Sharpe, an East Yorkshire schoolmaster, Margot Finn documents male consumption of a broad range of goods, basic and luxurious. Men were as acquisitive as women.[8] While Finn is surely right to lament historians' neglect of the male consumer (there is some important work on men's clothing but little else),[9] her sources and the situation of her subjects leave questions unanswered: it remains to be

---

J. Dahn, 'Material Culture, Abolitionism, and Dissenting Discourse (1791–1830): The Simplicity of a Quaker But Not Their Language', Conference paper at 'Women and Material Culture 1660–1830', University of Southampton and Chawton House Library 14–15 July 2004. On aristocratic display, see M. Henry, 'Keeping Up with the Beauforts: Consuming Passions', *Harvard Magazine* (Sept.–Oct. 1997) and M. Pointon, *Strategies for Showing: Women, Possession and Representation in English Visual Culture, 1665–1800* (Oxford, 1997). One of the earliest attempts to wrestle with the differences between male and female materialism based on inventory data is L.Weatherill, 'A Possession of One's Own: Women and Consumer Behaviour in England, 1660–1740', *Journal of British Studies*, 25 (1986), 131–56. On the language of bequests, see M. Berg, 'Women's Consumption and the Industrial Classes of Eighteenth-Century England', *Journal of Social History*, 30: 2 (1996). There are accounts of certain commodities which draw out a gender perspective, perhaps inevitably china. See B. Kowaleski-Wallace, 'Women, China and Consumer Culture in Eighteenth-century England', *Eighteenth-Century Studies*, 29: 2 (1995–6), 153–67, and id., *Consuming Subjects: Women, Shopping and Business in the 18th Century* (New York, 1997); S. Richards, *Eighteenth Century Ceramics: Producers for a Civilised Society* (Manchester, 1999).

[8] M. Finn, 'Men's Things: Masculine Possession in the Consumer Revolution', *Social History*, 25: 2 (May 2000), 133–55. The problem is also raised by De Grazia in the Introduction to V. de Grazia and E. Furlough (eds.), *The Sex of Things: Gender and Consumption in Historical Perspective* (Berkeley, 1996), 1: 'If women figure not only as the proverbial shoppers, the Ur-decorators, the perennial custodians of the bric-a-brac of daily life but also as objects of exchange and consumption, what then can be inferred about the relationship of man, males, and masculinity to the world of commodities?'

[9] See D. Kuchta, *The Three Piece Suit and Modern Masculinity: England 1550–1850* (Berkeley, 2002), C. Breward, *The Hidden Consumer: Masculinities, Fashion and City Life, 1860–1914* (Manchester, 1999), and C. Horwood, 'Keeping Up Appearances: Clothes, Class and Culture, 1918–1939' (Univ. of London Ph.D. thesis, 2003), a study that gives equal attention to men's and women's dress. For a fascinating glimpse of masculine passion for mechanical goods, especially bicycles, read K. Whitworth, 'Shop and Shop Floor: Men's Sense of Belonging in 1930s Coventry', in Putnam *et al.* (eds.), *Making & Unmaking: Creative and Critical Practice in a Designed World. Selected Proceedings Design*

seen, for instance, whether Parson James Woodforde would have run the grocery accounts had he been in possession of a wife.

On the basis of my previous research on northern letters, diaries, and account books I suggested that women's consumption was more daily and visible, while male consumerism in its nature escaped notice. Of course, the way spouses carved up their shopping lists must have varied from couple to couple. When the Londoners Bessy and William Ramsden fulfilled the commissions of a northern cousin in 1765, Bessy Ramsden bought the 'Gowns, Caps, Ruffles and such like female Accoutrements', while William was accountable 'for the Wafers, Paper & Pocket Book'. After all it would be remarkable if a schoolmaster had not been able to judge the quality of stationery. But William Ramsden was unusual among husbands in going to market to purchase humdrum groceries. Individual variations notwithstanding, while a wife's consumption was predominantly repetitive and mundane, a husband's consumption was by contrast characteristically occasional and impulsive, or expensive and dynastic.[10]

Business records confirm that men dominated the purchase of high-status, expensive luxury goods. Few business historians have bothered with a gender breakdown of the consumer market, but valuable research on the ledgers of a London art dealer, the Derby porcelain business, and the London silversmith Parker and Wakelin reveals the broad patterns of male and female formal patronage of the luxury trades.[11] Stark male dominance of

---

History Society Annual Conference 2000. (DHS/University of Portsmouth, 2000), and 'Men Changing Allegiance: From Workshop to Shopper in 1930s Coventry', in *History And Change: Selected Conference Proceedings* (University of Turku, forthcoming).

[10] A. Vickery, *The Gentleman's Daughter: Women's Lives in Georgian England* (New Haven, 1998), 166–8. Sophie White finds an identical gender division of consumer labour amongst the elite of colonial Louisiana in the 1750s, where a husband might place the actual order for his wife's taffeta summer gown, while she saw to ordinary clothing: S. K. White, 'This Gown was Much Admired and Made Many Ladies Jealous: Fashion and the Forging of Elite Identities in French Colonial New Orleans', in T. Harvey and G. O'Brien (eds.), *George Washington's South* (Gainesville, Fla., 2004), 86–118; 100.

[11] L. Lippincott, *Selling Art in Georgian London: The Rise of Arthur Pond* (New Haven, 1983), 66–9; J. A. Anderson, 'Derby Porcelain and the Early English Fine Ceramic Industry, c.1750–1830' (Univ. of Leicester Ph.D. thesis, 2002); L. Lippincott and H. Clifford, *Silver in London: The Parker and Wakelin Partnership, 1760–1776* (New Haven and London, 2004), 138. Only 37 of the 321 clients in the 1766–70 ledger were female: two 'Countesses', seven 'Ladys', twenty-two 'Mrs', and six 'Miss'. Only three women out of the 37 made large orders for investment goods such as entire tea services or gold and precious stone jewellery. Most of Parker and Wakelin's female customers bought smaller, less expensive items, like individual pieces of tea-ware, snuffboxes, and paste and silver jewellery.

luxury spending emerges in all three cases. Women do not figure as prominent patrons and collectors, in their own right, at the top end of the market. The satirists may have believed that female customers were spending a fortune on shiny geegaws, but ledgers studied so far do not bear this out.

Of course ledgers conceal as much as they reveal; they tell us who paid, and represented the family, not necessarily who truly chose. Women's desires undoubtedly lie concealed beneath the names of husbands, fathers, and brothers.[12] Sometimes, as a late eighteenth-century shop ledger from Penmorfa in North Wales reveals, women's transactions were concealed from their menfolk. The ledger includes repeated entries for purchases on men's credit by wives or maidservants which use phrases like 'handkerchief . . . wife, not to tell' or 'hat 11s. 6d., to tell 8s.'. Evidently, the purchase or its real cost was not to be divulged to the man of the house.[13] Lady Shelburne's account of an afternoon's luxury shopping suggests some of the matrimonial negotiation which underpinned a male to male commission:

> . . . we went first to Zucchi's, where we saw some ornaments for our ceilings, and a large architectural painting for our ante-chamber, with which however, my lord is not particularly pleased. From there to Mayhew and Inch [Ince] where is some beautiful cabinet work and two pretty glass cases . . . From thence to Cipriani's where we saw some beautiful drawings and crayon pictures and where Lord Shelbourne bespoke some to be copied for me, to complete my dressing room . . . From thence to Zuccarelli's where we also saw some large pictures doing for us and from thence home it being half past four.[14]

My reading of this account is that while Lord Shelburne placed the order, and indeed believed *he* had made the key decisions, it was in fact his wife

---

[12] A similar point is made by the art historian Kate Retford in 'Patrilineal Portraiture? Gender and Genealogy in the Eighteenth-Century Country House', in John Styles and Amanda Vickery (eds.), *Gender, Taste and Material Culture in Britain and North America 1700–1830* (New Haven, forthcoming). Retford's research in family correspondence reveals that Caroline Fox was primarily responsible for the new commissions and the hang in the gallery at Holland House in the early 1760s, but you would never know this from the family account books, or Reynolds's bills.

[13] University College of North Wales, Bangor, Dept. of Mss., MS 82, Penmorfa, Caernarvon, shop ledger, *c*.1788–*c*.1803: f. 4, account of Harry Evan of Tyddynfilin, 14 May 1792; f. 13, account of William Evans of Wern, 15 Aug. 1793. I thank John Styles for this reference.

[14] Letters quoted in Michael Snodin and John Styles, *Design and the Decorative Arts: Britain 1500–1900* (V&A, London, 2001), 272.

who had orchestrated his choices. For as one nineteenth-century wit put it, 'if the man was the head of the family, the woman was the neck, and often turned the head which way she liked'.[15]

Looking at the consumption of men and women in tandem offsets a tendency in the more celebratory accounts of consumer behaviour to glorify the individual economic actor, wrenching him or her from their household and familial contexts. We should not forget the lessons of the history of poverty—that the consumption of one almost always affects or responds to the consumption of the others closest to her. The flashy spending of young wage-earners on fashion and entertainment in the 1930s and 1950s was built on a parental subsidy of their shelter, fuel, food, and domestic utilities; while the unstraitened personal consumption of adult men, despite family poverty, in the nineteenth and twentieth centuries is notorious.[16] Indeed, the neglect of the household as a unit of consumption is especially odd for the early modern era when family and household loomed so large as living experience, organizational category, and ideological trope. Jan de Vries has urged researchers to look behind the myth of patriarchy, whereby the household speaks with one voice (and that voice the master's), to get a sense of the choices made *within* households about market participation.[17] Individual consumers rarely operate in a vacuum.

This essay uses men and women's account books to establish the interweaving of men and women's consumption in eighteenth-century England.

---

[15] This was said by a Mr Jordan to a meeting of working-men in Marlow in 1868 on the importance of wooing the disenfranchised wives of male voters. Quoted in M. Cragoe, 'Jenny Rules the Roost: Women and Electoral Politics, 1832–1868', in K. Gleadle and S. Richardson (eds.), *Women in British Politics, 1760–1869: The Power of the Petticoat* (London, 2000), 156.

[16] D. Fowler, 'Teenage Consumers? Young Wage-earners and Leisure in Manchester, 1919–1939', in A. Davies and S. Fielding (eds.), *Workers Worlds: Cultures and Communications in Manchester and Salford, 1880–1939* (Manchester, 1992); id., *The First Teenagers? Young Wage Earners Between the Wars* (London, 1996); A. Davies, *Leisure, Gender and Poverty: Working-class Culture in Salford and Manchester, 1900–1939* (Manchester, 1992); and see the brilliant essay by S. Bowden and A. Offner, 'The Technological Revolution That Never Was: Gender, Class and the Diffusion of Household Appliances in Interwar England', in de Grazia and Furlough (eds.), *The Sex of Things* 244–74.

[17] Jan de Vries, 'Between Purchasing Power and the World of Goods: Understanding the Household Economy in Early Modern Europe,' in Brewer and Porter (eds.), *Consumption and the World of Goods*, 118. The centrality of the household family is the key argument of N. Tadmor, *Family and Friends in Eighteenth-century England: Household, Kinship, and Patronage* (Cambridge, 2001).

Account books assume literacy and numeracy, creditworthiness, a regular income stream, and what we might term an accounting frame of mind. Double-entry bookkeeping famously arose in the counting houses of the city states of Renaissance Italy, and was quickly taken up by merchants and bankers in commercial centres across Europe. Household, as opposed to business, accounting seems to have been devised on the model of the stewardship of the large landed estate.[18] By the early eighteenth century there were several published guides to household accounting which offered standardized models for the aspiring administrator to follow, such as those in North's *Gentleman Accomptant* (1715), but most of these authors were prophets of double-entry bookkeeping, and simply laid out debt and credit on a month-by-month basis, offering advice to the novice on putting transactions in the right column. Few broke down the incomings and outgoings in any other way. Once the mysteries of double-entry were grasped, the accounting system on offer looked deceptively simple, and easy to adapt. It could be borrowed, bowdlerized, and elaborated. So although manuscript account books are not without their generic features, there was no fancy categorization into which the economic life of the household had to be forced, apart from debit and credit, month by month.

Account books were not written with historians in mind. They lack the emotional expansiveness of diaries and letters, and can give limited insight into attitudes and meanings. In the words of a candid local historian, 'accounts are boring to read as well as difficult to understand'.[19] Still, household account books are often the only surviving document of family fortunes, charting economic vicissitudes, family tensions, triumphs and disasters. The human story is belied by the terseness of the writing, yet the lists and numbers bear witness to drama nevertheless.

If account books were not written for the entertainment and instruction of posterity, what did practitioners think they were for? The purpose of accounts, according to contemporary exponents of the art, was above all financial security: 'making inspection into that, that is to keep me and mine from ruine and poverty.'[20] But Margaret Hunt suggests that the promise of bookkeeping was even more profound: a method of predicting and hence controlling the future, a mysterious art on a par with divination and

---

[18] S. Pollard, *The Genesis of Modern Management: A Study of the Industrial Revolution in Great Britain* (London, 1965), 209–49.

[19] C. E. Foster, *Seven Households: Life in Cheshire and Lancashire 1582–1774* (Arley Hall Press, Northwich, 2002), 1.

[20] This is a quote from *Advice to the Women and Maidens of London* (London, 1678), 2. See esp. J. Hoppit, *Risk and Failure in English Business, 1700–1800* (Cambridge, 1987).

magic.[21] Historians of management argue that for traders and manufacturers accounts could express a 'quest for order and regularity when dealing with overwhelming detail, perhaps without reliable managerial staff or settled routine'. It is in the very regularity of the system that bookkeeping assumes 'the colouring partly of a tool of management as well as a system of reckoning'.[22]

All of which raises the vexed question of how account books were used in particular families. Was an account book an aid or a weapon? A woman's account book, for example, could be read as a map of her jurisdiction, but it might also document a patriarch's surveillance of her time and spending. There are certainly manuscript account books where the father has audited and signed off his daughter's account books, monitoring the proper expenditure of her allowance.[23] Anne Brockman, a Kent gentlewoman, was an assiduous accountant, running the household books for nearly twenty years, but she was married to a formidable 'over busy' magistrate and Whig MP, notorious for the carefulness of his record keeping, who found time enough to check her calculations. In July 1719 Mrs Brockman was compelled to record: 'Miscounted in Mr Brockman's reckoning from London 0-10-0.'[24] Doubtless many readers will remember the scene in Louisa Alcott's *Little Women*, of 1868, when the monthly checking of the housekeeping account and personal pocket-book forced the newly-wed Meg to reveal to her hardworking husband the £50 she had spent on some shimmering violet silk: 'When John got out his books that night, Meg's heart sank; and for the first time in her married life, she was afraid of her husband.'[25] For one specialist

---

[21] M. Hunt, *The Middling Sort: Commerce, Gender and Family in England, 1680–1780* (Berkeley, 1996), 58.

[22] Pollard, *Modern Management*, 216.

[23] British Library, Add. Ms 62092, Account Book for Personal expenses of Margaret Spencer, with her father's notes throughout as auditor. I am indebted to Frances Harris for bringing these accounts to my attention.

[24] British Library, Add. Ms 45208; Add. Ms 45204; Add. Ms 45210, Anne Brockman's Household Accounts. See July 1719, f. 59. On William Brockman, see E. Cruikshanks, S. Handley, and D. W. Hayton, *The History of Parliament: The House of Commons, 1690–1715* (London, 1900), 332–5.

[25] L. M. Alcott, *Little Women* (1868; Harmondsworth, 1989), 282–3. See also pp. 280–1: 'She knew her husband's income and she loved to feel that he trusted her, not only with his happiness, but what some men seem to value more, his money. She knew where it was, was free to take what she liked, and all he asked was that she should keep account of every penny, pay bills once a month, and remember that she was a poor man's wife. Till now she had done well, been prudent and exact, kept her little account books neatly, and showed them to him monthly, without fear. But that autumn the serpent got into Meg's paradise, and tempted her, not with apples but with dress . . .'

in accounting history, domestic accounting systems helped sustain the operation of patriarchy in the Victorian middle-class home. Accounting is seen to be disabling, an instrument for controlling female consumption and containing women in domestic roles.[26]

An account book was always and ever a tool of domestic management, though whose management exactly may sometimes remain moot. Modern sociology draws a distinction between day-to-day management of family finances, and overall control, with final say in financial decision-making. In this reading, day-to-day management is not seen as a site of much power. Contemporary households where the wife controls the money and the husband manages it are rare; and in the even rarer cases where men both control and manage money there is a strong likelihood of extreme abuse.[27] However, this sociology is too pessimistic about the possible benefits of accounting expertise and consumer management, even within a framework of masculine control. If the management of money were not a significant freedom, then abusive husbands today would not seek to crush it. And in an era of written accounts, one could argue that the accountant who massages the figures accrues practical power thereby, even if they present the books to a higher authority. After all, fraud is a secret form of control. Men often had no choice but to trust to female knowledge, and knowledge, it scarcely needs repeating, is power.

Yet even where the ultimate control behind the account book is hard to ascertain, we can still conclude that account books were as much an active representation of domestic business as they were a record of it, and varied with the financial circumstances, business culture, and emotional climate of different families.

The account books that survive are emphatically not a systematic sample. Account books that were kept in attics and old chests, to be deposited in local record offices, tend to belong to solvent, organized families who have managed to reproduce themselves and bequeath their property. Although some survivals seem to be entirely serendipitous, in general the records of feckless and disorganized householders have rotted away. (When families went to the wall, the contents of houses were often brought under the hammer, and the

---

[26] S. P. Walker, 'How to Secure Your Husband's Esteem: Accounting and Private Patriarchy in the British Middle Class Household During the Nineteenth Century', *Accounting, Organizations and Society*, 23: 516 (1998), 485–516. Beverley Lemire argues that qualitative thought triumphed over older conceptions of household management by the nineteenth century. See B. Lemire, *The Business of Everyday Life: Gender, Practice and Social Politics in England, c.1600–1900* (Manchester, 2005), ch. 6.

[27] J. Pahl, *Money and Marriage* (London, 1989), 67.

papers to the bonfire, although some account books of the utterly insolvent can be sampled in the Chancery files at the National Archive in Kew.[28])

Household account books were not designed to answer the questions this essay sets. They are often either too broad or conversely too partial. The model estate account chronicles so much more than consumer spending and personal choices. Typically amongst the gentry, formal account books catalogue income from rents, investments, inheritance and allowances, loans, farm produce, sales. They tabulate outgoings on rents, annuities, allowances, taxes, dues, interest on loans, wages, services (e.g. doctors, tutors), as well as the running expenses of house, farm, stable and estate, travel expenses, pocket money, and cash in hand. However, in practice account books are rarely if ever utterly all-encompassing either in conception or in execution. Many ignored double-entry altogether, and kept separate record of incoming and outgoings.

Even keen accountants may have chosen to capture only one area of their lives in a record book. Two magistrates noted for their professional record-keeping, William Brockman of Kent and William Hunt of Wiltshire, had no one with whom to share the duties of domestic accountant at certain points in their lives. Yet as a bachelor in the 1690s and a widower in the 1730s, Brockman and Hunt often recorded only livestock and produce sold, wages paid, and large accounts settled. Young Brockman's accounts were roughly jotted into his old Latin exercise book.[29] Sir Charles Chesterfield, who recommended that the young gentleman about town 'keep an account in a book', rose above petty detail: 'I do not mean that you should keep an account of the shillings and half-crowns which you may spend in chair-hire, operas, etc.: they are unworthy of the time, and of the ink that they would consume; leave such minutia to dull, penny-wise fellows . . .'[30] Mathematical knowledge was uneven. Consumers with good memories and a flair for financial improvisation may have kept only the scantiest written accounts in the first place. Defoe complained about merchants who believed they could carry the whole history and future of their businesses in their heads.[31] Written accounting was not for everyone.

Yet on the rare occasions where manuscript accounts exist for both husbands and wives, the historian is offered a unique opportunity to examine

[28] National Archive, Chancery masters.

[29] Wiltshire Record Office, 1553/69, Personal Account book of William Hunt; British Library, Add. Ms 45213, William Brockman, Accompts 1696–1742.

[30] *Lord Chesterfield's Letters to His Son* (1774; Oxford, 1992), 132–3.

[31] P. Cline Cohen, 'Reckoning With Commerce: Numeracy in Eighteenth-Century America', in Brewer and Porter (eds.), *Consumption and the World of Goods*, 320–34; D. Defoe, *The Complete English Tradesman in Familiar Letters, Directing him in all the Several Parts and Progressions of Trade* (London, 1727), vol. 1, Supplement (separately paginated), 31.

the interrelationship of men and women's consumer responsibilities, services, and pleasures. Three unusual sets of eighteenth-century single-entry gentry accounts throw light on the distribution of consumer responsibility between women and men: those of the Cottons of Cambridgeshire, the Grimes of Warwickshire, and the Ardernes of Cheshire. None of them provide perfectly symmetrical his and hers account books, but each set reveals a distinctive form of accounting with, nevertheless, shared assumptions about male and female territories.

The Cottons of Madingley Hall, Cambridge, ran an accounting system which allowed female domestic management within a framework of male superintendence and surveillance. The Cottons were rich greater gentry, baronets, but not nobles, capable of spending a huge £4,153 in a single year.[32] Sir John Hinde Cotton was MP for Cambridge in 1765 and 1771. He married Anne Parsons in 1745, spending a princely £1,209 on the wedding. Miss Parsons was the daughter of an alderman, twice lord mayor of London. Anne Cotton's personal account books have not survived, but details from them were transferred into the master's book roughly every other month. This essay analyses the account books in detail for 1761, sixteen years into the marriage.[33] Seven times a year, Mrs Cotton cast up the house accounts, and Sir John recorded the transaction each time with a particular form of words: 'accounted with my wife viz. house book for may 30th to July 22nd £18.4.6.' Anne Cotton also ran another house book when they were in London.

In addition to the house-book payments, Anne Cotton paid the annual wages of ten female servants, her daughter's allowance, the salaries of the French master, the dancing master, and the writing master, though Mr Cotton paid his son's board at Westminster School. Mrs Cotton also ran the accounts with the butcher, confectioner, tallow chandler, and candle supplier, the brazier, turner, china man, and the glass man. She was the queen of the textiles; dealing with the mantua-maker, mercer, five different milliners, three haberdashers, two linen drapers, the coat woman, hosier, and a weaver, but she had no dealings whatsoever with the tailor. Mrs Cotton's spending in 1761 amounted to £933, 22 percent of expenditure recorded in her husband's account book.

---

[32] Sir John Hinde Cotton, a prominent Tory politician who repeatedly sat for the county and borough and was one of the last active English Jacobites, died in 1752. His son and namesake, John Hinde Cotton, left the accounts this study is based on. In 1791 financial difficulties forced him to transfer control of his lands to his eldest surviving son Charles, from 1799 an admiral and knighted, who died in 1812.

[33] Cambridgeshire Record Office, Hinde Cotton collection, 588/DR/A39, Account book of Sir John Hinde Cotton 1760–1767.

Account books aim to record the financial life of a household, and therefore have a much broader remit than shopping. Sir John Hinde Cotton was responsible for paying out on rents, annuities, taxes, tithes, fees, interests on loans, wages, estate supplies, and so on. Nevertheless, Sir John was also a beau. His bills to his tailor amount to a splendid £435 in 1761. Mr Cotton also liked special provisions. His one-off purchases included oranges and lemons, venison and snipe, brawn and sturgeon, rabbits, oysters, cheese, and a half hog of madeira. But his biggest single outlay was to the wine merchant, known chummily as 'Charlie'; his bill for 1759 to 1760 was a cheerful £154. Unique to himself were accounts with the peruke-maker, 'Pretorias', the hatter, the sword cutler, the saddler, horse dealers, and the coachmaker. Strikingly, Cotton's mandate allows personal consumer indulgence on the stable, travel, alcohol, luxury foodstuffs, newspapers, tailoring, and masculine accoutrements. Yet Cotton's overall surveillance accommodates his wife's management of key areas—particularly household provisioning, linens, the equipping of children, and the education of daughters.

My second case-study suggests a much more restricted female financial mandate. The most formal, structured, legible, and patriarchal accounting system I have come across so far is that set out in the Grimes account book.[34] The Grimes of Coton House, Warwickshire, were as rich as the Cottons, with income of £4,851 in 1781, £4,397 in 1782, and £3,086 in 1783. The household accounts of Abraham Grimes, Esq., 1781–8, are internally divided by category: the annual account, the house, stable, rent and taxes, miscellaneous, the debtor account, and finally, in a cordoned-off category of their own, Mrs Grimes and the children's account. It is not clear who was running the house account on a daily basis (Abraham's house account often gives summary totals, not a breakdown on foodstuffs, which suggests that another detailed house book was in operation), but if it was Mrs Grimes, then her husband was not giving her written credit for the effort. Of course, expenditure on children was always at the core of any matron's purchasing, but here mother and children are fused in a single category, as if both are dependants. Mrs Grimes's dispensation is reduced to its narrowest possible definition. The spending in this category of 'Mrs Grimes & children', or more often just 'Mrs Grimes &C' amounts to a relatively meagre £307 in 1781, £352 in 1782, and £242 in 1783, respectively 6, 8, and 9 percent of total recorded family expenditure in those years.

---

[34] Household Accounts of Abraham Grimes, Esq. of Coton House, Warwickshire, 1781–1788, Private Collection. I would like to thank Andrea Wulf for bringing this document to my attention.

However, this accounting system looks more formal and orderly than it actually is. The miscellaneous category is huge; miscellaneous spending in 1781 is £3,383—71 percent of the whole. Buried in this category are some of the consumer services Mrs Grimes performed for her husband. For instance, on 24 November 1782 Abraham records: 'Pd by Mrs. G for cambrick & c for self £2 2 0.' A husband's shirts again.[35] On her own account, Mrs Grimes dealt with three different linen drapers, a woollen draper, the glover, the mercer, the hosier, the shoemaker, the mantua-maker, the haberdasher, the lace man, the staymaker, the breechmaker, two milliners, a jeweller, a bookseller, and a man she unattractively calls a 'Mr. Jew-tailor' for a coat for herself and the children. She also paid the children's writing master, music mistress, dancing master, and later their schooling. Mrs Grimes is *credited* with a very limited terrain of consumer management—only that which pertains directly to herself and her children. Nevertheless, the Grimes household operates on a similar accounting system to the Cottons, that of discrete female accounting within a framework of masculine oversight, but interpreted much less advantageously to the wife. In fact, the account book constructs her more like an eldest daughter than a wife and mistress of the household.

The final case-study, that of the Ardernes of Cheshire, offers yet another financial model. John and Sarah Arderne were a gentry couple established at Harden Hall, near Stockport in Cheshire. Eleven notebooks document Sarah Arderne's personal and household expenditure over an eleven-year period between 1741 and 1752.[36] Unfortunately, her husband's account books do not survive, although the bills have been kept, so it is possible to identify the gaps in Sarah's own accounting, in order to ascertain some of the major areas which lay outside her jurisdiction.

---

[35] In December 1788 Mrs Grimes paid for £5-worth of shirt fabric for her husband, cambrick for ruffles, and muslin for nine neckcloths. Other rare references to Mrs Grimes's own consumption in the miscellaneous account include 'June 10 1783 By a black silk gown Mn Munier by Mrs G £3-5-0'; 29 Nov. 1783, 'By Mrs G for me £3-17-9'; 3 June 1784, 'Paid by Mrs G for me £1-10-6'; 27 November 1788, 'By paid by Mrs. G for Ho furniture £1-1-11 1/2'. As in Dec 1788, when Mr. G accounts for a list of items 'Pd by Mrs. G at sundry times. By Povers child £1-1-0. By a map of Yorkshire £1-4-0. By washing bills in Yorkshire £1-16-5 1/2. By les annales de la Porte £0-9-0. By White Callicoe for Drawing rm curtains £0 16-11 1/2. By a bottle fo blue 1/1/2 & thread 0.1/8 £0-2-9. By a piece of cloth for shirts/self/£5-0-0. By cambrick for ruffles £1-7-5. By muslin for nine neckcloths £2-10-0. By a purse £0-4-0. By toys for children at York £1-13-4. By netting box & c for Madlle de la L £1-7-6.'

[36] Cheshire County Record Office, DAR/B/14, Household and personal accounts of Sarah, wife of John Arderne of Harden esq., 1741–52.

Sarah Arderne's accounts record only outgoings; there is no record of income. Nevertheless her annual expenditure in 1745—a year I have broken down by category—is a liberal £546, less than the annual spending recorded in Anne Cotton's account for 1756, but more than the annual spending assigned to Mrs Grimes in the early 1780s. The Ardernes came from the north-of-England lesser gentry and were probably less well off than the Cottons and the Grimeses, but they were sufficiently prosperous to maintain a coach and horses. In 1745 the Ardernes were ten years into the marriage. John was a mature 36, but had still not yet come into his inheritance. Sarah was in the thick of child-bearing; she already had three girls and two boys, and would go on to have four more babies. For nine months of this account book she was pregnant.

Had they been a poor family, this would be a low point in the family poverty cycle; and even for a rich family the outgoings are prodigious. The shoe bill for six months in 1745 runs to thirty-two items—and totals £2.14s. 6d., roughly equivalent to the annual wage of a scullery-maid.[37] The expenses of running a large nursery are all apparent. The apothecary's bill to Mr Thornley was an impressive £40. The vouchers reveal that Mr Thornley supplied 570 individual items: from orange flower water, gripe water, purges, and frankincense to 'A large pott of cataplasm for Mrs Arderne's breasts and a linament to dress it with'. With three children, a toddler and two infants, the washing bill alone is £33—equivalent to the yearly wage of ten maids.[38] The account book is a drier ego document than the diary, but its details are still replete with concentrated emotion. The weeks leading up to the birth of Letitia in September were fraught with preparations. On 20 June 1745, for example, Sarah Arderne 'Pd for 14 yds of Diaper against my lying inn'.[39] From the account book, we are reminded that hemming baby linen was a soothing and ritual occupation for the last trimester.

But what of the gender comparison? Mr Arderne's account books are lost, though there are seventy-five bills for the year 1745.[40] We cannot know

---

[37] It was the shoe bill that crucified the Latham family of Lancashire smallholders when their children were young: see John Styles, 'Custom or Consumption? Plebeian Fashion in Eighteenth-Century England', in M. Berg and E. Eger (eds.), *Luxury in the Eighteenth Century: Debates, Desires and Delectable Goods* (London, 2003), 103–15.

[38] The heavy cost of washing when children are very small emerges in an earlier account book of the Cottons recording an era when the children were still in the nursery. The house washing bill for 29 May to 6 June 1751 was '£1-2-0', while the washing bill for the nursery was *four* times the amount: '£4-18-0.'

[39] Diaper is an unbleached linen with a diamond pattern on it, from which we must get the term 'diapers'.

[40] Cheshire County Record Office, DAR/C/20, Vouchers to account, Harden Hall, 1744–5.

whether all the bills survive, but there are enough to identify significant areas of personal and household consumption that lay beyond Mrs Arderne's jurisdiction. So how did Mr and Mrs Arderne manage their finances? Unusually, it appears that much family money flowed through the wife's account book, probably because as an heiress, married to a man who had not yet come into his property, the ready money was quite literally hers. John Arderne had to accept an allowance from both his father and his wife.[41]

Mrs Arderne's single largest outgoing in 1745 was to her husband; she paid him a hefty £169 in cash, in regular instalments. Like the pattern wife of the conduct book, Sarah Arderne passed a dollop of her settlement straight into the hands of her husband. Yet still not the whole. So she remained in a position to give her 'dear lord' spending money, like the £40 she gave him 'for Cheltenham' in June 1745, when she was heavily pregnant, authorizing his spree at the races. She paid some of his bills, and supplied him with all his linens. In April she 'Pd Mary Smith for making ten fine holland shirts for my Dear lord'. She sourced muslin for cravats and India handkerchiefs, and kept all his linens washed and mended. So in all, Mr Arderne's personal needs accounted for an outlay on his wife's part of £195 in that year, 36 percent of her annual expenditure.

Sarah Arderne's largest single category of expenditure in 1745, after her husband, is unsurprisingly the children. £47. 4s. 8d.—9 percent.[42] After that, the next largest amount was £42 on servants' wages, and then a monster £33 on washing. That which she designates as personal consumption ('for self') is very small in relative terms: £12, only 2 percent. She seems to have given herself up to her growing nursery, buying no new gowns, though she did have her christening gown retrimmed. The gown was getting hard use in those years, so she 'Pd Miss Shallcross for 7 yards of Edgin for my christning suit at 7 pr yard', to freshen it up a little. Mrs Arderne seems to have gone hardly anywhere, not even Stockport; though to the limitations of pregnancy must be added the disturbance of the Jacobite rebellion, which deterred many travellers in the north-west that autumn.

So what was Mr Arderne's province as a consumer? The vouchers which bear his name cover payments to the blacksmith, the gunsmith, the saddler, his tailor, a linen draper, the cobbler, the haberdasher, odd-job men, and the

---

[41] Cheshire County Record Office, DAR/I/21, The Booke of Accounts Harden Estate, 1726–1752, records the gifts of money that John Arderne senior gave to his son. Sarah and John Arderne seem to have been living as permanent guests within the household of Mr Arderne senior, for there is no evidence of basic household provisioning, though they did pay their own servants.

[42] Of that, children's clothes, both garments and accessories, amounted to £39.

glover. A huge category of consumption with which Mrs Arderne has no direct engagement is what one might loosely call men's tackle. There are sixty-eight items on saddler William Davenport's five-month bill to John Arderne, including dog collars, stirrups, bridles, halters, saddle straps, a martingale, curry-comb and brush, whipcord, dog whip, cart whip, springs for the landau, as well as payment for the mending of a pillion, saddle, bridles, and other household goods like a trunk and a footstool. The total came to £2. 11s. 3½d. Effectively, he was spending the equivalent of an annual servant's wage on leather. Interestingly, however, in January of 1745, when William Davenport put in a bill for a whopping £13. 13s., cash must have been wanting, as Sarah Arderne covered the cost. Crucially, she did not settle the account herself, but gave her husband the money to pay the bill. Presumably for her to have settled directly would have been profoundly embarrassing: it was for the man of the house to see to the horses, dogs, sport, and vehicles, even if his wife's inheritance oiled the wheels. The only thing Mrs Arderne bought for the horses was medicine; potions for their legs and hooves are included in her huge bill to the apothecary Mr Thornley. But here it seems the feminine responsibility for family health and medicine has overwhelmed the masculine responsibility for the stable. Physic has trumped horses as a category. Despite Mrs Arderne's control and management of much of the family's ready money, it was evidently important that her 'dear lord' appeared to the world as the uncontested master of their financial affairs, not a man who had to resort to his wife for spending-money.

Mr Arderne was happy to have his wife provide his personal linens, but he commissioned his own stylish main garments, paying a dandyish £6. 6s. 0d. for a Dresden-work waistcoat. The tailor, Daniel Downs, made breeches, drawers, and a coat for Mr Arderne, but also made coats and mended waist-coats for the coachman and other male household servants. At first glance, it is surprising that Arderne paid a tailor, John Sudlow, for making the children's coats, and a cobbler for their shoes. It seems that Mrs dealt exclusively with teams of female seamstresses and laundresses, while Mr traded particularly with the male tailor, even in the feminine matter of children's clothes. Who dealt with whom may be governed by conventions of propriety, as well as the convenience of drawing upon a pre-existing relationship between supplier and customer.

So what can the account books tell us about gender, accounting, and goods? Eighteenth-century account books are not a straightforward source for the history of consumer practices and consumer choices. At their baldest they are a list of payments. But they categorize those payments in a variety of ways, and that categorization in all three cases here is powerfully structured by gender. They are a representation of the way the allocation of financial responsibility between husband and wife was conceptualized in these families. The key here is notional responsibility, because the accounts do not necessarily reveal who decided on a purchase, or who eventually made the payment, or even who actually went to a shop. The accounts of the Grimes, Cotton, and Arderne couples reveal different ways of mapping financial responsibility, yet nevertheless broadly consistent assumptions about the appropriate division of labour is apparent in all three cases. A deep-seated notion about what women and men should control emerges. This idea of female responsibility varied from marriage to marriage in what it embraced at its fullest, as we can see from the contrast between Mrs Grimes and Sarah Arderne, but at its most circumscribed the female dispensation still covered personal dress, the clothing and education of children, especially girl children, and the provision of the family's personal linen.

The link between women and everyday textiles is strong and persistent. Of course, a female weakness for fine fabrics, especially silk, was a cliché of eighteenth-century commentary, as was the hypnotic allure of haberdashery. The variety and profusion of lady's linens was also a stock joke. Witness Campbell in the *London Tradesman*, on millinery, 'no Male Trade':

> The milliner is concerned in making and providing the Ladies with Linnen of all sorts, fit for Wearing Apparel, from the Holland smock to the Tippet and Commode; but as we are got into the Lady's Articles, which are so very numerous, the Reader is not to expect that we are to give an exact List of everything belonging to them; let it suffice in general that the Milliner furnishes them with Holland, Cambrick, Lawn, and Lace of all sorts, and makes these Materials into smocks, Aprons, Tippits, Handkerchiefs, Neckaties, Ruffles, Mobs, Caps, Dressed-Heads, with as many *Etceteras* as would reach from *Charing-Cross* to the *Royal Exchange*.[43]

Yet while such commentary emphasizes a woman's fetishistic self-indulgence in linens, in stark contrast, the account books chart a story of emotional responsibility and consumer service, not selfishness, through the ongoing provision of linen garments for others, especially men.

Mr Arderne's personal linen and cotton was Sarah Arderne's concern. It is clear that Mrs Cotton had batches of shirts made up for her husband; while Cotton's aunts kept him in linen and muslin in his bachelorhood ('Pd

[43] R. Campbell, *The London Tradesman* (1747; New York, 1969), 207.

my aunt Polly for linnen, lace &c 89-14-0).[44] Even Mrs Grimes sourced some of the cambrick for her husband's shirts and ruffles, and the muslin for his neckcloths. Making a husband's shirt was widely seen as a fundamental matrimonial duty. Women's plain sewing had an emotional symbolism which carried over even when a mistress did not ply the needle with her own fingers. In gentry families, wives did not expect to make shirts and shifts in bulk themselves.[45] Yet *administering* the production of personal linens, from buying the Holland and sourcing the thread, to employing the neat seamstresses and overseeing the making-up and washing, perhaps personally finishing them, off and labelling them, was one of the key ways that women serviced the needs of their men.

The link between women and men's linen is confirmed by other sources. 'Pray let me know what order your shirts are in?' is a leitmotif of women's letters to bachelor sons.[46] Elizabeth Shackleton, the wife of a Lancashire callimanco merchant, was sorting out her sons' linen shirts well into their twenties, and long after they had left home. Though they scoured London for the *dernier cri* in fashionable waistcoats, they still wrote home to their

---

[44] See Cheshire County Record Office, 588 Dr/A/26, Personal Account book of Sir J H Cotton, 4th Bart, unpaginated. See entries for 1745.

[45] Even conservative writers imagined that ideally ladies would supervise the plain sewing of others, having mastered the mechanics first. As Dr Gregory lectured the elite seamstress, J. Gregory, *A Father's Legacy to His Daughter* (1774), 22: 'the intention of your being taught needle-work, knitting and such like, is not on account of the intrinsic value of all you can do with your hands, which is trifling, but to enable you to judge more perfectly of that kind of work, and to direct the execution of it in others.' See also Lady Sarah Pennington on plain work, in *An Unfortunate Mother's Advice to Her Absent Daughters* (2nd edn., London, 1761), 42: 'All kinds of what is called Plain-work (tho' no very polite Accomplishment) you must be so well versd in, as to be able to cut out make or mend, your own linen: some Fathers, and some Husbands, choose to have their daughters, and their wives thus attired in the Labour of their own hands; and from a mistaken Notion believe this to be the great Criterion of Frugal Oeconomy; where that happens to be the Inclination or Opinion of either, it ought always to be readily complied with; but exclusive of such a Motive I see no other that makes the practical Part at all necessary to any Lady; excepting indeed, such a narrowness of Fortune as admits not conveniently the keeping of an Abigail, to whom such Exercises of the Needle much more properly appertain.'

[46] Lancashire County Record Office (hereafter LRO), DDB, Jane Pedder, Lancaster to son John Pedder, Blackburn, 16 Apr. 1785, 'pray let me know what order your shirts are in and if you want a new set against the summer that I may have them in readiness against your next vacancy. I bought you two pair of silk stockings in London but as I think you can't yet be in want of them they May as well remain here.'

mother requesting eleven new shirts without a blush.[47] Sophie White's case-study of Louisiana also identifies the link between women and this most hard-wearing of fabrics. White finds that while Chevalier Pradel

> commissioned his important purchases, whether of clothing or furnishings, from men in France, he addressed his mundane requests for household linens and underwear to women there. What's more the men charged with his important commissions were all professionals—agents or merchants—while the women tended to be his female relatives . . . he wrote to his brother to ask that his niece negotiate the purchase of the fabric for napkins, tablecloths and sheets, which he expected his daughter to hem on their arrival in New Orleans from France.[48]

One of Lady Sarah Cowper's self-righteous grievances against her tyrannical Hertfordshire husband in 1701 was his refusal to give her the key to the linen cupboard, a symptom of his wider campaign to undermine her due authority as housekeeper.[49] And while linens may sound a mundane province, it is a province that was ever-enlarging in this century, as Mark Overton argues on the basis of inventory data for Kent and Cornwall.[50]

---

[47] Long after Elizabeth Shackleton's sons left home, they continued to avail themselves of her services both managerial and technical. John and Robert Parker wrote from London requesting 11 new shirts without a qualm, while Elizabeth Shackleton was more than happy to oblige her sons. She told Robin in 1774 that she 'wo'd take particular care to have all his shirts done as he directed & desired his acceptance of the making of them'. Her efforts to make recompense with John Parker after a damaging quarrel are suggestive of the wider uses of her skills: 'I am Happy to have [John] here. Mended up slightly some shirts & night Caps, all his things much out of repair. God knows he will find it a great & expensive difficulty to renew them.' LRO, DDB/81/21 (1774), f. 37. On maternal attentions, see DDB/72/306–7 (1777), E. Shackleton, Alkincoats, to J. and R. Parker, London. For filial requests, albeit indirect, see DDB/72/328 (7 June 1774), J. Parker, London, to T. Parker, Alkincoats. The enthusiastic consumption of waistcoats is a major theme of DDB/72/322, 328 and 331 (1773–7), J. Parker, London, to T. Parker, Alkincoats.

[48] White, 'This Gown', 100.

[49] Anne Kugler, *Errant Plagiary: The Life and Writing of Lady Sarah Cowper, 1644–1720* (Stanford, 2002), 55

[50] M. Overton with J. Whittle, D. Dean, and A. Hann, *Production and Consumption in English Households 1600–1750* (London, 2004). I am indebted to Professor Overton for showing me his findings before publication.

But if women were responsible for linen and cotton, it seems men had most oversight of wool, a point made in jocular fashion by the *London Tradesman* when distinguishing between the Mercer and the Woollen draper: 'they are as like one another as two eggs, only the Woollen draper deals chiefly with the Men, and is the graver Animal of the two, and the Mercer trafficks most with the Ladies, and has a small Dash of their Effeminacy in his Constitution.'[51] Of course, gentleman did not live by broadcloth alone, and there were occasions when they had to strut in silk and velvet (in fact men probably wore more velvet than women), but for this they resorted to the tailor. Men almost invariably ran a separate account with the tailor, who was always a man. The relationship between a gentleman and the trader who had his measurements may already have been a distinctive one. In the seventeenth century tailors made men's *and* women's clothes, but the rise of the mantua-maker led to a bifurcation of the trade by the sex of the customer.[52] A good tailor, according to *The London Tradesman* again, was able 'not only to cut for the Handsome and Well-shaped, but to bestow a good Shape where Nature has not designed it . . .'.[53] A tailor could achieve a position of considerable intimacy and trust. Certainly, all research on nineteenth- and twentieth-century tailors suggests the length the trade went to in making the shop a homosocial sanctum for gentlemanly customers, in discouraging female intervention, and fostering a clubby, confidential relationship between male consumer and male supplier.[54] The raw consumerism of male clothes-shopping was hereby cloaked in a mantle of discretion and service, protecting the dignity of the male consumer, and maintaining the lowered profile of masculine materialism. For all the caricatures of male consumers flirting pleasantly with pretty shopgirls, men may, in fact, have found it far more congenial to deal with other men. Indeed, the hypermasculine decor of successful men's shops (from dark wood panelling to suspended biplanes) and the provision of men's side entrances to department stores in the twentieth century do

---

[51] Campbell, *The London Tradesman*, 197.

[52] Ibid., 227. The mantua-maker 'must be a sister to the Tailor and like him, must be a perfect Connoisseur of Dress and fashion'. She was responsible for making 'Night-Gowns, Mantuas, and Petticoats, Rob de Chambres etc. For the Ladies'. In the seventeenth century the seamstress was consigned to making linen underwear and accessories.

[53] Ibid., 192.

[54] C. Breward, *The Hidden Consumer: Masculinities, Fashion and City Life, 1860–1914* (Manchester, 1999), 106–7, 162–5; C. Horwood, *Keeping Up Appearances: Fashion and Class Between the Wars* (Stroud, 2005), 77–82.

suggest a certain reluctance on the part of the average male consumer to run the gauntlet of femininity.[55]

Nevertheless, we know that eighteenth-century tailors continued to perform occasional services for women, often making a lady's riding habit or travelling dress which echoed the lines of men's coats. Anne Lister, who wore almost nothing but masculinized riding habits, had habitual dealings with her Halifax tailor, but perhaps the mannish lesbian romantic is the exception that proves the rule. Some milliners specialized in riding habits and masquerade dress for ladies, while 'coat-women' appear in directories and account books.[56] Mrs Grimes resorted to a 'Mr. Jew-tailor' for a coat for herself and the children, but her scorn suggests he was a less prestigious tradesman than her husband's regular tailor. Mr Arderne accounted with the tailor to make his children's coats, despite the assumption that clothing the children was a female concern. It was intercourse between a gentleman and his tailor which was customary.

A conspicuous object of male consumer desire, indeed *the* most flamboyant masculine accoutrement, was the coach. All three families studied here maintained one. The vehicle was always ultra-expensive in itself, but the running of it demanded coachmen, postillions, horses, stables, feed, farriers, and so on, and could be ruinous. The full Monty ate up so much capital that in modern terms the coach's equivalent would be less the proverbial sports car than a helicopter. Abraham Grimes's stable account cost him £418 in 1781. Over £80 of this he laid out to the coachmaker, over £213 on new horses, and the rest on coach tax, feed, the farrier, and the saddler. Which brings us to a major area of *repetitive* male shopping—tackle. Of course, one might guess that tackle for horses, dogs, sport, and vehicles would be a significant male interest, but what is truly surprising is just how infinitely

[55] B. Lancaster, *The Department Store: A Social History* (1995). Similarly, Catherine Horwood, finds of shopping between the wars in 'Keeping Up Appearances', 81–2: '. . . general department stores were not as successful in luring men as women. Their percentage of total sales nearly doubled during the interwar period but were still only 6.6 per cent of the total market by 1939. Men, it was believed, did not enjoy such a frivolous occupation as shopping and even today one will invariably find the menswear departments of larger stores on the ground floor safely surrounded by exits for a quick getaway.'

[56] A. Buck, *Dress in Eighteenth-Century England* (London, 1979), 52. The riding habit was a petticoat, jacket and waistcoat, or waistcoat fronts attached to a jacket, following the lines of men's coats until the 1780s, of camblet (a closely woven worsted sometimes mixed with silk), and later broadcloth. On female producers of riding habits and tailored clothes, see Campbell, *Tradesman*, 207.

varied this equipment could be, and how recurrent a man's visits to the saddler. In fact, one can read John Arderne's bill from the saddler as a summary of many hours spent fingering an astounding array of whips, combs, collars, and bits of horses' tackle; so many etceteras, so oddly named, from norzel and sirsingle, to rowlers and cruppers. The month of September alone saw the purchase or mending of twenty-nine items, on seven different occasions. It seems that John Arderne comforted himself in an utterly masculine, dark brown territory of goods, while his wife laboured away to produce his sixth child.[57] If women adored the infinite variety of the haberdashery counter, then the multifariousness of horse furniture was probably equally magnetic for men. In fact, it was even known in some trade directories as horse millinery.[58] Yet men handling a plethora of leather and buckles were never satirized by critics or captured by cartoonists. Gentlemen were lucky that their fetishism could be presented to the world as an altogether practical concern with transportation.

Expensive household refurbishment also seems dominated, if not determined, by men. In two of the three accounts major redecoration is itemized, and in both cases it is listed under the male account. Abraham Grimes and John Hinde Cotton both employed an upholder on account. Whether gentleman and upholder consulted or perhaps even responded to the mistress's taste is not recorded for posterity,[59] although misogynistic eighteenth-century commentators like Lord Torrington were apt to identify certain kinds of decorative scheme as evidence of female agency: 'The parlour was (ill)

---

[57] The month of September alone sees the purchase of 'one best hunting bridle, one new collar & flap lettered for dog, a backband & links, norzels & straps, mussil & aeany, one collar & two rains, one crupper, one best bridle, one headstall for a martingale, new penneling a saddle, leather & making saddle cloth, mending sirginle & saddle, One curry comb, one strong night collar, two illicit leathers to a martingale, one strap to a rowler, one new 4 strap rowler, three straps to a rowler, mending a rowler, one strap to Cupples & mending a girth, one new pad for behind a sale lined.'

[58] *A General Description of All Trades* (1747), 119, 'HORSE-MILLINERS ARE a sort of Ironmongers, who chiefly deal in all sorts of Tackling for the Sadlers and Collar-makers Use.'

[59] An upholder was someone like Thomas Chippendale who provided an all-inclusive interior decoration and furnishing service—a professional with an even broader remit than an interior designer and decorator today. The influence they had on taste is open to interpretation, and needs further research. *A General Description of All Trades*, 214, described them thus: 'UPHOLDERS MOST frequently called Upholsterers, who are the absolute necessary Tradesmen for decently or sumptuously furnishing an House, and a large branch of Business it is, the working Part of which is not hard, but clean and genteel; (and if it were not so, what would the nice ladies do with them?)'

furnish'd in the modern taste, with French chairs, festoon'd curtains, and puffed bell ropes; this and his keeping in bed informed me that the gentleman was not master of his own house.'[60] Yet in the account books studied here, purchases of decorative household goods allocated to the wife's account are restricted to a handful of smaller items, like the two china dogs and the pair of china figures Mrs Cotton bought in 1756, probably either Meissen or, if English, Bow or Chelsea, and the black-and-gold teapot, probably Staffordshire, that Mrs Arderne bought in 1745. Interestingly, these are exactly the kind of new, small decorative wares that manufacturers and moralists alike regarded as 'feminine'.

Poor Mrs Grimes, however, got to buy very little of this kind of thing on her own account, perhaps because her husband was particularly controlling, but probably because of his own personal interest in consumption. Abraham Grimes seems to have been obsessed with the gadgets and novelties of the 1780s. Unusually, he bought a Bramah water closet (patented in 1778) and Argand lamps (patented in 1784), as well as a regulator stove, an array of Wedgwood earthenware, and plated silver candlesticks and tea urns. It is perhaps significant that Grimes, the most adventurous individual consumer in the three account books, was the one who accorded his wife the least financial room for manoeuvre. Men, like women, varied in their willingness and desire to engage with the new world of goods, as eighteenth-century inventory data on the qualitatively different consumerism of yeomen, craftsmen, professionals, and merchants makes clear.[61]

This essay has wrestled with the interrelationship of men and women's consumer responsibilities and consumer pleasures, emphasizing where men's hands were freed, and women's were tied. None of this is to suggest that the mistresses studied here were materially deprived. Rather, their consumption should be seen as an element in a bigger system, locked in relationship with the consumption of their husbands and households. Married gentlemen were able to rise above daily dealings with the grocer and the butcher only because their wives handled these tedious accounts for them. The explicit contract recorded in 1758 by Mary Delany, then wife of the dean of Down in Ireland, is suggestive of a division of labour recognized in most propertied households. 'The Dean has now settled my allowance for housekeeping at six hundred a-year, which I receive quarterly, and out of

---

[60] J. Beresford (ed.), *The Torrington Diaries, containing the Tours through England and Wales of the Hon John Byng* (London, 1934), i. 24.

[61] L. Weatherill, *Consumer Behaviour and Material Culture in Britain, 1660–1760* (London, 1988).

that pay everything but the men's wages, the liveries, the stables, wine cellar and garden, furniture and all repairs.'[62] Wives were unlikely to trespass on the masculine preserves of horse furniture and port.

Geographical mobility is a factor which contoured male and female engagement with the world of goods. Gentlemen were inevitably far more mobile than their wives. The nursery years were particularly immobilizing for young matrons. Meanwhile, gentlemen characteristically led peripatetic lives as sportsmen and local administrators, easily combining a swift survey of the shops in a county town with a session on the local bench or a jaunt at the races. Of course, much could be acquired from a distance. This was an era when a high percentage of provisioning was done by order, and an array of goods could be commissioned by letter. Many women were adept at describing the design, pattern, and ornament of luxury goods (particularly china, fabric, and dresses) in words. However, it took a seasoned eye to select the prettiest lawn, and judge the newest pattern, and one had to visit the showroom in person to discover the chance curiosity or unexpected novelty sitting on the counter. Women's irritation with the inept choices of proxy consumers speaks to the frustrations of distance.[63] Husbands often acted *faute de mieux* as their wives' consumer agents, and so again the account books must underestimate the extent of women's procurement.

His and hers accounts tell a distinctive story. They offer a particular construction of financial allocation within households. It is striking that the precise allocation of financial responsibility varies in all three instances studied here. We should not find this too surprising; modern sociology on methods of money management within marriages reveals that today, despite potentially equal access to banking and credit, and public professions of total equality, there exist four major systems of managing household finances, each with different implications for power and personal

---

[62] Lady Llanover (ed.), *The Autobiography and Correspondence of Mary Granville, Mrs Delany* (London, 1861), iii. 530.

[63] R. K. Marshall, 'Costume and Conscience in Seventeenth-Century Scotland', *Costume*, 6 (1972), 32–5: From the 1670s the duke of Hamilton went to London once a year taking his wife's measurements with him and a list of her orders. In 1689 he failed even to identify the garment she wanted: 'your "sallantine" I nether [*sic*] know what it is you mean by it, nor can I find anybody that knowes what it is, so explaine yourself by the next.' On another occasion, the duchess told her husband to go to a London tailor called Mr Renne to make her a black gown and mantua and a petticoat of 'verie grave cullers'. Imagine her horror, when the goods finally arrived, at discovering 'a scarlet satin petticoat with silver and gold lace on it, a coloured flowered silk gown, and a flowered gown trimmed all over with lace'.

spending.[64] Yet, despite the variation from family to family, the eighteenth-century account books expose deeply held and consistent categorizations of material responsibility, propriety, and expertise. Greater recourse to shopping did not undermine women's material obligations. Women had long been responsible for children's material needs, among which clothing loomed large. It would be a mistake to presume that the emotional investment diminished as the balance shifted away from domestic to retail provisioning. Recent anthropology reveals the extent to which modern wives and mothers see shopping for the family as a practical exercise in caring.[65] Nor should we underestimate the expertise required by eighteenth-century shoppers as the range and quality of products like linens diversified.[66]

Georgian retailers who targeted the male consumer as a desirous individual, and not just as the representative of his household, were plentiful. Wigmakers, barbers, hatmakers, watch-makers, tailors, tobacconists, stationers, wine merchants, saddlers, sword cutlers, horse dealers, and coachmakers, among many others, prospered by attending to the personal needs of both bachelors and patriarchs. Models of Scottish Highland soldiers standing to attention outside tobacconists and of naval officers guarding scientific-instrument shops proclaimed the unambiguous manliness of the treasures within.[67] Men's ornaments and accoutrements were as varied as women's. 'A fool cannot withstand the charms of a toy-shop . . .', Lord Chesterfield warned his son, 'snuff boxes, watches, heads of canes, etc are his destruction.'[68] It is a cruel irony that the consumer self-indulgences of eighteenth-century married men so often went unnoticed: the dandy and the fop singled out in satire are almost always young bachelors. Yet a wife's responsibility for basic provisioning exposed her to accusations of vanity, avarice, extravagance, materialism, and even fetishism. It was the big spender

---

[64] The four most common systems are female-management of the couple's entire wage, female management of a housekeeping allowance, joint-pooling and joint management, and independent management arrangements: Pahl, *Money and Marriage, passim*. See also C. Vogler, 'Labour Market Change and Patterns of Financial Allocation within Households', ESRC, working paper, 12.

[65] Miller, *A Theory of Shopping, passim*.

[66] For the decline of linen manufacturing in gentry households, see John Styles, 'Clothing the North: The Supply of Non-Elite Clothing in the Eighteenth-Century North of England', *Textile History*, 25 (1994), 139–66. On the proliferation of linens, see M. Spufford, *The Great Reclothing of Rural England: Petty Chapmen and their Wares* (London 1995).

[67] Claire Walsh, 'Shops, Shopping, and the Art of Decision Making', forthcoming.

[68] *Lord Chesterfield's Letters to His Son*, 132.

Sir John Hinde Cotton who traded with 'Charlie' the wine merchant and 'Pretorias' the peruke-maker, while his wife made him dutiful presents of full sets of Holland shirts. Women's consumer services remained deeply indebted to an older economy of virtuous, productive housewifery, despite the decline of manufacturing within the household, the proliferation of goods available for purchase, and the multiplication of shops.

Gender and Welfare in Modern Europe

Jane Lewis

Modern states have always constructed social provision around the twin poles of paid work and welfare, a system that largely distinguished it from needs-based and arguably universal, but punitively deterrent poor-law systems. Governments have always been concerned about the conditions for providing welfare—policy analysts use the language of entitlements while governments are really concerned with conditions of receipt of cash or services. There has been a longstanding firm conviction too that wages are the best form of welfare. In the United Kingdom almost a hundred years ago the Labour Party fought for a legislative proposal called the Right to Work Bill more fiercely than it did for pensions, while it was not at all keen on the new idea of social insurance because trades unions feared state intrusion into the territory of mutuality. What was at stake of course was the fight for the old-style labour contract, securing regular, full-time work for men, to which social insurance was successfully joined in a range of Western countries between the 1890s and the 1930s, and which is now under profound review.[1]

At the heart of the modern welfare state was the settlement between capital and labour. Feminist critique[2] and recent comparative work on social provision has shown how equally important is the settlement between men and women and the changing nature of family and gender relations.[3] Welfare

---

[1] A. Supiot, *Beyond Employment* (Oxford, 2001).

[2] For example, J. Lewis, 'Gender and the Development of Welfare Regimes', *Journal of European Social Policy*, 3 (1992), 159–73; A. Orloff, 'Gender and the Social Rights of Citizenship. State Policies and Gender Relations in Comparative Research', *American Sociological Review*, 58 (1993), 303–28.

[3] C. Crouch, *Social Change in Western Europe* (Oxford, 1999); G. Esping-Andersen, *Social Foundations of Post-Industrial Economies* (Oxford, 1999); G. Esping-Andersen *et al.*, *Why We Need a New Welfare State* (Oxford, 2002); E. Huber and J. Stephens, *Development and Crisis of the Welfare State: Parties and Policies in Global Markets* (Chicago, 2000); W. Korpi, 'Faces of Inequality: Gender, Class, and Patterns of Inequalities in Different Types of Welfare States', *Social Politics*, 7 (2000–2), 127–91.

states have deployed models of individual 'survival' based on relatively firm assumptions about family organization and gender relations. Every welfare system has made assumptions about what 'the family' looks like and how earning and caring are organized. But both the assumptions and the social reality are now in the process of transformation.

The old labour contract was designed first and foremost for the regularly employed male breadwinner, with provision made alongside it for women. The gender settlement meant that those marginal to the labour market got cash cover through dependants' benefits. Alain Supiot has described the labour/capital settlement in terms of security traded for dependence. A similar set of arrangements can be said to have marked the gender settlement. The male-breadwinner family model was based on a set of assumptions about male and female contributions at the household level, with men primarily earning and women caring for the young and old. The male-breadwinner model built into the post-war settlement assumed regular and full male employment *and* stable families, in which women would be provided for largely through their husbands' earnings and their husbands' social contributions.

However, a pure male-breadwinner model never existed in reality, since women always engaged in the labour market. Following the Second World War in many Western countries, people of the middling sort in the United Kingdom (as in United States in the late nineteenth century), together with large tracts of the middle and respectable working classes, lived lives which to a large extent reflected this model. In the second half of the twentieth century increased numbers of women entered the labour market. Indeed, this has become one point of convergence between EU member states. Family change, which has resulted in family breakdown, more fluidity in intimate relationships, and a large increase in single-person households, has also contributed to the erosion of the male-breadwinner model at the behavioural level. As a result, strong arguments have been made that change in family and labour markets may be characterized in terms of increasing 'individualization,'[4] with the erosion of traditional family bonds (manifested in the last quarter of the twentieth century in low fertility, higher rates of divorce, extramarital births, lone parenthood, and increasing numbers of single-person households) and more economic independence among women. In part the existence of 'welfare states' and social provision has permitted more risk-taking in individual relationships, for example in the case of women with dependent children leaving unsatisfactory marriages. However, welfare-state restructuring in the last decade or so seems in large measure to have been *premised* upon the idea of

[4] See, for example, E. Beck-Gernsheim, *Reinventing the Family* (Cambridge, 2002).

increasing individual autonomy, and much greater emphasis has been placed on the responsibility of all adults, both men and women, to enter the labour market. This is highly problematic because gender inequality in respect of both employment and the unpaid work of care remains so marked.

This chapter first reviews the changing nature of the relationship between families, labour markets, and social provision before outlining, in broad-brush fashion, the different models that exist for reconciling work and family in modern Western states. It then returns to the issues raised by trends in welfare-state restructuring at the beginning of the twenty-first century.

Gender and the Changing Relationships Between Families, Labour Markets, and Welfare States

Until the end of the 1950s the ideal of a male-breadwinner model family was widely accepted by policymakers and by men and women more generally. Men endorsed it because it provided a rationale for wage bargaining on the basis of a 'family wage'; women, for whom pregnancy was frequent and household labour hard, accepted it because they depended on their husbands' incomes and allowances. In such circumstances adding on paid work was often regarded more as a misfortune than an opportunity.[5] The male-breadwinner model persisted in the post-war period to very different degrees in different countries.[6] In Germany, the Netherlands, and Ireland it has remained relatively strong, whereas in the Nordic countries it has been almost completely eroded. In North America women's employment has reached levels comparable to the Nordic countries, and the lifelong housewife has become rare. However, unlike in Nordic countries, the strength of conservative cultural politics, particularly in the United States, continue to make 'wife and motherhood' a powerful symbol. The traditional male-breadwinner model assumed a clear division between the public and private spheres of responsibility of men and of women, based on a family wage and a gendered separation of responsibility for paid work and unpaid care.

Family change has been both rapid and dramatic in the last quarter of the twentieth century, with a much larger range of possibilities in intimate relationships. Beck Gernsheim has argued that the family has become an 'elective relationship' rather than 'a community of need'.[7] However, the

[5] J. Lewis, 'The Working-Class Wife and Mother and State Intervention, 1870–1918', in J. Lewis (ed.), *Labour and Love: Women's Experience of Home and Family 1850–1940* (Oxford, 1986).

[6] Lewis, 'Gender and the Development of Welfare Regimes'.

[7] E. Beck-Gernsheim, 'On the Way to a Post-Familial Family: From a Community of Need to Elective Affinities', *Theory, Culture and Society*, 15 (1999), 53–70.

gendered pattern of responsibilities for the care of young and old dependants in the family has showed much less change, with the gendered division of labour in care work remaining intact in all western countries. Women curtail their labour-market activities most often by working part-time to accommodate care, but also by refusing promotion opportunities that may entail longer hours and more responsibility. Most women, but few men, face challenges in reconciling paid and unpaid work.[8] Time-use studies show that while women have added paid work to unpaid work, with comparatively little reduction in unpaid working hours, men have made rather small changes in the balance of paid and unpaid work.[9] Even in the Nordic countries, which have the highest levels of formal participation in the labour market, many mothers of young children who remain in the labour force are on parental leave; men very rarely take up their full entitlement to such leave, especially if they are working in the private sector.[10] To some extent the care of young children and older people has been 'defamilialized' and shifted to formal institutions outside the family, but women's care work remains critical to the well-being of families and individuals. Indeed it is very difficult to measure the extent of formal (institutional) as opposed to informal (familial) care work. In the late 1970s Michael Anderson showed that there was little evidence to support the idea that the proportion of elderly people in institutions had increased over the twentieth century.[11] Evidence regarding welfare-state change at the end of the twentieth century, and in particular processes of marketization, decentralization, and fragmentation, suggests that more rather than less informal care is needed in many countries (for example, to get the young child from the daycare centre to the childminder).[12]

---

[8] Penny Becker and Phyllis Moen, 'Scaling Back: Dual-earner Couples' Work-Family Strategies', *Journal of Marriage and the Family*, 61 (1999), 995–1007; J. Rubery *et al.*, 'National Working-Time Regimes and Equal Opportunities', *Feminist Economics*, 4 (1998-1), 71–101; Gillian Pascall and Jane Lewis, 'Emerging Gender Regimes and Policies for Gender Equality in a Wider Europe', *Journal of Social Policy*, 33 (2004–3), 373–94.

[9] J. Gershuny, *Changing Times* (Oxford, 2000).

[10] P. Moss and F. Deven, *Parental Leave: Progress or Pitfall? Research and Policy Issues in Europe* (Brussels: NIDI/CBGS Publications, 1999); U. Bjornberg, 'Ideology and Choice Between Work and Care: Swedish Family Policy for Working Parents', *Critical Social Policy*, 22 (2002–1), 35–52

[11] Michael Anderson, 'The Impact on the Family Relationships of the Elderly of Changes Since Victorian Times on Government Income Maintenance Provision', in E. Shanas and M. B. Sussman (eds.), *Family, Bureaucracy and the Elderly* (Durham, NC, 1977).

[12] Jane Lewis (ed.), *Gender, Social Care and Welfare State Restructuring in Europe* (Aldershot, 1998).

Thus the gender division of paid and unpaid work has not disappeared, but has rather changed, as women, particularly mothers, go into the paid labour force and stay on. There is a good case to be made that gender differentiation is increasingly based on time.[13] In Western European countries in particular, couple families commonly participate in the labour market, with women working part-time and men full-time. This gendered distinction has in large measure replaced the older division between women as full-time carers and men as full-time earners. It is increasingly expected that women will work, although there is less consensus as to the desirability of mothers' employment. There are debates among policymakers and academics as to whether the mothers of young children should work part-time or full-time, and whether they should have access to childcare services that enable them to work or to leaves that enable them to exit the workforce to care. The social-science literature on the effects of mothers' employment on children has swung between negative and positive assessments over the past fifty years.[14] As the male-breadwinner model family has been eroded and the proportion of lone-mother families has increased, so also more attention on the part of academics and, in some countries, policymakers has turned to the issue of fathers' 'involvement' with their children. It is now more likely to be expected that fathers will be involved with their children in the sense of nurture and care, as well as earning; again, there is debate about the extent to which mothers' and fathers' roles should converge, and if they should, what is the role of social policy in helping men to take up care.[15]

Despite common trends, there are large differences among countries in terms of the overall rate of women's participation, patterns of participation over the life course, and part-time versus full-time employment. While in virtually all countries the trend since the Second World War has been for women's labour-market participation to rise and for men's to fall, women's employment rates in Southern Europe (except Portugal), but also in the Netherlands, are still very low compared to any English-speaking or Scandinavian country. The differences become more complicated still when

---

[13] Ellen Mutari and Deborah Figart, 'Europe at a Crossroads: Harmonization, Liberalization, and the Gender of Work Time', *Social Politics*, 8 (2001), 36–64; O. Hufton and Y. Kravaritou (eds.), *Gender and the Use of Time* (London, 1999).

[14] For example, H. Bowlby, *Maternal Care and Mental Health* (Geneva: World Health Organization, 1951); J. Belsky and J. Casidy, 'Attachment: Theory and Evidence', in M. Rutter and D. Hay (eds.), *Development Through Life: A Handboook for Clinicians* (Oxford, 1994); P. Gregg and E. Washbrook, *The Effects of Early Maternal Employment on Child Development in the UK* (London: CMPO Working Paper, 2003).

[15] B. Hobson, *Making Men into Fathers* (Cambridge, 2002).

the nature of women's labour-market participation is examined more closely. A large proportion of European women, especially in the United Kingdom, the Netherlands, and Germany work part-time, as is the case in Australia and New Zealand. In addition, women in these countries are likely to work relatively short part-time hours. In the Scandinavian countries, however, they are likely to be working 'long' (30+ hours) part-time. Female labour-market participation in the United States and Canada is not only high, but also consists mainly of full-time work. In Southern Europe, while fewer women are in the labour market overall, those who are employed tend to work full-time. In Eastern Europe women's employment rates are now in the medium range, after having been as high or higher than in Scandinavia prior to 1989. There, women are facing new and explicit forms of discrimination and higher rates of unemployment than are men, while supports for employed mothers are cut back; whether this will remain the case as these countries complete their economic transitions is still an open question. Although many women want to remain employed, some political forces are pressing for a return to 'traditional' gender roles, that is, women's housewifery,[16] a trend that suggests a measure of convergence to a one-and-a-half breadwinner model across the continent. Such changes suggest a need for caution in describing women's work in the second half of the twentieth century in terms of a 'revolution'.[17]

People's practices with respect to fertility, partnering, and household formation also vary across countries, as well as within them. Both divorce and non-marital childbearing have become widespread in the Nordic and English-speaking countries over the last thirty years, but cultural and political responses to such practices have varied. While in recent years commentators in the United Kingdom and the United States have been agonizing over the growing proportion of lone-mother families, formed because of divorce and unmarried motherhood, in the Nordic states similar phenomena excite much less political and cultural concern.[18] These rates are more moderate in continental Western Europe and low in Southern Europe, with the exception of Portugal, which, as late as 1995, had a higher extramarital birth rate than Germany. Fertility is now highest in the United States and United

---

[16] Jacqueline Heinen, 'East European Transition, Labour Markets, and Gender in the Light of Three Cases: Poland, Hungary and Bulgaria', Paper presented at the 5th TSER Seminar of the European Network 'Gender and Citizenship' at the Georg-August Universität, Gottingen, Germany (Feb. 1999); Pascall and Lewis, 'Emerging Gender Regimes and Policies for Gender Equality in a Wider Europe'.

[17] C. Hakim, *Key Issues in Women's Work: Female Heterogeneity and the Polarisation of Women's Employment* (London, 1996).

[18] J. Lewis (ed.), *Lone Mothers in European Welfare Regimes* (London, 1997).

Kingdom, where female labour-market participation rates are also high (albeit with very different rates of part-time employment), where family formation and dissolution are most fluid, and where there are very high rates of *young* motherhood, married and unmarried.[19]

While behavioural changes in the family and the labour market have been dramatic over the last thirty years, the precise relationship between such changes and the state is much harder to work out. For example, the rapid increase in lone-mother families, particularly in English-speaking and in many of the Nordic countries, has led American conservative commentators such as Charles Murray to argue that welfare benefits *caused* lone motherhood.[20] Subsequent research has shown this claim to be simplistic,[21] and at most we can say that benefits may *facilitate* changes in family form. Although women's increasing economic independence *is* important in explaining changes in family form,[22] women's low pay makes it hard to credit family change to this particular economic variable alone. More recently still, family change has been seen as the key *independent* variable explaining the erosion of the male-breadwinner model, and hence also expectations regarding female labour-market participation.[23]

The key point to note is that 'individualization' is far from complete when it comes to behavioural change. This is important because the assumptions underpinning social policies have also changed in response to family and labour-market change, as well as to the perceived downward pressure on public expenditure exerted by population ageing and 'global' competition. There is a danger in regard to policymaking that the simple male-breadwinner model is being replaced by an equally simple 'adult-worker model family', which is no better at matching today's complex social reality than its forerunner.[24]

Models for Reconciling Work and Family at the National Level

The ways in which paid and unpaid care work are treated at the national level are very different. Only in the United States and the Nordic countries have models been based on the assumption that men and women will be

---

[19] Jane Lewis, *Should We Worry About Family Change?* (Toronto, 2003).

[20] Charles Murray, *Losing Ground: American Social Policy, 1950–80* (New York, 1984).

[21] M. J. Bane and D. T. Ellwood, *Welfare Realities: From Rhetoric to Reform* (Cambridge, Mass., 1994).

[22] V. K. Oppenheimer, 'Women's Rising Employment and the Future of the Family in Industrialised Societies', *Population and Development Review*, 20 (1994–2), 293–342.

[23] Esping-Andersen, *Social Foundations of Post-Industrial Economies*; Esping-Andersen *et al, Why We Need a New Welfare State.*

[24] J. Lewis, 'The Decline of the Male Breadwinner Model: The Implications for Work and Care', *Social Politics*, 8 (2001–2), 152–70.

fully engaged in the labour market. However, these models work in very different ways. In the United States, women must enter the labour market because of a residual, even punitive, welfare system, whereas in Scandinavia women are supported by entitlements that help them care for children and older people. The position of lone mothers is revealing,[25] because as a group they focus the problem of combining unpaid care work and employment. Since 1996 the United States treats these women as citizen workers, mandating a work-first policy and imposing time-limited benefits. Employment rates for lone mothers are high in the United States. Employment rates are even higher in Sweden and Denmark, but lone mothers' poverty rates are much lower than in the United States, because the state provides as much as one-third of their incomes.[26] The Nordic model treats women as workers, but then makes allowance for difference,[27] grafting on transfers and services for partnered and unpartnered mothers alike that take account of their unpaid work of caring. Hobson has described the Swedish variant as a 'gender participation model', focusing as it does on promoting gender equality in employment and providing 'supports' via cash (for parental leaves) and services (in the form of care for children and elderly dependants).[28]

Thus, the United States continues to operate a fiercely gender-neutral, equality-defined-as-sameness adult-worker model, with very few supports for care work,[29] although the market provides good access to affordable (but not necessarily good-quality) daycare services for children. Recent American feminist literature is replete with references to the 'care crisis'[30] and to family stress.[31]

---

[25] K. Kiernan, H. Land, and J. Lewis, *Lone Motherhood in Twentieth Century Britain* (Oxford, 1998).

[26] Lewis (ed.), *Lone Mothers in European Welfare Regimes*.

[27] J. Lewis and G. Astrom, 'Equality, Difference and State Welfare: Labour Market and Family Policies in Sweden', *Feminist Studies*, 18 (1992–1), 59–87.

[28] B. Hobson, 'The Individualised Worker, the Gender Participatory and the Gender Equity Models in Sweden', *Social Policy and Society*, 3 (2004–1), 75–84

[29] Equality-as-sameness has a long historical tradition in the USA and has been supported by feminists, who in the early twentieth century were not inclined to support even basic legal recognition of care work in the form of maternity leave: U. Wikander, A. Kessler Haris and J. Lewis (eds.), *Protecting Women. Labor Legislation in Europe, the United States and Australia, 1880–1920* (Urbana and Chicago, 1995). There are, however, tax allowances for childcare.

[30] A. Hochschild, 'The Culture of Politics: Traditional, Post-modern, Cold-modern and Warm-modern Ideals of Care', *Social Politics*, 2 (1995–3), 333–46.

[31] T. Skocpol, *The Missing Middle: Working Families and the Future of American Social Policy* (New York, 2000), J. Schor, *The Overworked American* (New York, 2001); S. Hewlett, *When the Bough Breaks: The Cost of Neglecting our Children* (New York, 1991).

Scandinavia operates what is in practice, but not in name, a gender-differentiated 'supported adult-worker model', with both highly developed services for child care and generous cash transfers in respect of parental leave. As a result, moderately high proportions of women work (long) part-time hours, exercising their right to work a six-hour day when they have pre-school children, as well as leaving the labour market for up to three years if they have two children in rapid succession. As a result, the Swedish labour market is the most sexually segregated in the Western world. Swedish women have more choice about combining work and care, but at the expense of equality in respect of vertical and horizontal labour-market segregation. Despite its long historical tradition of full-time work for women, Finland introduced a flat-rate homecare allowance in 1990 (added on to parental leave) for care of children under 3, which is offered as an alternative to public daycare. Salmi has argued that this effectively brings Finland closer to the more mixed continental European norm, with employment rates for women falling since 1990.[32] The introduction of the 'daddy quota' in the Scandinavian countries, whereby men are obliged to take part of the parental leave allocation (usually a month) or lose it altogether, was aimed at promoting greater gender equality in unpaid work, something that would also begin to tackle labour-market inequalities.[33] However, the new Danish right-wing government abandoned the 'daddy month' in 2002 because of the way in which it explicitly tries to change behaviour in the private sphere of the family. The development of the adult-worker model in the Scandinavian countries shows the extent to which the politics of choice are interleaved with those of gender equality.

Other Western European countries have moved substantially towards assuming the existence of an adult-worker model family, but in practice still operate a mixed model of 'partial individualization'. Thus the Netherlands and the United Kingdom changed the nature of entitlements for lone-mother families in the mid-1990s, with the result that governments encouraged women with school-age children to seek employment in order to limit cash transfers to this group. However, incentives to partnered women to enter the labour market are ambiguous. In the United Kingdom, for example, the operation of means-tested social assistance provides an inbuilt disincentive

[32] M. Salmi, 'Analysing the Finnish Homecare Allowance System: Challenges to Research and Problems of Interpretation', in L. Kalliomaa-Puha (ed.), *Perspectives on Equality— Work, Women and Family in the Nordic Countries and the EU* (Copenhagen: Nordic Council of Ministers, Nord v, 2000).

[33] A. Leira, 'Caring as Social Right: Cash for Child Care and Daddy Leave', *Social Politics* 5 (1998–3), 362–79.

to partners of unemployed men to enter the labour market. The United Kingdom has opted to move towards a 'supported' rather than an 'unsupported' adult-worker model, but much more attention has been paid to investing in child-care services, which are more likely to result in women's employment, than in cash transfers. These will pay for parental leave or long home-care leaves, which are more likely to result in women 'choosing' to stay at home to care.[34] In the Netherlands part-time work still remains the preferred way of reconciling work and family.[35] The 'combination scenario' launched by the Dutch government in 1991 envisaged men's employment patterns conforming to those of women, so that all adults would work long part-time and carry out care work. In Germany too, providing women (but not men) with the 'choice' to work or care is high on the political agenda.[36]

Ideas about women and their relationship to work and care can be discerned in these various models. In some countries the desire to promote an adult-worker model is stronger in relation to some groups of women (particularly lone mothers) than to others. The point is that first, policymakers in different countries operate with different assumptions about the contributions that men and women should make to families, and second, that choice in all these models is profoundly structured by social policies. In the United States and Scandinavia it is assumed that adults will be in the labour market, but only in Scandinavia do sufficient 'policy supports' in the form of cash enable women to choose to care, with the result that these countries operate a 'one-and-three-quarter-earner model'. The 'policy supports' are gender neutral, so that men may care, but labour-market segregation here as elsewhere means that men are more likely to be in better-paying jobs and to experience work cultures that are often unsympathetic to care leaves. In the United States women can choose to work, but it is much harder to choose to care (especially when the real fall in male manual workers' earnings during the 1980s and 1990s is also taken into consideration). In the mid-1990s in the United Kingdom and the Netherlands lone mothers were encouraged to become workers, so that in these countries and in Germany recent increases in social expenditure on care promote service rather than cash provision.

Just as the male-breadwinner model represented a set of assumptions about what the contributions of men and women to households ought to

---

[34] Lewis, *Should We Worry About Family Change?*

[35] T. Knijn, 'Challenges and Risks of Individualisation in the Netherlands', *Social Policy and Society*, 3 (2004–1), 57–66.

[36] I. Ostner, 'Individualisation: The Origins of the Concept and its Impact on German Social Policies', *Social Policy and Society*, 3 (2004–1), 47–56.

look like, so has the uneven shift towards a set of assumptions based on the notion of an adult-worker family model. For women the problems are two-fold: first, it is always problematic when policies address an 'ought' rather than an 'is'; and second, it is likely that policies based on what in many countries are prescriptions rather than the social reality will militate against the exercise of what might be termed 'genuine' or 'real' choice.[37]

Trends in Welfare-State Restructuring

The governments of developed countries increasingly sponsor the idea of 'active' rather than 'passive' welfare, based on the assumption that all able-bodied adults should be in the labour market. The European Commission stresses the importance of adult labour-market participation to increase competitiveness,[38] while both the EC[39] and the OECD[40] emphasize the importance of policies to 'make work pay', and in the words of the EC, of strengthening 'the role of social policy as a productive factor'.[41] Reviewing the policy changes in European countries since 1990, Goodin has empha-sized the importance of what he terms 'a new constellation of work-and-welfare variables'.[42] Policies to promote labour-market participation have included a variety of 'welfare-to-work' programmes, as well as minimum wages and tax credits to make work pay.

Assuming universal employment for adults can create problems for gender equality and for the quality of care.[43] Usually these assumptions are made

[37] Jane Lewis and Susanna Giullari, 'The Adult Worker Model Family, Gender Equality and Care: The Search for New Policy Principles and the Possibilities and Problems of a Capabilities Approach', *Economy and Society*, 34 (2005–1), 76–104.

[38] CEC, *Growth, Competitiveness and Employment—The Challenges and Ways forward into the 21th Century* (Luxembourg: CEC, 1993); CEC, *Equal Opportunities for Women and Men—Follow-up to the White Paper on Growth, Competitiveness and Employment* (Brussels: DGV, 1995); CEC, *Report on Social Protection in Europe 1999* (Brussels: CEC, 2000); CEC, *Communication from the Commission to the Council, the European Parliament, the Economic and Social Committee and the Committee of the Regions: Social Policy Agenda* (Brussels: CEC, 2000).

[39] CEC, *Report on Social Protection in Europe 1999*.

[40] OECD, *Economic Studies*, 31 (Paris, 2000–2).

[41] CEC, *Communication from the Commission to the Council, the European Parliament, the Economic and Social Committee and the Committee of the Regions: Social Policy Agenda*, 2.

[42] R. E. Goodin, 'Work and Welfare: Towards a Post-productivist Welfare Regime', *British Journal of Political Science*, 31 (2001–2), 39.

[43] Lewis, 'The Decline of the Male Breadwinner Model'; Lewis, 'Gender and the Development of Welfare Regimes'.

without sufficient concern for the unequal division of unpaid care work between men and women, and women's unequal position in the labour market, which is due to their responsibility for unpaid care work, to the low value attached to paid care work, and to workplace-based discrimination. In addition, it is noteworthy that such assumptions are often applied more rigorously to some groups, for example lone mothers, than to others. Anything to do with care tends to be poorly valued. Wages in the formal care sector are low and benefits and allowances for carers in the informal sector are also low. This means that in a world in which individualization *and* the capacity for self-provisioning is increasingly being assumed by policymakers, carers are profoundly disadvantaged, for example in respect to pension entitlements. Care also continues to be associated with women rather than with both sexes. Putting some limit on working hours, and encouraging men to share the unpaid work of care, are both necessary if there is to be 'time to care' and if women are to avoid the stress of the 'double day'.

Today, supporters of full-time mothering and women's lifelong non-employment are few. But many contemporary feminist reformers do want to see employment shaped to fit women's—or men's—care work, rather than the other way round, and further, want to see care work accepted as a valid form of social participation entitling persons to full citizenship rights.[44] A range of policy proposals flows from these concerns, from caregivers' allowances and reduced workdays for caregivers to citizen's basic income grants, that is, benefits that are provided to all citizens and residents and are not conditional on employment, care, or other requirements.[45] Some feminists have joined campaigns for a citizen's basic income, arguing that such a benefit would have emancipatory effects for women who perform the bulk of caregiving, offering them a genuine choice about whether or not to participate in employment.[46] (Whether such a benefit would give them a genuine choice about whether or not to care is another matter.)[47] Given concerns about the amount of employment available in some societies, such proposals might at some point be given serious political consideration.

Women's employment is on the rise, but is only unevenly supported by welfare states, and there are parallel concerns being expressed about the care

[44] For example, J. Tronto, *Moral Boundaries: A Political Argument For and Ethic of Care* (London, 1993).

[45] A. B. Atkinson, *Public Economics in Action: The Basic Income/Flat Tax Proposal* (Oxford, 1998).

[46] Ailsa McKay and Jo VanEvery, 'Gender, Family and Income Maintenance: A Feminist Case For Citizens' Basic Income', *Social Politics*, 7 (2001), 266–84.

[47] J. Lewis, 'Gender and Welfare Regimes: Further Thoughts', *Social Politics*, 4 (1997), 160–77.

needs of the young and the old. Some analysts[48] call attention to an emerging 'care crisis'—a shortage of care for the growing numbers who need it. In the industrialized countries equal-treatment initiatives have, by and large, provided social security to women on the same basis as that of men. But welfare regimes are far from unbiased in dealing with the problems of how men and women can combine caregiving and paid work. Participation in and of itself is not sufficient to advance women's interests; the quality of jobs in terms of pay, hours, conditions, locations, and how compatible jobs are with caregiving are critical. Many worry about whether women's equality can flourish under the new conditions of globalization, given pressures by many employers and allied political forces for maximum workers' 'flexibility' and the decline of traditionally well-paid, secure, and unionized jobs in the manufacturing sector.[49] Workers have a very different view of 'flexibility' from that of their employers. They would prefer greater control over when and how long they work, as well as greater social protection.[50] The rapid expansion of women's employment in Southern European countries has consisted very largely of short-contract jobs. While such employment can be a way for women to gain entry to labour markets (after all, becoming 'commodified' has historically been difficult for women in many countries), it can also become a dead-end.

The issues are different in different countries, and different strategies may be pursued to enhance women's employment, while reducing poverty and economic vulnerability and ensuring caregiving activities are supported. An 'adult-worker model family' holds out considerably more promise for women and for gender equality than the old 'male-breadwinner model', but much depends on the terms and conditions on which it is introduced. The welfare of dependants—young children and the increasing number of frail elderly people—also depends in large measure on *how* countries move towards securing the more equal involvement of men and women in the labour market. The US case, with its well-established opportunities for employment and equally well-documented high rates of family stress, shows the dangers of neglecting care policies. If all are expected to be (paid) workers,

[48] For example, Hochschild, 'The Culture of Politics'; T. Knijn and M. Kremer, 'Gender and the Caring Dimension of Welfare States: Toward Inclusive Citizenship', *Social Politics*, 4 (1997–3), 328–61.

[49] J. O'Connor, A. Orloff, and S. Shaver, *States, Markets, Families* (Cambridge, 1999); Jane Jenson *et al.* (eds.), *Feminization of the Labor Force: Paradoxes and Promises* (New York, 1988).

[50] S. Lewis, 'Restructuring Workplace Cultures: The Ultimate Work-Family Challenge?', *Women in Management Review*, 16 (2001–2), 21–30.

it must be understood that workers have caring obligations which should be supported and/or compensated. In Scandinavia, where workers who are caregivers have excellent supports but employers discriminate on the basis of caring responsibilities, it is women's opportunities in employment—rather than simply their participation in the labour force—that must be affirmed, while assuring that services and leaves are not cut back. Here, where men remain workers first and foremost, despite the rhetoric encouraging them to take up care, and women remain the main carer-providers, it is women's rights as workers that must be emphasized while continuing to make it clear that men should be carers as well. While the Nordic countries have the longest and most impressive record of implementing policies to reconcile work and family, gender equality in the labour market and and in care work remains elusive. What emerges from this account is the fact that there is no 'magic bullet' for achieving gender equality in both paid and unpaid work. Rather, it is important that policies address workplace-based discrimination (via equal-opportunities legislation) and the gender division of care work, via a range of policies to provide both cash and services, time to care and time to work, and which are directed at the household level as well as the collectivity.

Too often, however, the focus has been an instrumental one, emphasizing that continuing economic growth and healthy tax revenues, on which robust systems of social provision are based, depend on drawing more women into the labour force, keeping more women working longer and more continuously, and fully tapping women's human capital.[51] If this is to be accomplished without sacrificing women's capacities to bear and rear children and to care for others, it is then argued that there is a need for policies to help women to 'reconcile' work and family responsibilities. The focus of this literature thus becomes *women's* ability to reconcile work and care, rather than the much more complicated issues that are raised by the goals of gender equality, promoting the responsibility of men and women to both care and work, and developing women's social inclusion and full citizenship.

In 1998 a European Foundation for the Improvement of Living and Working Conditions' survey on employment options for the future showed that 71 per cent of respondents (from all EU member states) wanted to work a thirty–forty hour week, with convergence between male and female respondents towards a preference for long part-time working. This suggests that there may be general support for the Dutch 'combination scenario', which encourages men and women to share both paid and unpaid work.

---

[51] For example, Esping-Andersen *et al., Why We Need a New Welfare State.*

This is official government policy in the Netherlands, although the efforts to implement it have proved disappointing. France has sought to shorten working hours, and as we saw above, the Scandinavian countries have tried to encourage men to share care work by designating a month of parental leave as 'daddy leave'.

Putting some limit on working hours and encouraging men to share the unpaid work of care would seem to be necessary if there is to be 'time to care', and if women are to avoid the stress of the 'double day'. Both may also be necessary to boost fertility, although the causes of fertility decline are much more complicated than this diagnosis would suggest. Thus far, the main focus of government policies designed to reconcile work and care has been on de-familializing care (via the collective provision of childcare services in particular) in order to facilitate female labour-market entry. This is the approach taken by the European Commission, and has also characterized the recent major efforts to expand family policies in the United Kingdom and Germany. But sharing care between men and women also requires a fundamental transformation of the male-employment model, through the regulation of working time and the promotion of policies designed to change behaviour at the individual level of the household (for example, the 'daddy leave'). If gender equality matters, we need more than the de-familialization of care work. Policies that aim to redistribute cash and time between men and women are crucial. In brief, the policy grid to enable genuine choice would require action on the following:
— time: working time and time to care;
— money: cash to buy care, cash for carers;
— services for (child and elder) care;
and all in relation to both:
— the household level (in terms of the provision of cash and time for men and women);
— the collective level (in terms of services and cash, and workplace-based changes especially in respect of measuring the work accomplished, rather than the 'face-hours' devoted to it).

The ultimate solution to the problems of reconciliation of employment and care and women's economic dependency in all systems may be a 'universal caregiver' model: to induce 'men to become more like what most women are now—that is, people who do primary care work'.[52] This would dismantle the gendered opposition between breadwinning and caregiving. It would also

---

[52] N. Fraser, *Justice Interruptus: Critical Reflections On The 'Post-Socialist' Condition* (London, 1997).

necessitate changing workplaces to accommodate caregiving, and would call upon income-security systems to ensure that people can take time to care and have access to care services. Encouraging *men's* caring is essential, as is encouraging women's integration into paid employment while allowing their continued care work.

Women's equality movements have often advocated women's enhanced employment opportunities and reconciliation policies, but they have had a somewhat different orientation from politicians and policymakers. Their main concern, of course, has been gender equality, over and above fertility, economic productivity, or tax revenues. Equality is linked to women's economic independence, to be secured partially through employment. But gender equality also demands attention to care, and to the relations between men and women; in particular, to the ways men do or do not participate in care activities, and the ways in which the workplace accommodates those with caring responsibilities or fails to do so. From this perspective, one may point to both advances and new difficulties in the policy models developing in a world in which employment is expected for all and women's economic independence is increasingly assumed (and sometimes facilitated), yet too frequently without sufficient regard for the concerns of carers and those who need care. Thus, a key question on the agenda of twenty-first-century advocates of gender equality is whether we can find ways to support both autonomy and care—and, if we are practical, whether this can be done in the context of straitened state budgets, newly powerful neo-liberal ideologies, and globalizing labour and capital markets.

Rooms to Share: Convent Cells and Social Relations in Early Modern Italy

Silvia Evangelisti

> The 30th October 1675. I, *Donna* Armenia Poepanni, a nun in the Most Serene Monastery of Saint Giulia of Brescia . . . donate my room and its annex to *Donna* Regina Savoldi to be kept and possessed in my company for the rest of my life and after my death she can do as she pleases with it.[1]

Donna Armenia addressed these lines to the father superiors of her convent. The cell she wanted to bequeath to her companion, with whom she was already sharing it, was located right above the *loggie* of this huge Benedictine complex of Lombard foundation, which developed around three cloisters and a large garden at the bottom of the hill overlooking the city. A few years before, Armenia had inherited this cell from another nun, who had in turn inherited it from a third sister who had built it using generous private funding from her brother. Now Armenia intended to extend this chain. In her request to the superiors she made clear that she was the 'owner' of the cell and that no one but the nun she had chosen as her successor could claim any rights over this space. Whether Armenia, a member of the powerful local elite, actually wrote this note herself or—more likely—had it written by someone else on her behalf, she wanted it to have 'the same function as if it were written by the hand of a public notary'.[2] Indeed, her name and the date appear at the bottom of her paper, like in any other official document or will.

Cells undoubtedly provided the nuns with personal comfort, the company of a restricted circle of peers, as well as an appropriate retreat for the

---

[1] Archivio di Stato di Brescia (ASBs), *Ospedale, S. Eufemia*, b. 102, 129, c. 3r. This essay builds on work started years ago with my dissertation on nuns and material culture in early modern Italy, under Olwen Hufton's supervision; see Silvia Evangelisti, ' "Farne quello che pare e piace . . ." L'uso e la trasmissione delle celle nel monastero di Santa Giulia di Brescia (1597–1688)', *Quaderni Storici*, 88 (1995), 86–110.

[2] ASBs, *Osp. S. Eufemia*, b. 102, 129, c. 3r.

spiritual exercises and prayers which were the primary obligations of monastic life.[3] They allowed nuns to lead a partially private existence, and maintain a standard of living similar to the one they had been used to before entering religion, even though this was in deep contrast with the rule of religious poverty and the regime of communal property that they were bound to follow. The daughters of rich families in particular benefited from the use of one or more cells, furnished with the most amazing variety of material objects of domestic and devotional use, such as linens and woollen cloths, dressing items, furniture, crockery, sacred objects, paintings, and images made of clay, wood, or fabric. Nuns lived in these cells individually, or in small groups of relatives, servants, or friends, sometimes sharing their personal allowances in cash or food.

In those rare cases where historians have focused their attention on nuns' cells they have emphasized how these spaces materialized the dynastic management of convents.[4] Elite families moved entire 'clans' of their women—sisters, aunts, and nieces—into female monastic institutions which they endowed with rents, alms, or sumptuous works of art. Convents provided important connections with local ecclesiastical politics, and above all an honourable and economically advantageous home for 'surplus' daughters.[5]

---

[3] On nuns and the material world, see e.g. Eileen Power, *Medieval English Nunneries, c.1275 to 1535* (London, 1922), 96–130; Roberta Gilchrist, *Gender and Material Culture: The Archaeology of Religious Women* (London, 1994); Kathryn Burns, *Colonial Habits: Convents and the Spiritual Economy of Cuzco* (Durham, NC, 1999); and my 'Monastic Poverty and Material Culture in Early Modern Italian Convents', *Historical Journal*, 47 (2004), 1–20.

[4] For the 'cell system' see Carla Russo, *I monasteri femminili di clausura a Napoli nel secolo XVII* (Naples, 1970); Gabriella Zarri, 'Gender, Religious Institutions and Social Discipline: The Reform of the Regulars', in Judith C. Brown and Robert C. Davis (eds.), *Gender and Society in Renaissance Italy* (London and New York, 1998), 193–212, and 'Monasteri femminili e città (secoli XV–XVIII)', in *Storia d'Italia. La chiesa e il potere politico. Annali*, 9 (Turin, 1986), 359–429; Gaetano Greco, 'Monasteri femminili e patriziato a Pisa (1530–1630)', in *Città italiane del '500 tra riforma e controriforma* (Lucca, 1988), 313–39.

[5] Jutta G. Sperling, *Convents and the Body Politics in Late Renaissance Venice* (Chicago and London, 1999); Elisa Novi Chavarria, *Monache e gentildonne. Un labile confine: poteri politici e identità religiose nei monasteri napoletani secoli à (XVI–XVII)* (Milan, 2001); Judith Brown, 'Monache a Firenze all'inizio dell'età moderna. Un'analisi comparata', *Quaderni storici*, 85 (1994), 117–52; P. Renee Baernstein, 'In Widow's Habit: Women Between Convent and Family in Sixteenth Century Milan', *Sixteenth Century Journal*, 25: 4 (1994), 787–80; Richard Trexler, 'Celibacy in the Renaissance: The Nuns of Florence', in *Power and Dependence in Renaissance Florence*, vol. 2 (Binghamton, NY, 1993), 6–30;

Religious dowries paid to the convent for each woman who entered were substantially cheaper than the ever more expensive marriage dowries, and therefore more congenial to the patrimonial strategies of patrician groups seeking to keep family property within the male line.[6] All this is undeniably true, and the interaction between family history and convent history opened up new paths for looking at how gender and family strategies determined the functioning of female monastic institutions, and how convents played a role in consolidating the local power of the elites.[7] But while scholars analysing social networks have recognized the variety of clienteles and non-kinship ties operating together with kinship ones, studies of convents have adopted a narrower interpretation. These studies have focused on family relations, and glossed over the key role played by personal relations inside monastic communities. To be sure, convents were subject to extensive family influence and control. Furthermore, they reproduced symbolic families made of 'sisters', 'mother abbesses', and 'father superiors'. Nevertheless they belonged to the society that had created them, and non-family relations represented a meaningful component in the social organization of the cloistered world, just as they probably did in the many other religious and lay institutions where early modern men and women spent part or all their lives, such as monasteries, hospitals, orphanages, and houses for the poor. In order to assess fully the social role of convents in the early modern world we need therefore to look further into their internal structure, as well as their osmotic links with society outside.

Building on the assumption that the study of material culture—including space, objects, and property relations—is deeply revealing of social networks

---

Sara Cabibbo e Marilena Modica, *La santa dei Tomasi. Storia di Suor Maria Crocefissa (1645–1699)* (Turin, 1989). On Spain see Magdalena S. Sanchez, *The Empress, the Queen, and the Nun: Women and Power at the Court of Philip III of Spain* (Baltimore and London, 1998).

[6] On families' patrimonial strategies in late medieval and early modern Italy, see Christiane Klapish-Zuber, *Women, Family and Rituals in Renaissance Italy* (Chicago, 1985); Thomas Kuehn, *Law, Family and Women: Toward a Legal Anthropology of Renaissance Italy* (Chicago and London, 1991); Antony Molho, ' "Tamquam vere mortua": Le professioni religiose femminili nella Firenze del tardo Medioevo', *Società e storia*, 43 (1989), 1–44; Stanley Choinackj, *Women and Men in Renaissance Venice: Twelve Essays on Patrician Society* (Baltimore, 2000).

[7] See e.g. Renata Ago, *Carriere e clientele nella Roma barocca* (Rome and Bari, 1990); Sandra Cavallo, *Charity and Power in Early Modern Italy: Benefactors and their Motives in Turin, 1541–1789* (Cambridge, 1995); Benedetta Borello, *Trame sovrapposte. La socialità aristocratica e le reti di relazioni femminili a Roma (XVII–XVIII secolo)* (Naples, 2003).

and relations,[8] this chapter considers some of the ways in which nuns used their cells to interact with their peers, and what this reveals about the composition and the internal dynamics of the monastic community. My analysis will draw on the case of Saint Giulia in post-Tridentine Brescia between 1597 and 1688, a period well documented by the sources. My concern is not so much with the cells' shape and interiors, but with their distribution within the community. My essay, I hope, will offer the opportunity to rethink the functioning of the complex convent machine, and explore different patterns of community and social organization in a gendered perspective.

Records from the Congregation of Bishops and Regular Orders provide abundant information about the management of cells. One of the main bodies charged with ruling on monastic institutions, this Congregation was created in the wake of the Tridentine disciplinary reform, and extended its power to monastic institutions in the entire Catholic world. Its documents attest that, although according to the monastic model everything was meant to fall under common ownership, in practice cells did not. The ideal communal monastic space was in fact a fragmented composition of different spaces, or cells, which nuns often considered as their own property. This fragmentation was universal to convent life, in Spain, Portugal, Latin America, the Dalmatian territories, and Italy. The roots of this situation partially lay with a basic economic problem of funding. Female monastic communities were traditionally less productive and more prone to economic weakness than male ones. Nuns were bound to enclosure, which was compulsory for them only. Enclosure limited their contacts with outsiders, prohibiting them from leaving the convent and unlicensed outsiders from entering it. This inevitably impinged on their economic exchanges with the city, and reduced their already limited profitable activities.[9] The reform programme approved by the Council of Trent in 1563 tightened the discipline of enclosure, thus creating even more pressure on the strained budgets of

---

[8] For an insightful discussion on the use of material culture in social sciences, see *The Social Life of Things: Commodities in Cultural Perspective*, ed. Arjun Appadurai (Cambridge, 1986). See also Luke Syson and Dora Thornton, *Objects of Virtue: Arts in Renaissance Italy* (London, 2001); Moira Donald and Linda Hurcombe (eds.), *Gender and Material Culture in Historical Perspective* (Basingstoke, 2000).

[9] On the economically negative effects of enclosure on medieval convents, see Penelope D. Johnson, *Equal in Monastic Profession: Religious Women in Medieval France* (Chicago and London, 1991), 158; Jane Tibbetts Schulenburg, 'Strict Active Enclosure and its Effects on the Female Monastic Experience (ca.500–1100)', in John A. Nichols and Lillian Thomas Shank (eds.), *Distant Echoes: Medieval Religious Women* (Kalamazoo, 1984), 51–86.

convents.[10] Pushed by the imperative need to solve this long-standing problem, the Roman ecclesiastical authorities sought to increase private incomes from families and patrons.[11] They adopted formal measures to encourage and even require from families charitable offerings and personal allowances for nuns, while willingly accepting their contributions to building-works and the creation of spatial extensions to convent buildings: cells for the nuns to live in, as well as common rooms like infirmaries reserved for the sick and dying, and working rooms in which part of convents' meagre incomes originated.

Although convents relied on a mixed economic regime, partially communal and partially private, the Church set up strong limitations on families and individual nuns claiming ownership of what they had contributed to fund and build. These restrictions made the distribution of empty cells the exclusive prerogative of the abbess, according to the principle of individual need and the seniority of each nun. It was forbidden for nuns to decide for themselves to share, sell, or bequeath their cells to other nuns, or to give them away in the form of gifts. These prohibitions applied also to blood relatives within the convent, even when their families had paid for the cells.[12] Such utilitarian approach aimed at neutralizing any interference with the Church's control of convent cells. Inevitably, though, it fostered the conditions that favoured their private management.

How did all this play out at Saint Giulia? This rich convent had rooms for many of its residents, though probably not for all of them, and some slept in the communal dormitory. Founded around 757 by the king of Lombardy, Desiderius, and Queen Ansa, for their daughter (and first abbess) Anselperga, this nunnery was a major monastic institution in Northern Italy. It enjoyed imperial protection, and was endowed with lands, farms with animals and renters, and an extraordinary collection of relics, including the body of the

---

[10] *Canons and Decrees of the Council of Trent*, ed. H. J. Schroeder (St Louis and London, 1960), ch. 5: 'Provision is made for the enclosure of nuns.'

[11] See Pope Gregory XIII's bull 'Deo Sacris' (1572), n. 5.

[12] I have examined the decisions of the Roman Congregation between 1600 and 1647, Biblioteca Apostolica Vaticana (henceforth BAV), ms. Borg. Lat. 71, *Breve Compendio di Decreti et Ordini fatti dalla Sacra Congregazione de Regolari spettanti a Monache (1604–1644)* and ms. Borg. Lat. 77, *Indice di decreti della Sacra Congregazione de'Vescovi e Regolari*. For the licences given to nuns for building and buying rooms, and for prohibition of selling, exchanging, or bequeathing them, see Archivio Secreto Vaticano, Sacra Congregazione dei Vescovi e Regolari (henceforth ASV, SCVR), *Registra Regularium*, 3, ff. 31v and 24r; 4, f. 30v; 5, f. 7r; 18, f. 42v; 20, f. 193r; 25, f. 478r; 28, f. 270r; 39, f. nn. On Tridentine legislation concerning monastic poverty see *Canons and Decrees*, ch. 2, 'Private ownership is absolutely forbidden to regulars'.

Christian martyr Giulia, all of which added to the community's renown.[13] By the mid-seventeenth century Saint Giulia was the richest of all Brescian female monastic houses and one of the most expensive, filled with the women of the aristocracy and rich patricians.[14] Here, between 1597 and 1688, at least a third of the nuns had private cells—fifty nuns on a total average of 147. This group included two boarders who lived in cells rather than the usual dormitory separate from the nuns.[15] The picture projected by an early nineteenth-century inventory, drawn up after the convent's Napoleonic suppression, is that of several large 'apartments', sometimes on two floors, with kitchens, latrines, and attics.[16]

In such a wealthy environment cells were managed like very small estate properties. They were often sold to those who could afford them and were able to pay the money directly to the convent, rather than being distributed to nuns according to their neediness or seniority, as recommended by the Roman authorities. The abbess and the Benedictine superiors of Saint Eufemia supervised their sale and allocation. Following a 'very ancient' medieval consuetude the abbess had greater authority, and she enjoyed exclusive powers over all the properties and cells.[17] The father superior

---

[13] On the history of S. Giulia's convent see Susanne Fonay Wemple, 'S. Salvatore and S. Giulia: A Case Study in the Endowment and Patronage of a Major Female Monastery in Northern Italy', in Julius Kirshner and Susanne Fonay Wemple (eds.), *Women of the Medieval World* (Oxford, 1985), 85–102; Giovanni Spinelli, 'La storiografia sul monastero nell'età moderna e contemporanea', in *Santa Giulia di Brescia: archeologia, arte, storia di un monastero regio dai Longobardi al Barbarossa* (Brescia, 1992), 21–38; G. Pasquali, 'S. Giulia di Brescia', in A. Castagnetti, G. Pasquali, M. Luzzatti, and A. Vasina (eds.), *Inventari altomedievali di terre, coloni e redditi (secc. IX–X)* (Rome, 1979), 41–94.

[14] ASBs, *Osp. S. Eufemia*, b.115, 167 (census 1657). ASBs, *Notarile*, 2978, 2979, 3368, for a comparison between the dowries in S. Giulia and in other convents.

[15] ASBs, *Osp. S. Eufemia*, b.104, 143; b.105, 146, which contains fifteen lists of nuns (1616–1655). In 1581 Carlo Borromeo fixed the maximum number of nuns at 350. As the documents only concern conflicts between nuns about cells, they underestimate them, so the actual number was likely to be higher.

[16] ASBs, *Intendenza di finanza, Soppressioni*, b. 97.

[17] ASBs, *Osp. S. Eufemia*, b. 102, 130, c. 55r. On the power of the abbess see *Historia Patriae Monumenta. Codex Diplomaticus Langobardiae*, 13 (Turin, 1873), 294–5; Fonay Wemple, 'S. Salvatore', 90 n. 31. For the list of S. Giulia's abbesses see Andrea Valentini, *Codice necrologico-liturgico del monastero di S. Salvatore e S. Giulia di Brescia* (Brescia, 1887), 261–3. On the power of abbesses, Merry Wiesner Hanks, 'Ideology Meets Empire: Reformed Convents and the Reformation', in A. C. Fix and S. Karant-Nunn (eds.), *Germania Illustrata: Essays on Early Modern Germany Presented to Gerald Strauss* (Ann Arbor, Mich., 1992), 181–95.

simply ratified her decisions, or intervened to arbitrate in cases of conflict. The value of each cell was established on the basis of material conditions, and prices were set in accordance with the cells' facilities and comforts, and their size, structure, and position within the building. For example, cells close to the garden were more desirable and therefore might be more expensive than others. According to a widespread practice, which in some convents was known as 'expropriation', the sale of empty cells could include everything that was found inside. Comparative analysis shows that sometimes cells came with rents deriving from investments or lands. Nuns using such cells benefited from their incomes too, although they were obliged to pay a portion to the convent.[18] In Saint Giulia cells were 'non-profitable' and probably had a limited economic value, whatever their price was. This might be one of the reasons why most of the time nuns managed to exercise a significant degree of control over their distribution. For instance, in one sample of ten requests to bequeath cells to other nuns, permission was only denied twice. More generally, nuns were allowed to bequeath, sell, and exchange cells. By doing this, not only did they accomplish those actions that legally defined the notion of property, prohibited by monastic rules, but they also denied the convent the opportunity to control the use of cells or make money out of selling them.

As Sherrill Cohen pointed out in her work on the Florentine *Convertite*—a convent hosting ex-prostitutes who 'redeemed' and entered religious life—the nuns shared their cells in groups of three or four, and bequeathed them to their relatives or friends in the same convent.[19] In Saint Giulia too the distribution of cells followed a similar pattern, something that gave way to endless and bitter conflicts, which on occasion reached the point of physical violence.

The logic of family ties was an efficient arrangement for allocating cells. Indeed, the abbess herself allocated cells to relatives of the previous occupiers, and individual nuns inherited their relatives' cells, and in turn bequeathed them to other relatives. Nuns claimed or received cells even when they already enjoyed one or more of them and had little immediate need for extra space. Regina Savoldi received a cell from her aunt even though she had already had a cell from the day of her profession.[20] As we have seen from the

---

[18] Sherrill Cohen, *The Evolution of Women's Asylums Since 1500: From Refuges for Ex-Prostitutes to Shelters for Battered Women* (New York and Oxford, 1992), 61–100; I would like to thank Gianna Pomata for this suggestion. Archivio di Stato di Pisa, *Corporazini religiose soppresse, S. Marta*, 1286, and 1287. On convent cells as ecclesiastical *benefici*, or rents related to ecclesiastical offices, see Greco, 'Monasteri femminili', 335.

[19] Cohen, *The Evolution*, 67–100.

[20] ASBs, *Osp. S. Eufemia*, b. 102, 129, c. 49r.

opening quotation, she also inherited another cell, thus managing three in total—though we do not know whether these cells were contiguous, so as to form a proper quarter. Fulgenzia Ottonella, who already had a cell, laid claim to the cell of her deceased aunt, which another nun was then using.[21] However, the documents attest that: although kinship ties were strong, nuns had to justify their claims on the basis of non-kinship reasons too. In the case of Fulgenzia, the claim on her aunt's cell was grounded on two lines of argument: that the nun living there did not actually use the cell, and that the cell was—like other cells in that corner of the convent—too exposed to the outside world, and therefore a cause of scandalous and immoral behaviour. Her claim therefore did not rely on kinship ties, but was instead justified on general grounds which she probably perceived as more effective for pushing her case.

A way to ensure that cells remained in the family line was by buying them. In October 1651 Aquila Martinengo bought, for 100 *scudi*, the cell of the deceased Corona Martinengo; probably her aunt, given the large numbers of aunt–niece couples found in convents. She added 12 *scudi* as an 'alms' for the sacristy, and made a quite specific request: she wanted 'the said room to always pass on to her successors . . . who will be *pro tempore* in the Reverend Monastery'.[22] Her request for the room to be used by her future relatives was granted. The money was counted before the notary and witness, and the abbess, the sister chancellor, and the sister bursar signed the contract. With this investment Aquila ended up paying a high price for one cell, given that a couple of years earlier cells had been sold for half as much. Maybe the cell she wanted was worth more, but it appears that by paying this high price she intended her investment to serve her family as a whole. Aquila pursued a broader project to acquire more cells. Three years later she came into conflict with another nun over a cell once occupied by Tarquinia Terzi, the latter's aunt. Tarquinia had left oral disposition that she wished to bequeath her cell to both of them. As both now claimed exclusive access to and use of the cell, the abbot was called on to intervene. He first questioned the abbess, who explained that Tarquinia had left her cell to both nuns precisely because 'one was her long-time friend and the other was her niece'.[23] Then he consulted fifteen nuns from the convent. Most of them backed the niece, as it was the consuetude of their convent for cells to be passed on to relatives after death. Only three nuns argued that both nuns were entitled to the cell.

---

[21] Ibid., b. 103, 136, c. 34r, and b. 102, 129, c. 4r.

[22] Ibid., b. 102, 134, c. 29r.

[23] Ibid., b. 103, 136, 20r and 25r–26r.

Finally, one nun thought the cells should 'return' to the convent to be distributed in the usual way, according to the principle of seniority. As things did not look good for Aquila, she attempted to turn the situation around by producing her personal accounts, which showed that Tarquinia was in debt to her for a loan of money and furniture which had not been settled. On this basis she now claimed the cell as a form of compensation for her financial generosity. In the end the strict family logic won. The abbot allocated the cell to the niece, but ordered her to repay her debts to Aquila, confirming the priority of blood ties over non-blood ones.

In those years the superiors were continually busy with other women from the Martinengo family. Several Martinengo women lived in Saint Giulia, in their own cells. Between 1650 and 1671 at least nine of them took part in the family's attempt to colonize convent space by marking specific areas of the building with their presence. In 1651 Orizia Martinengo, supported by the abbess, wrote to the father superior asking to share a 'little room', which she had inherited from her aunt, with Lucidea Martinengo, a relative. The room was contiguous to where Lucidea already lived, and the two nuns were planning to turn it into their own kitchen.[24] About twenty years later two boarders, Lelia and Margherita Martinengo Cesaresco, became involved in a litigation concerning their cell. The two daughters of the Count Cesare, once the protector of the convent, had obtained this empty cell some years before. Their father had offered to pay the convent for this cell, but the nuns had refused and the two 'Martinenghe' had been using it as a kitchen. In 1671 a relative of the nun who previously inhabited the room laid claim to it. A quarrel began and the Martinengos' father threatened to appeal to the bishop if his daughters were not allowed peaceful use of their kitchen-cell. The father superiors intervened and—unwilling to confront Martinengo's rage—passed 'the mess' over to 'another competent judge'. Though we do not know how the whole matter ended,[25] it clearly shows that, in Saint Giulia, the cell system was monopolized by a few clusters of nuns, some of them from the same kin-group. With the exception of this family, however, there seem to have been no other open examples of direct intervention of relatives in the distribution of cells. Most likely they offered their indirect support by acting unseen from backstage.

Despite the clear primacy of family networks, there were occasions when they were not acknowledged. Cells could be given to nuns on the basis of personal relationships, even against the claims of relatives. Such was the case

[24] Ibid., b. 102, 129, cc. 10r–11r.
[25] Ibid., b. 102, 130, cc. 12r–13r, c. 19r, cc. 21r–22 r, c. 25r, cc. 27r–28r.

of Fulgenzia Ottonella. Fulgenzia inherited a cell from another nun, who was her 'friend', but some years later the dead nun's niece also claimed the same cell. In this case the abbot ruled that the cell should go to Fulgenzia; by excluding the niece, he privileged personal relations over family ones.[26] Interestingly, families also acknowledged personal relations, and sometimes backed their women when they chose to leave their cells to nuns who were not relatives. Archbishop Marcantonio Martinengo, the brother of Orizia Martinengo, wrote a letter to the abbot after her death recommending that 'certain rooms . . . left by Mother *Donna* Oritia my sister as a sign of her gratitude to . . . Giustina Oliva *benemerita* of my said sister'[27] should indeed be allocated in this way. The archbishop's intervention in support of his sister's last will probably sought to reinforce Orizia's memory within the monastic community, as well as asserting his own authority and his aristocratic family's power within Saint Giulia.

The coexistence of family and non-family ties, and appeals to notions of gratitude as grounds for distributing or claiming rooms, are hardly surprising in a monastic context. The Christian tradition placed great emphasis on the primacy of spiritual kinship over blood kinship. Blood ties were transitory and divisible; spiritual ties, on the other hand, were eternal and indivisible. Blood sisters were related by nature, spiritual sisters were related by 'divine grace'.[28] In this light, gratitude became a legitimate principle for governing human relationships. As St Thomas contended, gratitude, or the adequate compensation for a favour received, was a 'moral debt' and one of the potential 'virtues' of justice.[29] Thus, in buying, selling, or bequeathing their cells, nuns may have subverted the imperative obligation of poverty, but by sharing them with their spiritual sisters—who were sometimes preferred to blood ones—they were asserting some of the main principles of monastic ideology.

So blood and spiritual kinship did not fully cover the complexity of the interpersonal dynamics which united or divided nuns. In a mixed economic regime such as the monastic one, where individuals were not completely dependent on the convent for their living, cells could be allocated on the basis of friendship—a word that frequently recurs in the documents. This notion of friendship, however, reflected a diversity of relationships, which

---

[26] Ibid., b. 103, 136, c. 34r.

[27] Ibid., b. 102, 129, c. 12r.

[28] Paolo Richiedei, *Regola data dal Padre S. Agostino alle monache* (Brescia, 1687), 42.

[29] Thomas of Aquinas, *Summa Theologica*, XIX, 2, 2, q.106. On law and human relations see Michael Clanchy, 'Law and Love in the Middle Ages', in John Bossy (ed.), *Disputes and Settlements: Law and Human Relations in the West* (Cambridge, 1983), 47–67; personal relations—including love—played their part in legal disputes.

ranged from mutual economic support, such as the sharing of money, through full-blown domestic service and care in illness and old age, and finally to spiritual guidance and direction.

As we have seen, Aquila Martinengo motivated her claim to the cell of the deceased Tarquinia Terzi on economic grounds. Tarquinia received an income from her family that was insufficient to meet her needs, and so Aquila had, in her own words, provided her with 'food and clothes for twenty-eight years'.[30] Now Aquila wanted her cell. In 1649 another nun, Massimilla Ganassona, bequeathed part of her 'capital' to Lucina Zamara, her 'confidant', as a mark of gratitude towards a sister who had provided some 'services'. The two of them had previously shared a room which they had purchased together, paying 25 *scudi* each.[31] In other cases, gratitude was extended to servants, as in the case of the abbess Prassede Savoldi, who bequeathed her kitchen-room to the servant-nun Nicolosa, in return for the 'services that she received, receives, and hopes to receive' from her.[32] The only condition laid down was that Nicolosa share this kitchen-room with Abbess Prassede's protégées. In the last two cases, the nuns' magnanimity towards their servants reflected the protective attitude in exchange for domestic service characteristic of patron–servant relations which the nuns reasserted within the cloister's walls.

Caring for ill or dying nuns was also very important to cloistered women, and constituted a reason for claiming and allocating cells. Enclosure deprived nuns of the care their relatives would have provided, and restricted visits to doctors, who needed an official licence in order to enter the convent. They therefore became completely dependent on other nuns to care for them. For example, in 1682 Regina Savoldi came before the abbot to make her claim for a furnished cell once used by Armenia, contesting another nun's claim on the same cell. Her request was justified in terms of her long-standing companionship with Armenia with whom—she reported—she had lived 'for twenty years continuously, and even more, until her death, and I cured her infirmity'. Whilst Regina had willingly fulfilled her caring duties, her rival had shown no interest in her or Armenia and 'abdicated our company about a month after she took her profession'.[33] The abbot, who supposedly knew how important physical care was to nuns, assigned Regina the cell, and praised her caring role, stating that she had 'for a long time faithfully . . . assisted and served the said Mother Donna Armenia, so . . . she should be preferred to other nuns'.[34]

[30] ASBs, *Osp. S. Eufemia*, b. 103, 136, c. 20r.

[31] Ibid., Notarile di Brescia, 5198 (Ercole Piacenza), 20. 03. 1649.

[32] Ibid., b. 102, 134, c. 3r.

[33] Ibid., b. 102, 129, c. 52r.

[34] Ibid., b. 102, 129, c. 5r.

Finally, the allocation of cells sometimes reflected roles of spiritual guidance and nuns' relationships with their spiritual mothers. The aristocratic Angelica Baitelli had a cell located near the servant-nuns' dormitory, which she left to two younger sisters. Angelica—whose brother was a member of the city council, ambassador in Venice, and one of the protectors of the convent—was one of the 'illustrious women of Brescia', known for being the author of two celebratory works on the history of the convent of Saint Giulia. The learned Angelica had won authority within the community as a spiritual mother,[35] and she bequeathed her cell to her two spiritual daughters (although one of the two was also her niece). After Angelica's death the usual battle began. Again the abbot questioned those nuns who had witnessed her death and could therefore confirm her last will, and then interrogated the abbess who, with her own trembling hand, wrote a statement confirming that both nuns should have the cell, as this was Angelica's last wish. Nevertheless, after having listened to all the nuns and examined the contested space, the abbot opted for a slightly different, almost bizarre, solution: he declared that a wall should be built to divide the cell into two parts of equal size, leaving the key in the niece's half.[36] Primary access was therefore allocated to the niece only, leaving the material and symbolic value of Angelica's inheritance, and the hopes of both nuns, in tatters. As all these cases suggest, spiritual ties, and various forms of economic and material exchange, at times competed with kinship ties on an almost equal footing.

The distribution of convent cells provides insights into a crucial aspect of convent life which has been neglected by scholars. Two different 'classes' of nuns existed in convents: choir-nuns and servant-nuns, in other words, the rich and the poor.[37] This class distinction was the most crucial form of social discrimination within what should be, in theory, an egalitarian

---

[35] Angelica Baitelli, *Vita martirio e morte di Santa Giulia Cartaginese Crocefissa* (Brescia, 1644); ead., *Annali Historici dell'Edificazione Erettione e Donatione del Serenissimo Monasterio di S. Salvatore e S. Giulia di Brescia* (Brescia, 1657). On Angelica Baitelli see Gianbattista Rodella, *Le donne bresciane per sapere, per costume e per virtù eccellenti*, Brescia, Biblioteca Queriniana, ms. Di Rosa 15, cc. 131–8 (which includes her portrait), and Vincenzo Peroni, *Biblioteca Bresciana*, I (Bologna, 1818–23), 75.

[36] ASBs, *Osp. S. Eufemia*, b. 102, 130, c.37r. and b.102, 129, c.2r.

[37] See 'Classi di religiose', in G. Pelliccia (ed.), *Dizionario degli istituti di perfezione*, 2 (Rome, 1975), coll. 1154–8. On the normative distinction between choir- and servant-nuns, see my 'Ricche e povere: classi di monache nelle comunità monastiche femminili tra Cinque e Seicento', in Margareth Latzinger and Raffaella Sarti (eds.), *Celibi e nubili nella società moderna e contemporanea* (forthcoming, 2006).

monastic world in which everything was to be shared collectively. The distinction applied to female as well as male members of the regular clergy, and was codified, and thus legitimized, by convent regulations. Choir-nuns—usually of wealthy origin—prayed, took up the highest monastic offices, and ruled the community. Servant-nuns—often from poorer backgrounds—served the choir-nuns and performed domestic duties, deprived of the opportunity of following any monastic career or of being involved in convent decision-making. The differences between these two groups were underpinned by external signs. Religious symbols on the nuns' habits were different: for instance, in the military order of Malta the choir-nuns wore the full cross of Malta whilst the servant-nuns wore a half cross. Differences in daily routine were also prescribed. For instance, servant-nuns ate their meals after the choir-nuns had theirs. Cells differed according to status, the 'best' being reserved for the oldest 'mothers', the next best to the choir-nuns, and finally the 'infamous' cells to servant-nuns.[38] These regulations, however, were not always strictly applied. As we have seen, in Saint Giulia choir-nuns and servant-nuns lived together in the same cells, either at the same time or in succession. The occupants of the cell built by Celeste Averoldi, for example, were a servant-nun and two choir-nuns. Another servant-nun, Nicolosa, had two cells. One was a kitchen-room given to her by the abbess Prassede Savoldi, and the other was a 'vacant room' given to her by the Chapter of Saint Giulia for her 'great services, and charity' towards the nun who previously lived there.[39] Nicolosa was to share this room with two other nuns, one of whom was Prassede, this time a beneficiary of the cell rather than her benefactor, as had been the case four years before.

It is clear that in the convent, as in other social contexts, private space acted as an important element of distinction within the community, and an indicator of the wealth, prestige, and status of the nuns living there. Sharing the same space meant sharing the rights over it and may be the status of the previous occupant. As Armenia Poepanni wrote to the father superiors, the choir-nun to whom she wished to leave her room would maintain her 'place, state, and grade'. We do not know what happened when cells passed from choir-nuns to servant-nuns. It is likely that servant-nuns were required to maintain their role and provide their services and work to the choir-nun with whom they lived. However, through cell-sharing servant-nuns developed close relations with nuns of higher status, something that

---

[38] Paolo Richiedei, *Pratica di coscienza per tutte le religiose claustrali divisa in ventidue trattati* (Bologna, 1710), 88–9.

[39] ASBs, *Osp. S. Eufemia*, b.106, 147, c.15r.

must have had an impact on their own life and position within the community. Living together did not eliminate economic differences amongst nuns, and particularly the difference between choir- and servant-nuns. But it did probably blur them somewhat.

The convent therefore reproduced the typical dynamics of outside society, such as class difference and privileges. On the one hand, the status of each nun was conferred by birth and family name, by the official monastic hierarchy, and by the symbolic capital of relations that they entertained with each other—in other words, their social capital. On the other hand, the internal network of relations based on personal ties as well as blood ties which organized the monastic community probably contributed to smoothing these differences, giving way to informal dynamics of internal social mobility, and helping to mitigate its structural inequalities.

The preceding discussion has shown how the distribution and management of cells, often the subject of long and bitter quarrels, contributed to the internal organization of convents. But their importance for those inhabiting the cloister also must be understood in terms of the highly disciplined structure of convents, and the power relationships this generated.

Some of the contemporaries of the nuns of Saint Giulia were already aware of the implications of convent discipline. In his work on the precepts of painting, the painter and writer Giovan Battista Armenini (1530–1609) described the appropriate decorations for nuns' and monks' cells.[40] Nuns' cells should be painted with frescos depicting edifying sacred images of the Virgin and saints. Frescos on the walls were ideal for nuns' permanent cloistered condition, which denied them the opportunity to leave their convent. Monks, on the contrary, were better opting for paintings to hang on their walls, as they were likely to live in different religious houses and might want to take the paintings with them. Armenini was a well-travelled man, who worked in Milan and Rome, where he made copies of artworks to be sent to King Philip II of Spain. His writing drew on his direct visits to many monastic buildings of monks and nuns. Although his main concern was artistic and devotional, he also identified one of the most striking features of monastic space: its profoundly gendered nature, mainly determined by the obligation, for nuns only, to observe enclosure.

Enclosure and strict monastic discipline had an impact not only on the interiors of cells, as suggested by Armenini, but also on their meaning for nuns. In Saint Giulia, rigid Tridentine enclosure seems to have been fully implemented. Visits from outsiders—in particular doctors treating ill and

---

[40] Giovan Battista Armenini, *De' veri precetti della pittura* (Ravenna, 1586). I would like to thank Caroline Murphy for drawing my attention to this text.

dying nuns, wetnurses breast-feeding them, and workers burying dead bodies—were closely regulated by licences. There is no evidence of nuns ever going out of the convent or escaping from it. This physical segregation aimed at cutting off nuns' relations with the outside world and their families and acquaintances, permanently restricting them to a shared communal space, delimited by walls and governed by their superiors. Against this normative backdrop, nuns' cells—their only individual space—became a means of regaining control over the material and symbolic space of their community and their lives, and fully asserting their 'ownership' of the convent.

But cells also became an arena for confrontation between the nuns and the superiors, in which issues of power and authority over the monastic community were at stake. Indeed, quarrels over cells even provoked (albeit rarely) the direct intervention of the ecclesiastical authorities, to whom the nuns sometimes appealed if the father superiors denied their requests. On one unspecified date, 'the nuns of Saint Giulia' sent two letters to their abbot asking him to stop Teodora Chizola from building a new room, and warning that if necessary they would appeal to 'another judge in order to obtain that grace which we hope to receive from your fatherly affection'.[41] In some other cases the nuns went beyond verbal threats and directly initiated legal action. Regina Savoldi presented her claims to the superiors of the Benedictine orders, the fathers of the Congregation of Saint Giustina in Padua. She was determined to assert her rights over the room inherited from Armenia Poepanni. When, after Armenia's death, another nun claimed the use of this cell on the grounds that Regina already had two, they had a violent quarrel, 'to the point of hitting each other'. Unable to solve the problem, the monks denied the use of the cell to both of them. In response, the implacable Regina—'a hard and stubborn woman', protected by the bishop—hired a legal advisor who brought her case before the Apostolic Nunzio in Venice, the direct emissary of Roman power in the Venetian republic of which Brescia was part. According to the sources, no one had 'in the sacred cloisters ever heard of or done [such a thing] before'. Thus began the 'Savolda case', which went on for years without any agreement being reached. In the end the procurator of the nuns in Venice suggested a strategic solution. The disputed cell was to be given to a third nun, previously persuaded to put in a request on the grounds that she did not have a cell herself. Regina was forced to renounce her claims, and beg for pardon before her superiors.[42] Conflicts such as these uncovered all the complexity of internal and external power

---

[41] ASBs, *Osp. S. Eufemia*, b. 102, 134, cc. 6r.–7r.

[42] Ibid., b. 102, 129, cc. 16r–18r, cc. 21r and v, and c. 87r and b. 102, 130, cc. 40r–45r.

relations, and confirmed the inability of the regular clergy to govern the female branch of their order, forcing them into dealing with the centralized power of the Roman Church.

I would like to conclude with two vignettes. One of the best-known portraits of the celebrated seventeenth-century Mexican poet, playwright, and intellectual Sor Juana Inés de la Cruz (1648–1695) was attributed to Juan de Miranda (died 1714). The painting offers visual documentation of this nun's monastic cell, and presents her standing in front of a desk at the centre of a closed book-lined space. There is no doubt that 'Sor Juana'—as she was known—was an extraordinary gifted mind. Trained in Latin, literature, and poetry, she wrote, studied natural phenomena, and put together her own library and set of scientific instruments, which she kept in her cells where she lived with servants and a slave donated by her mother.[43] In close touch with the Mexican court and a personal friend of the viceroy's wife, she was published during her lifetime, producing a vast array of poems and plays, and an elaborate tract in defence of the female sex which spread her fame on both sides of the Atlantic. Miranda's portrait celebrated this intellectual dimension of her life, and conveyed a very straightforward message: a nun's cell was her study.

We find a more contemplative and less learned vision of cells in a much earlier work, a diptych painted by the Belgian artist Jean Bellegambe before 1534. The diptych was commissioned by the abbess of the convent of Flines for the Cistercian superiors. The external wing of the painting displays her image, kneeling in adoration of the host, with a prayer-book before her. Behind her, in the right upper side, another scene presents two nuns standing in a room furnished with a bed, fireplace, and benches. One of them is guiding the other as she reads from a book. Conceived in the midst of the disciplinary reform of Cistercian nuns, this Belgian painting declared their acceptance of the new disciplinary requirements and celebrated the leading role of the abbess in the accomplishment of the reform. This visual representation of monastic life points to yet another, mainly religious, meaning of cells: that of quiet places for meditating on spiritual teachings.[44]

---

[43] There is a vast bibliography on Sor Juana—including online texts—much of which is quoted in *Sor Juana Ines de la Cruz: The Answer/La Respuesta: Including a Selection of Poems*, ed. Electa Arenal and Amanda Powell (New York, 1994).

[44] For a close reading of this work, in the light of its devotional context, see Andrea Pearson, 'Nuns, Images, and the Ideals of Women's Monasticism: Two Paintings from the Cistercian Convent of Flines', *Renaissance Quarterly*, 54 (2001), 1356–402. Post-Trent directives addressed to nuns sponsored this devotional meaning of cells as 'small heavens' for praying to God in solitude and silence; see e.g. Richiedei, *Pratica*, 66–137.

The evidence discussed in this chapter adds to these two images, showing that there was a great deal more than intellectual and contemplative life going on in cells. There were other ways for nuns to use their cells and for us to understand them. Cells, like all the cloistered space, were symbols of the deeply gendered nature of the monastic experience. They testified to the convent's mixed, collective and individual, economy,[45] which—in the rich monastic houses like Saint Giulia—consisted of individual allowances, furnishings, private catering in kitchen rooms, and the work of servants. Cells materialized the presence in the sacred cloisters of worldly dynamics of privilege and exclusion which were rooted in society beyond the walls, thus attesting once again to the deeply intertwined connections between religious and lay life. Taken further, the nuns' quest for cells tells us something about the weak position of women in property relations. In theory nuns were completely precluded from any access to property. As women they enjoyed very restricted rights to property, and had little chance of inheriting a share of their family's patrimony; as nuns they were denied property rights by the obligation to profess the vow of poverty on entering the convent. The internal organization of convents, and the nuns' possessive attitude towards their cells, provided some redress for gender discrimination and women's exclusion from property rights. Finally, cells became means of expressing the nuns' individuality, and acted as a focus for the small networks of power, care, and sociability that revolved around family and non-family relations. As such, they offer important insights into the degree to which the family was able to shape convent life, and into the diversity of alternatives to family influence in the organization of communities.

---

[45] Mario Rosa, 'La chiesa e la città', in Elena Fasano Guarini (ed.), *Prato, storia di una città* (Florence, 1986), ii. 525–33.

Concubinage and the Church in Early Modern Münster

Simone Laqua

From the moment priestly concubinage was discussed at the Council of Trent, the Church made its position clear: 'How shameful and how unworthy it is of the name of clerics who have dedicated themselves to the service of God to live in the filth of impurity and unclean cohabitation.'[1] A detailed list of measures to be applied against concubinaries was drawn up. First, the cleric was to be admonished by his superiors. If that had no effect, he was to lose a third of his salary. If he persisted, the fruits and revenues from his benefices were forfeit, and if he still failed to dismiss his concubine, he was to be stripped of all his ecclesiastical benefices, portions, offices, and salaries. As a last resort, 'chastisement with the sword of excommunication' was threatened.[2] Such measures and threats of punishment not only prove the Church's determination to wage war against concubinage but also show that it fully expected to meet with difficulties or even opposition. Clearly, a single rebuke from the ecclesiastical authorities would not be enough to make clerics give up their lovers.

Considering the emphasis the post-Tridentine Church placed on raising the moral standards of its priesthood, it is surprising how little research has been done on this issue.[3] An examination of concubinage must consider all

---

[1] Session XXV reform, ch. XIV: 'The manner of proceeding against clerics who keep concubines is prescribed', in H. J. Schroeder, *Canons and Decrees of the Council of Trent* (Rockford, Ill., 1978), 246–8.

[2] Ibid., 247.

[3] The exception is August Franzen's *Zölibat und Priesterehe in der Auseinandersetzung der Reformationszeit und der katholischen Reform des 16. Jahrhunderts*, Katholisches Leben und Kirchenreform im Zeitalter der Glaubensspaltung, 29 (Münster, 1969), which examines the theological discussions of the issue of celibacy from the early days of Christianity until the end of the sixteenth century. However, Franzen is solely concerned with the viewpoint of the Churches, Catholic and Protestant, and their leaders, while the experiences of the clerics and their concubines remain untold. Other studies, such as H. Kamen, *The Phoenix and the Flame: Catalonia and the Counter Reformation* (New Haven

three parties involved: the Church, clerics, and women. This chapter is based on an analysis of archival material covering the episcopate of Ferdinand of Bavaria (1612–50), who spearheaded the introduction of the Counter-Reformation in Münster. I want to concentrate on three issues: first, the measures the Münsteran Church took to abolish concubinage— and here I am especially interested in why the Church attached so much importance to this issue. Secondly, I will explore the position of the other 'half' of these relationships, the guilty clerics. Their response to the Church's reforms will tell us how they saw their role and status in the parish community. Finally, I shall consider the women hidden behind the term 'concubine'. Fortunately, letters written by the concubines themselves or by people close to them have survived, allowing us direct access to their personalities, perceptions, and strategies of defence.

The Bishop

How great a problem was concubinage for the Church? Reporting back to the pope after his tour of German lands in May 1561, the papal nuncio Giovanni Francesco Commendone repeated the duke of Cleve's claim that there were 'not even five priests in his lands, who did not live in public concubinage'.[4] The same was true of Bavaria, where, in the same year, a visitation had revealed that, 'of a hundred priests hardly three or four can be found who did not publicly live in concubinage or in a clandestine marriage, or had even got married in public'. And when Pope Pius V gave orders in 1566 to the bishop of Münster to 'sternly admonish the clergy to live an honourable life and eliminate concubinage', Bernhard of Raesfeld (1557–66) resigned rather than take up the task. This was probably a wise move on his part, for, as the first post-Tridentine visitation of the *Oberstift* revealed, the moral behaviour of the clergy in the territory was lamentable: everywhere, except in only two parishes, Überwasser and St Lamberti, clerics admitted to living with women.[5] Bishop Ernst of Bavaria (1585–1612) was the first to tackle the problem, setting up an ecclesiastical court (*Geistlicher Rat*) in 1601, which, among other things, prosecuted cases of concubinage. But its success was limited, as a 1607 report to Bishop Ernst's Roman superiors revealed:

---

and London, 1993), and R. Pörtner, *The Counter-Reformation in Central Europe: Styria 1580–1630* (Oxford, 2001), mention concubinage only in relation to the wider reform package that the Church tried to implement in the decades after Trent.

[4] Franzen, *Zölibat und Priesterehe*, 166.

[5] According to Franzen's calculations about one-third out of 500 clerics were concubinaries, ibid., 167.

Not only canonized canons, but also prelates, pastors, curate priests, members of the religious orders, and even their abbots take part at public events together with their concubines . . . The women call themselves prelatesses (*Pröpstinnen*) and abbesses, and make sure they are called thus on their gravestones and other public inscriptions.[6]

So when Ferdinand of Bavaria was elected bishop of Münster in 1612, he faced a daunting challenge. His task was to implement the prescriptions of Trent to reform his diocese, lay and clerical, and thereby revive early Christian values like celibacy. On 28 June 1612 Ferdinand issued his first order prohibiting concubinage, proof of his serious desire to tackle the problem; on a practical level, however, Ferdinand had to balance a reformist programme designed to break long-standing clerical habits and lifestyles with the need to keep the clergy upon whom he relied for his power and authority on side.

In his very first communication on concubinage Ferdinand urged the ecclesiastical officials and the city council to instruct Münster's archdeacons strictly that they must end the 'highly prohibited and offensive' concubinage:

Because it is repulsive in the face of our most High, Almighty God and diminishes our clerical standing and, even if taken on its own, it is against our honour that those who have once freely pledged through their oath to commit themselves to God and who are bound by their highly sacred benefices, should live their lives in dangerous public concubinage and immorality; this arouses widespread anger and degrades the clergy too . . .[7]

Ferdinand reminded his clergy that those living a sinful life in the company of a woman had freely chosen to bind themselves to the service of God, and were dedicated to chastity. But this argument had dubious moral weight: parents sought to provide a respectable career for their offspring by assigning one or two sons to the Church without consulting them in the matter. Ferdinand's own case reflects this tradition. When he was still in his infancy his father started to negotiate with his influential Bavarian relatives and, later, even with the pope, to obtain a profitable position for his third son in the German Church. Ferdinand himself must initially have had other plans, because he only consented to remain unmarried in 1609, at the age of 32, years after his family had started to make such plans for him; and even then,

---

[6] A. Hüsing, *Der Kampf um die katholische Religion im Bistum Münster nach der Vertreibung der Wiedertäufer 1535–1585* (Münster, 1883), 351.

[7] Staatsarchiv Münster (hereafter StAM), Fürstentum Münster, Landesarchiv, 2a Nr. 16 Bd. 5, 1612.

he did not receive priestly consecration. This hardly looks like a decision based on free will.

Yet there were other reasons why concubinage aroused the bishop's condemnation. Concubinage posed a serious threat to the Catholic Church, for the return to the early Christian value of chastity was one of the cornerstones of the post-Tridentine reform movement. Failure on so visible a level would not go unnoticed by Protestant propaganda, which had already exploited the stereotype of the lewd Catholic priest. Ferdinand knew that concubinage harmed the reputation of the clerics involved in it and damaged the credibility of the Tridentine Church's much vaunted claim to have reformed itself. How could this assertion be sustained if even the Church's own personnel did not see the point of following the most basic Catholic principles?

On a more personal level, too, concubinage undermined the bishop's position. As he put it, laying his authority on the line: 'to elude divine just wrath, and because of what we owe to our episcopal office and to our Christian conscience we cannot watch this any longer and do not want to either.'[8] Ferdinand came into office with a clear desire to change the state of religious affairs in his episcopacy. His vision was to restore Catholicism in those areas won over to heresy and to expand the influence of the Church in the northern parts of the Holy Roman Empire. He wanted nothing less than a religious transformation, and to accomplish this he was willing to take unpopular decisions. One of his first decrees abolished the ecclesiastical court (*Geistlicher Rat*). This institution had been introduced on a permanent basis by his predecessor Ernst of Bavaria to exercise control over all spiritual matters, to discipline and to administer all ecclesiastical business during the many absences of the bishop from Münster.[9] By abolishing the court Ferdinand removed some influence from the archdeacons and the cathedral chapter, placing important decision-making powers in his own hands or in those of carefully chosen trustees such as the vicar general. At the same time he increased the powers of the vicar general considerably by giving him extensive visitation rights, allowing him to travel the diocese to uncover potential problems and report them to Ferdinand. This remoulding of local power to allow speedy discipline to be meted out did not go uncontested, as the career of Dr Hartmann, the first vicar general, shows.

---

[8] K. Schafmeister, *Herzog Ferdinand von Bayern, Erzbischof von Köln als Fürstbischof von Münster 1612–1650* (Haselünne, 1912), 31.

[9] Ibid., 63–4. The protocols of the ecclesiastical council have been published by H. Immenkötter as *Die Protokolle des Geistlichen Rates 1601–1612*, Reformationsgeschichtliche Studien und Texte, 104 (Münster, 1972).

In Hartmann, Ferdinand had chosen a well-trusted and ambitious follower. However, if the abolition of the ecclesiastical court did not go down well with the members of the cathedral chapter, the decision to give the position of vicar general to an outsider, a foreigner from the city of Bonn, caused even greater ructions. The cathedral chapter consented only very reluctantly to Ferdinand's choice, knowing full well they would have little influence on Hartmann. The vicar general, a former pupil of the Collegium Germanicum in Rome, took his responsibilities very seriously and used a firm hand against local clergy living with concubines.[10] His intervention soon led to quarrels with the archdeacons, who felt their traditional rights had been impinged upon by the interloper. The disagreements continued for another three years until, in 1615, Ferdinand finally conceded that the ecclesiastical jurisdiction traditionally belonged to the archdeacons. From now on, instead of dealing with problems in person the vicar general had to report the results of his visitations to the archdeacons, who were obliged to deal with the short-comings within four weeks. Should this not be done satisfactorily, the general vicar held the right to step in. Both sides were thus forced to compromise, but the workability of the compromise varied from archdeacon to arch-deacon and case to case. Given that the right to discipline now lay in the hands of those who hithero had not been noted for their antagonism towards clerical concubinage, the question arises of whether there was any realistic chance of winning the battle against loose morals.

One example which helps to illustrate the behaviour commonly encoun-tered by ecclesiastical officials in their campaign against concubinage is the case of Johannes Wiggers, pastor of Ennigerloe, a village about 50 kilometers west of Münster. In 1611 Wiggers had repeatedly been told to abandon his concubine and to stop seeing her. Threatened with 'serious punishment' Wiggers did so, but 'only temporarily and as a pretence', because, as the report explains, Pastor Wiggers subsequently, 'in a shameless manner readmit-ted her so that she could force her way back in'. Spurred on by this blatant disregard of their authority, the officials decided to get tough. 'We are now determined to proceed with a serious punishment against the said concubine and we cannot permit her to stay with the pastor in the future.'[11] Wiggers was given an ultimatum of three days to bid farewell to his woman and to make her move out of the territory of his parish. However, before we discuss those proceedings, let us examine the terminology applied in the

[10] Schafmeister, *Herzog Ferdinand*, 64.
[11] StAM, Fürstentum Münster, Landesarchiv, 2a Nr. 16 Bd. 5, 1611.

written communication between the Münsteran ecclesiastics and the officials carrying out Ferdinand's orders in the parishes.

The word most commonly employed in the records to describe the abandonment of concubines is *dimittiren*, a word whose core meaning concerns a person's dismissal from employment.[12] In our context *dimittiren* suggests concubinage was viewed as a kind of work: a concubine was a woman who performed certain services in the clerical household and the clerical bed, and in return received remuneration in kind, free board and lodging. The possibility of an emotional bond between the two was discounted—a misconception, as we shall see later. A concubine was not regarded as a lover but as a servant to love. This is also the logic behind the categories assigned to women in the reports of the ecclesiastical officials in which women were either cooks, servants, housekeepers, or concubines. Despite a reality filled with clandestine marriages, children, and long-term relationships, theory made the Church authorities think only in black-or-white categories. Hence, women working in clerical houses could at best be regarded as plain servant girls. But, as we shall see, even the seemingly straightforward professional identity of a servant harboured potential dangers for a girl's moral and social standing.

On taking up her job in a household, a servant girl had to leave the protection of her parents' house to live under the roof of strangers. Temptations and dangers, like getting carried away with her new-found freedom away from home, or the (unwanted) sexual advances from male members of the new household, were traps for a young woman's moral integrity. Generally, it was the task of the mistress of the house to avert any such danger through her strict regime and sharp eyes. But what if there was no housewife, as was the case in clerical households?[13] For single maidservants, the prospect of dishonour was perilously close.

There was, however, a more subtle reason for the precariousness of the maids' situation caused by an insinuation of the German language. The roots of the word *Dienstmagd* lie in the Middle High German word *dierne*. During the middle ages *dierne* described a young woman as well as a servant girl, with *dienen* meaning 'to serve' and *Dienst*, 'service'. In the later sixteenth century these roots were still visible in the term *Dienstmagd*, but the medieval word *dierne* had acquired a much more dubious double meaning, signifying not only a young girl but a prostitute. Obviously, early modern people would

---

[12] Cf. *Deutsches Rechtswörterbuch: Wörterbuch der älteren deutschen (westgermanischen) Rechtssprache*, Bd. II, 1932–5, (Weimar, 1914–2001).

[13] The Council of Trent had decreed that clerics were only allowed to have female servants of the age of 40 or over, but this regulation was obviously not followed in Münster.

have drawn a clear distinction between *Dienstmagd* and *dierne*, between the servant girl and the prostitute. Yet the suggestive connotations implied in the antecedents of the early modern *Dienstmagd* left room for ambiguity, and, as elsewhere, prostitution in Münster was mainly undertaken by servant girls and casual workers.[14] The indirect connection between the two professions is clear. This tacit ambiguity between 'maidservant' and 'concubine' is also evident in a letter written by the *Commissarius* of Freckenhorst where he mentions servant girls and concubines in the same breath, stating that 'suspicious servant girls and concubines should be prohibited on the pain of serious punishment'.[15]

As the language of the reports reveals, the authorities presumed ulterior motives rather than genuine affection behind lay–clerical partnerships. This presumption considerably simplified their task, because it precluded any discussion of the issue of celibacy itself. If the authorities had allowed love and partnership to be considered, this could potentially have opened the doors to a debate on Tridentine strategies in general and Münsteran realities in particular, especially since many married clergymen lived just a few kilometres across the Dutch border. There, they practised officially what the Münsteran clergy had done unofficially for decades.

Visiting the clergy's houses in person, the officials usually managed to get the clergyman to comply reluctantly with the bishop's orders. The concubines were dismissed and moved to neighbouring villages or towns, some even finding refuge with the relatives of their former lovers.[16] Solemn celibacy reigned in clerical quarters until, after a while, the concubines gathered their belongings together and returned home, or as it was put in the report on Pastor Wiggers, they 'sneaked [back] in'.[17] The reunion had to be secret, since the authorities carried out occasional checks to make sure their orders were followed. Given the small size of the parishes, it seems unlikely in any case that the relationship would have remained undetected for long. Some of the authorities' knowledge came from gossip and local rumours, other cases were detected because the concubinaries were anonymously denounced by disgruntled parishioners. Most of what the authorities knew, however, came from the visitations carried out by the archdeacons. Once detected, the authorities moved in and the whole procedure began again: the cleric was

---

[14] S. Alfing and C. Schedensack, *Frauenalltag im frühneuzeitlichen Münster*, Münsterische Studien zur Frauen- und Geschlechtergeschichte, 1 (Bielefeld, 1994), 130.

[15] StAM, Fürstentum Münster, Landesarchiv, 2a Nr.16 Bd. 16, July 1620.

[16] Ibid., Bd. 5, 25 Dec. 1612.

[17] Ibid., 1611.

reprimanded and his woman dismissed; and often, once the storm had blown over, she returned once more.

This cycle of reprimands, break-ups, and returns was bound to create frustration. So, for example, in Werne, another archdeaconry of the bishopric:

> Hövel and Bockum: the priest *dimittirt* his concubine but when times were safe again, she was seen with him again in secret . . . Nortkirchen: she returned and spent a while with the priest again, the archdeacon returned to the house and questioned him, now she lives about an hour away by foot . . . Sendkirchen: the concubine was dismissed, she spent some time in Münster in the house of his brother but has recently returned again, fourteen days ago, now she has disappeared again . . .[18]

There are many similar accounts until at least the late 1620s.[19] It proved difficult to expel the concubines from the bishopric and to persuade the clergymen to buy into Ferdinand's talk about divine wrath and the need to reform their lifestyles. Victory, it seems, could not be achieved through the ordinary governmental techniques of legislation and execution. Why was this so?

One reason was that the ecclesiastical authorities lacked an effective punitive system. This might seem surprising in view of the frightening Tridentine punishments listed at the beginning of this study, ranging from admonitions to confiscation of salary, from dismissal to excommunication. Laid down in 1563, such punishments had still not been put into practice in Münster fifty years later. Apart from repeated verbose admonitions, none of the penalties laid down by Trent were actually used to support the enforcement of the bishop's orders. Aside from imprisonment, the most severe punishment documented in the Münsteran sources is the *Brüchte*, a fine payable to the archdeacon himself, who set its level. Many of the Münsteran archdeacons discovered that this was a lucrative source of income.[20] The introduction of money into the process made it possible for the more affluent clergy to buy their way out of punishment. The application of *Brüchten*, moreover, potentially transformed ecclesiastical jurisdiction from a respected means of correction into a bargaining tool, as is clear in the case of Johannes Bocholtt, a priest from Wesülbe. On 14 February 1617 he wrote a letter to the privy council (*heimgelassener Rat*) to complain about the size of his *Brüchte*. The

---

[18] Ibid., 25 Dec. 1612.

[19] See e.g. StAM, Domkapitel Münster, Akten Nr. 846, 20 April 1627.

[20] G. Ebers, *Die Archidiakonal-Streitigkeiten in Münster im 16. und 17. Jahrhundert: Sonderabdruck* (Weimar, special edn., n.d.), 371.

priest, who because of 'human weakness and stupidity' had engaged in an affair with his cook, was ordered to pay 50 *Reichstaler*. In Bocholt's eyes this sum was too high. As he pointed out in his letter he had already done 'enough of penance' when he had been in prison and 'lived on water and bread'. Bocholtt pleaded with the authorities to follow '*ad exemplum Christi* and give mercy now', adding in his support that he 'had improved so far and, with God's mercy, intended to remain abstinent in the future too'.[21]

His appeal to Christian values was not his only argument. Bocholtt also advanced plain material considerations, asserting that the penalty was so high that he would be unable to live according to his clerical status. It might seem unfitting for a man of the Church to adduce his own material needs and comforts, but this was a shrewd argument. Even the Church fathers at Trent had busied themselves with the importance of presentation and appearance. Clothes, as the Church authorities recognized, functioned as a marker of a person's social position in the community, allowing people to distinguish between high and low, proper and improper, honourable and dishonourable. The image their clergy projected, their appearance and life-style, was therefore not merely a matter of the propriety of the clerical dress code but an important part of Catholic propaganda.

Bishop Ferdinand himself had informed his priests that he expected them always to 'dress in the prescribed priestly clothing with the black cloak of knee length, that they avoid overly worldly ruffs and be tonsured'. He also ordered that 'the priests should not only dress according to their status, their reputation and their honour, but they should also distinguish themselves from lay folk through their appearance. If necessary he would enforce this order with the help of the punishments of the Tridentinum.' This was what Johannes Bocholtt exploited in his argument. The *Brüchte*, he wrote, would make it impossible for him 'to live according to my priestly status as I should', because it would make him 'come down completely and reduce me to beggary'.[22] Bocholtt suggested the penalty be reduced from 50 *Reichstaler* to 22 or 24, and included the additional bait of 'prayers every day for the rest of my life' for the members of the clerical council.[23]

The use of fines meant that the prosecution and punishment of clerical offences was transformed into a matter of negotiation, where, with a bit of

---

[21] StAM, Fürstentum Münster, Landesarchiv, 2a Nr. 16 Bd. 12, 14 Feb. 1617.

[22] A. Schröer, *Das Tridentinum und Münster* (Münster, 1951), 364.

[23] '. . . quod ut fiat jura canonica et SS. Concilium Tridentinum praescribit, et Ecclesiae Catholicae utritas requirit . . .', StAM, Fürstentum Münster, Landesarchiv, 2a Nr. 16 Bd. 12, 14 Feb. 1617.

luck, the penalty could be reduced. This lenience on the part of the Church reveals a measure of preferential treatment towards its own people, a tolerance for which ordinary sinners against Church law could not hope. Münsteran concubines, for example, were forced to leave the bishopric even if their priestly lovers had left the episcopacy in the meantime. The administration of justice, as carried out by some of the Münsteran archdeacons, was discriminating, partial, and variable. Consequently the legal process failed to achieve one of its initial goals: the inculcation of a consciousness of sin within the clergy. This effect has been described by Heinz Schilling as a consequence of what he calls the 'criminalization of sin'. Although Schilling developed his thesis for the Protestant Netherlands, where political conditions were very different, his assessment of how punishment degenerates when what he calls 'compensatory deals' are introduced applies equally to Catholic Münster: 'Unmistakable signs of church discipline having degenerated were fines and prison sentences. In this way conversion and repentance were substituted by punishment in the sense of secular punitive jurisdiction or rather by a compensatory deal as had been typical of medieval criminal justice.'[24]

Ferdinand was aware that the archidiaconal administration of justice posed a danger to the progress of reform. His failure in 1615 to take the prosecution of ecclesiastical offences away from the archdeacons now came home to roost. Because his archdeacons were unwilling to 'get tough', his attempt to reform was considerably slowed down. Nor did Ferdinand himself make use of the weapons given to him by the Council of Trent. None of the Münsteran clergy ever had to fear long-term reduction in wages, confiscations of benefices, or even excommunication. These punishments remained only paper threats, as his clergy probably knew.

Here again, one of Ferdinand's biggest problems is evident: in reforming the Münsteran Church in general and in prosecuting concubinage in particular, the bishop had to rely on the support of his clergy. Their knowledge of local conditions together with their power in the localities were indispensable in pushing through his reforms. Yet Ferdinand's reform programme did not meet with their unconditional support, and many episcopal orders express his dissatisfaction with what he felt was their lack of determination. In July 1613, for example, the *heimgelassener Rat* requested the officials to

---

[24] H. Schilling, ' "History of Crime" or "History of Sin"? Some Reflections on the Social History of Early Modern Church Discipline', in Tom Scott (ed.), *Politics and Society in Reformation Europe* (Hampshire, 1987), 304.

pay more regard to the prosecution of the concubines and less to their own convenience:

> Concubines have sneaked back in, living with their masters or in a village or town close by. Through this not only the common man is annoyed but also His Grace could be easily moved to disfavour. In order to elude public scandal the most serious distress requires to employ all our sincerity and diligence to carry out the orders of His Grace and to inquire most diligently, and should a concubine have returned, she should be pursued without regard to convenience . . .[25]

This complaint was merely one amongst many. In 1615 the *heimgelassener Rat* warned the officials that 'His Grace's orders shall be truly effected so that He might not be moved to disfavour and other thoughts because of the manifest laziness and negligence'.[26] This warning was given against the background of the familiar problem of concubines returning to their lovers: 'concubines have sneaked back in after they had been under pretence sent away for some time just to return shortly afterwards and to be taken back willingly by the clergy without any care for these goings-on or for His Grace's orders.'[27] The lack of real determination to carry out the bishop's decrees is obvious. This was because, amongst other things, Ferdinand's attempt to reform clerical lifestyles clashed with existing networks of patronage and established power structures. At local level these conflicts could usually be resolved by the officials with the help of some well-applied pressure in the form of verbal warnings or the threat of the bishop's anger. Matters became more complicated when the officials themselves did not cooperate with the bishop but instead worked hand in glove with the offenders, as the following report reveals: 'the lower officials (*Unterbeamten*) do not work to the effect to take the concubines to the local administration but collude with the clerics and their persons.'[28]

Higher up in the ecclesiastical hierarchy it was even harder to get matters to move more quickly. When, for example, the case of Johannes Borckhorst, a canon of the cathedral chapter, came to the boil in 1616, the vicar general was faced with a complex web of patronage. Borckhorst had already been accused of concubinage three times, and was denounced yet again. On top of this, Dr Hartmann, the vicar general, had repeatedly protested to the deacon

[25] StAM, Fürstentum Münster, Landesarchiv, 2a Nr. 16 Bd. 7, 18 July 1613.
[26] Ibid., Bd. 9, 31 July 1615.
[27] Ibid.
[28] Ibid., Bd. 12, date unknown.

of the cathedral chapter, 'not only once or twice but six times, orally and in writing', about Borckhorst's behaviour. The deacon, however, showed no willingness to take any action. On the contrary, instead of telling Borckhorst to mend his ways, the deacon exerted his connections amongst other members of the cathedral chapter to make them halt any proceedings against one of their own. When the case could no longer be postponed, the deacon insisted on a rather complicated and inefficient procedure to drag out the proceedings against Borckhorst, by establishing that he would only act 'in the presence of a number of prelates which he assigned to the case'. Yet, as Hartmann complained, 'whenever one of them is absent the rest do not want to proceed'. This meant that progress remained slow, since absenteeism was widespread amongst the higher clergy of the city. The strategy of delays was intended to distract Hartmann's attention from the case until his reformist energies were diverted elsewhere. When Hartmann realized what was afoot, he reminded the chapter that 'speedy process is needed to comply with the requirements of the Tridentinum, otherwise no permanent improvement can be expected'.[29] Networking and patronage also characterize a case from 1627, when the deacon and archdeacon of Überwasser reported his 'manifold suspicions and denunciations against Georg Kerstiens, the vicar here'. The archdeacon continued:

> Because of the powers of my job I wanted to visit him and after the examination to correct his shortcomings . . . When I let him know of the visitation Kerstiens used all sorts of elaborate excuses, which he put on paper with the help of the right kinds of people, this is why I grew all the more suspicious . . . Kerstiens then went to the spiritual vicar and the keeper of the seal and made a testimony on 22 June 1626 . . . Then he also used the vicar, *fiskal*, and *pater* to attest for him . . . All this made me even more suspicious of Kerstiens.[30]

The archdeacon continued his investigations until finally Kerstiens agreed to be questioned, though only in the presence of a notary. When interrogated, Kerstiens admitted to almost all the points, from concubinage to '*fraudulentiam*'. Although the archdeacon would have been authorized 'to punish Kerstiens harshly', he decided instead 'to give him only a small fine, which Kerstiens tried to reduce even more with sure words . . . and then appealed

---

[29] Ibid., April 1617.

[30] StAM, Domkapitel Münster, Akten Nr. 846, 20 April 1627. The context of the accusation of 'fraudulentiam' is not explained further in the text. It shows, however, that concubinage was often not the only moral transgression of the cleric in question.

against it'.[31] But the archdeacon did not give in to Kerstiens. As a result, Kerstiens took the matter one step further, appealing to the *Officialis* although, as the archdeacon pointed out sourly, he did not even 'have the right to appeal at all'. It was the fact of the appeal which sparked the archdeacon's complaint, for he simply could not allow his authority to be undermined in this way. Kerstiens' strategy was clearly to involve as many people in high places as possible, getting them to exert influence on his behalf. Ultimately, their interference was intended to remove decision-making powers from the archdeacon, placing them with those who might be more sympathetic to Kerstiens and might bring about a favourable outcome to his case. By mobilizing 'the right kinds of people', insisting on notaries and other jurists, and formalizing every detail of the proceedings, Kerstiens kept the bureaucratic machine busy. This was a ploy favoured by many concubinaries higher up in the ecclesiastical hierarchy. Just as Bishop Ferdinand issued an increasing flood of orders and decrees, of bureaucracy and officialdom, concubinaries also used paper to defend their liberties.[32]

Ronnie Hsia has pointed out that the canons of the cathedral chapter all came from the Westphalian nobility. Only a minority would have met the spiritual standards and obligations of Trent. Most could be accused of absenteeism, neglect of their spiritual responsibilities, and many even kept common-law wives. According to Hsia, the cathedral chapter can be seen as the main focus of opposition to the implementation of the Tridentine decrees of reform in Münster.[33] Moreover, there was no formal code of morality or any other form of self-discipline applied to the members of the chapter. The canons were not willing to make any concessions regarding their own freedoms, and even mocked Hartmann and his attempts to tidy up concubinage: 'Some men think that they have done enough to carry out the bishop's orders . . . and wonder whether the spiritual vicar wants to

---

[31] Ibid.

[32] The growing importance of the legal professions in seventeenth-century Münster has also been noted by Ronnie Hsia, who states that litigation together with linen weaving represented the two fastest-growing sectors in Münster's economy: R. Hsia, *Society and Religion in Münster, 1535–1618* (New Haven, 1984), 114.

[33] Ibid., 32–3. For more literature about the cathedral chapter, see for example, Heinrich Spieckermann, *Beiträge zur Geschichte des Domkapitels zu Münster im Mittelalter* (Emsdetten, 1935); Ulrich Herzog, *Untersuchungen zur Geschichte des Domkapitels zu Münster und seines Besitzes im Mittelalter* (Göttingen, 1961); Alois Schröer, 'Das Münsterer Domkapitel im ausgehenden Mittelalter. Ein Beitrag zur Kirchengeschichte Westfalens', in id., *Monasterium. Festschrift zum 700jährigen Weihegedächtnis des Paules-Domes zu Münster* (Münster, 1966).

master them.'[34] Hartmann, on the other hand, did not shy away from taking on some of the most powerful ecclesiastics of the Münsteran Church.

The results, however, were mixed, because concubinage touched the very core of ecclesiastical hierarchy. The impact of its prosecution was noticeable among all sections of the clergy, from those living in the localities to the members of the cathedral chapter. Ferdinand's decision to place more power into the hands of the vicar general meant that no concubinary of whatever background or status could be sure that his lifestyle would not be scrutinized by the bishop's officials. This knowledge must have helped to form alliances and support networks amongst those members of the clergy who resented the interference from above or simply refused to give up their ways.

Ferdinand's lack of success was also conditioned by the limited time and personnel available to prosecute concubinage. The years leading up to the outbreak of the Thirty Years War, when Münster joined the Catholic League in 1613 and later the war itself, diverted some of the bishop's energies to international politics. More importantly, however, concubinage was essentially about a constant renegotiation of power. This renegotiation took place between the prince-bishop and his officials on one side and competing authorities, such as the archdeacons or the canons of the cathedral chapter, on the other. Concubinage thus had little to do with morality but far more with authority and influence over spiritual territories, rights, duties, and responsibilities.

The Clerics

Concubinage was more than just an embarrassment for the Catholic Church. Its consequences, particularly on the spiritual level, were very severe. Most serious was the damage it caused in the relationship between the human and the divine. A cleric's susceptibility to the flesh was seen by the Church as a threat to the Christian ideal of virginity and the charisma that was associated with a life of undivided service to God. It was popularly believed that mass said by a sinful priest was not fully effective. Concubinage jeopardized his position as a mediator between God and his people, a role that had been bestowed on him through holy ordination. The solution lay in a return to the early Christian ideal of virginity as required by the Tridentine decrees, in which the priest had to renounce the intimacy of marriage and family for the universal love of his flock. Free from worldly cares and demands, he would then be able to fulfil his service to his fellow Christians wholeheartedly. Even philosophers like Aristotle had regarded marriage, family, and sex as

---

[34] StAM, Fürstentum Münster, Landesarchiv, 2a Nr. 16 Bd. 12, April 1617.

obstacles to reaching self-perfection and wisdom.[35] But would the Münsteran clergy be able to grasp the theological significance and impact of celibacy?

The sources frequently mention *humana fragilitas* or human weakness as a reason why clerics broke their vows of chastity when faced with carnal temptation. The Münsteran material suggests that many concubinaries saw celibacy as applying to nuns and monks, but not to them. They had chosen the clerical life in the way that others became teachers or farmers, on the basis of family traditions and practical considerations. Living out their normal human desires, therefore, did not make them feel guilty, as the following example shows:

> I was reminded of the bishop's orders a couple of times through the official of Horstmar and also threatened with punishment to leave my servant girl without any further ado and to bring her away . . . Although it is my duty to observe his Grace's order with subservience, it is nevertheless right and true that I have been in the clerical estate for forty-seven years . . . that I can take the responsibility before God Almighty and hopefully thus also before my high superiors too, forty-one years I have been the innocent shepherd and have taken care of the spiritual welfare of the people of Appenhülst whilst losing my health and as my body became pitifully broken, thus because of my great age and physical frailty, I cannot help myself without my housekeeper . . . I have an old maidservant who served me forty years for the yearly wage of a servant girl and who looks after my household loyally and, moreover, she does not do any other loose things (which do not have to be referred to here any further) so that I can be sure of her loyal honest service and have to praise and thank her. If I should now let her go from me without any reason, but after much effort and work from her side, and hire a new one, it would bring me much harm and scolding; in order not to get into discredit and suspicion with my prince-bishop and master and the *heimgelassene Räte* I am making this very friendly request for you to speak to the officials about my case . . . Johannes Kerlvinck.[36]

This letter, sent by the priest of Appenhülst to Matthias Duffertz, the judge of Bilderbeck and Kerlvinck's 'very special friend', demonstrates how

---

[35] Franzen, *Zölibat und Priesterehe*, 8–11.

[36] Ibid., Bd. 7, 24 Aug. 1613.

theological ideals clashed with the realities of clerical life in the parishes. Kerlvinck tried to exploit his friendship with Duffertz and his connections in the council to keep his female servant. As the reason why the council should grant him this exception, Kerlvinck adduced his great age and his 'pitifully broken body', which meant he needed personal care. He also underlined the old age of his maid, thus implying a diminished interest in sexual matters. In arguing thus, however, Kerlvinck did not explain the presence of the woman in his house for the past four decades.

More striking, however, is the emotional bond evident between the priest and his maid. The strong attachment to a woman conflicted with the asexual image the Church wanted its priesthood to project. And yet, priests lived and practised their profession in a local community. Emotional attachments between the two sexes outside the sanctioned confessor–penitent relationship were bound to arise. A cleric was supposed to be sufficiently involved in the affairs of his parish to know the behaviour and concerns of his flock, yet sufficiently removed to preserve his charisma as vicar of Christ. But the reality of shared housekeeping and personal attachment looked different. To these clerics, the actions of the bishop and his officials were an overreaction which unjustly extended suspicion to each and every woman. Nor were they alone in this view. In a letter from 1615 Gerhard Crane, the archdeacon of Langenhorst, wrote to the authorities:

> I, the *commissario archidiaconatus* . . . have been miserably, wretchedly told by Mr Heinrich Lodrigs, a vicar of Ochtrup, 85 years old, that he had hired a maid for many years, who helped him in his housekeeping as an honest, pious servant girl should, that she has until recently served him, but the other day it has happened that the official of Ochtorpe took the same maid (as if she were living with him in concubinage and in breach of duty) from his house, and after much discussion the official kept her imprisoned in his house and this, as he says, because of his Grace's severe orders . . . Although it is right to watch out for vice and to follow his prince-bishop's orders with all seriousness, I am nevertheless of the opinion that his Grace's orders cannot not be understood in any other way but to be directed against those persons who are guilty of such an immoral life, but not those honest servant girls who are in the service of the clergy and who behave honourably, otherwise no honest maid would want to serve a cleric any more because of the dangers and innocent denigration . . . it is my wish that Your Honour should let the said person go without a fine but also let her work for her master again and because he would be offended and dishonoured in front of everyone . . . it should be

proven instead that she had been the concubine of the said Mr Henrichen, that's how you deal with the good and punish the evil ones, that's what I have to tell you . . .[37]

The archdeacon demanded better proof through a more formalized procedure. Gossip, rumours, and denunciations were not sufficient. He may also, of course, have been complaining because the officials' speedy intervention had interfered with his rights and powers.

The Church aspired to a morally impeccable clergy, well educated and tireless in carrying out its spiritual duties. The Council of Trent had confirmed the special function of the clergy as role models for the laity, calling on the clergy to terminate any illicit sexual affairs:

Wherefore, that the ministers of the Church may be brought back to that continency and purity of life which is proper to them, and that for this reason the people may learn to reverence them the more, the more honourable they see them in their conduct, the holy council forbids all clerics whatsoever to presume to keep concubines or other women concerning whom suspicion can be had in their house or elsewhere, or to presume to have any association with them; otherwise they shall be punished with the penalties imposed by the sacred canons or the statutes of the churches.[38]

Religious men and women alike should follow a life of inner and outer perfection, not only for its own sake but because of the effect that their lifestyle would have on others. It was hoped that this would help to turn the laity into devout believers. 'There is nothing that leads others to piety and to the service of God more than the life and example of those who have dedicated themselves to the divine ministry.'[39] Yet, as the Münsteran ecclesiastical authorities realized, a clergy of such immaculate religiosity was hard to find. Meanwhile, behaviour like that of a priest from Warendorf inspired mockery and disrespect rather than piety and religious devotion. The anonymous writer of the following satirical poem, composed in about 1612, vented his rage about the priest on paper:

---

[37] Ibid., Bd. 10, 14 Sept. 1615.

[38] Session XXV reform, ch. XIV: 'The manner of proceeding against clerics who keep concubines is prescribed', in Schroeder, *Canons and Decrees*, 246–8.

[39] Session XXII, ch. 1: 'Decrees concerning the life and conduct of clerics are renewed', in ibid., 152.

> Come all ye honest people and listen to this
> About a real rogue, the priest of the new church
> Hellebrandt is his name, well known in Warendorf . . .
> But the worst is still to come, one has to endure this
> What he did anno 1612 on Sacrament's Day,
> That after he with due manner and honour dignity
> Goes off soon to [the tavern] drinks himself full
> would be the pity of all devils
> Then he becomes sick: spits out his god at the wall
> This is known to the sacristan and many people of Warendorf.
> Let this be proper Catholic style.[40]

At a time when strict fasting was prescribed, the drunken priest vomited just after the celebration of the sacrament of the Eucharist, and spat 'his god at the wall'. Such behaviour made the Catholic doctrine of transubstantiation a laughing stock. No Protestant propaganda could have done more harm than the behaviour of this local priest: 'Let this be proper Catholic style.'

Yet this was not all. Three years later Hellebrandt caused a major scandal in Warendorf when he tried to elope with the 'daughter of an honest burgher, called Heinrich Tomckens, about 15 years old and very pregnant (*grob schwanger*) . . .'. The two were caught and the girl was instantly returned to her parents. Hellebrandt had to await his trial living on 'water and bread or thin beer in the evening only for three days, the following day he should be fed on common servants' food twice a day only, in between meals he should not be given any drink'.[41] These were the instructions of the vicar general himself. Hellebrandt received this rare punishment at the hands of his superior because of his public disregard for authority, ecclesiastical but also parental, and because the town of Warendorf was well known for its strong sympathies with Protestantism, a mixture which did not allow for leniency.

The priest's entanglement in these scandals also demonstrated that tolerating one kind of immorality could lead to others. It would be wrong to suggest that concubinaries were guilty of all sins. Yet in many cases, keeping a concubine was just the most visible failing amongst a host of others. This also becomes clear in a report by the city council of Münster itemizing the loose behaviour of members of the cathedral chapter:

---

[40] StAM, Fürstentum Münster, Landesarchiv, 2a Nr. 16 Bd. 5.
[41] Ibid.

The abuse has grown so far that a few years ago various children born in concubinage organized big wedding parties once the time for this had arrived (to which were invited a large number of secular men, women, apprentices, and virgins who all came along); the funds for these parties came from the honourable cathedral chapter to the not small anger of those watching in public . . .[42]

The list of failings is long: cathedral canons cohabited, sired children, and allowed their offspring to mix freely with laypeople of both sexes—and had gone unpunished by the cathedral. Yet of course promoting one's offspring, legitimate and illegitimate, was practised everywhere in such aristocratic circles. The anger of the city council stemmed from the fact that this was so public, and that all these people, together with their servants and children, lived within the immunity of the cathedral chapter where they were safe from punishment by the town council, and enjoyed clerical perks, namely 'being free from the obligations of the burgher people', without actually being clergy.[43] In an earlier synodal decree of 1613 Ferdinand had already tried to institute a general reform package for the clergy:

In order to terminate the abuses, the bishop, on the basis and with the approval of the cathedral chapter, institutes the decrees of the Council of Trent and demands that the clergy does away with all suspicious women. The clerics should abstain from visiting public taverns. Tonsure and clerical dress shall be worn. Those enjoying the income of ecclesiastical benefices shall be 'ordained to the clerical orders'.[44]

Bishop Ferdinand knew he had to tackle clerical immorality on all fronts, in whatever shape or form. The indifference Ferdinand faced was the biggest enemy of Catholic reform in Münster. The Church seemed unable to sell its programme as something positive and desirable. Few clerics would have followed the intellectual arguments about concubinage and its consequences with interest. To most, parting with their maidservants seemed like excessively harsh punishment, not reform. Nevertheless, the bishop was sure that the fight against concubinage was only one of a series of changes he needed to push through if a Tridentine clergy were to be established in Münster.

---

[42] Schafmeister, *Herzog Ferdinand*, 97.

[43] Ibid.

[44] StAM, Fürstentum Münster, Landesarchiv, 2a Nr. 16 Bd. 7, 24 Aug. 1613.

The Women

Because it proved so difficult to discipline the clergy, the ecclesiastical authorities increasingly turned their attention to the women themselves as the most effective means of prosecuting concubinage. At the beginning of his episcopacy Ferdinand used strong language against concubines: 'each and every cleric regardless of whatever their rank may be, if they are known or suspected of having women with them in concubinage, that they, on threat of serious punishment and disfavour, chase them out of their towns and the bishopric within four weeks, so as to escape much justified punishment from God.' Yet he was aware that ultimately human determination rather than divine intervention was needed to deal with the problem, and the decree continued: 'In case this does not work, you should grab them [the women] by their heads and place them publicly at the pillory and then have them removed from the bishopric.'[45] Two motives lay behind these measures, punishing sin and deterring other women, as is evident in an episcopal decree of 1615: 'The quasi-wifely concubines should be investigated with utmost diligence and in case they are keeping company with the clerics again to catch them at once and to display them publicly at the pillory to set an example and to disgust other people.'[46] The authorities used the pillory, imprisonment, and expulsion to demonstrate that cohabitation with a cleric would bring public humiliation. The unhappy fate of a concubine from Freckenhorst was clearly designed to teach a public lesson: 'because this is no cold and dangerous time the imprisoned concubine can be kept for another week in the local prison . . . Because the longer she sits [in prison] the greater her example will become known in the whole bishopric, and will thus hopefully deter others.'[47] In this respect the women were treated more severely than their partners, who, although also imprisoned, received spiritual guidance and comfort through the Church. Hellebrandt, the priest from Warendorf, was given a 'pater confessor to allow him a general confession and serious betterment' while in prison.[48] No comparable efforts were made to assist the spiritual welfare of the imprisoned women. Concubines could only hope to gain similar treatment if they joined the Magdalene category of fallen women, to whom the Church reserved its consolation. In a letter written in a female hand, a Münsteran woman described this process of reconciliation.

[45] Ibid., Bd. 5, 28 June 1612.
[46] Ibid., Bd. 9, 31 July 1615.
[47] Ibid., Bd. 16, 3 July 1620.
[48] Ibid., Bd. 10, August 1615.

I am a poor, burdened woman and cannot let it go unknown . . . that I too, God have mercy, through human weakness came to fall . . . and was for a while with Barthold of Raesfeld, canon of the collegiate church in Dülmen, and lived with him in the said manner . . . but I felt remorse and much regret, confessed and took communion and made a complete break . . . this is why the mayor and council of Dülmen admitted me to citizenship . . .[49]

Through the confession of her sins and the celebration of communion the repentant sinner sought absolution from Church and society. It was the only way a woman could re-enter society.

Another reason for the greater lenience of the Münsteran Church towards its own personnel lay in the general shortage of clerics in the bishopric, which forced the authorities to keep concubinaries in their posts. In Werne a known concubinary was 'tolerated', because of 'a shortage of persons and because he looks after the school and the organ at the same time'.[50] The lack of a proper seminary saved many a clergyman's tainted career. As Bishop Franz Wilhelm of nearby Osnabrück put it: 'One thing worries me deeply, and it slows progress too, I cannot remove these people with such offensive lifestyles, because I have no one to put in their place, because we lack the means for a seminary.'[51] Münster had to rely on a small makeshift seminary which also made it hard to recruit and train a more educated, devoted clergy.

Yet although the Church's punishments targeted the concubines, it was in fact uninterested in the women's minds and motives. In the documents the women are rarely mentioned by name but remain anonymous wrongdoers who are simply classified as *Concubinen*. During the sixteenth and seventeenth centuries the label underscored the ecclesiastical authorities' conviction that the women were the least important element in the triangle of women, Church, and clerics. Historians have so far continued this tradition, referring to the women only collectively as concubines without ever examining the realities of their lives. One reason for this lies in the paucity of archival material. This is also why the popular image of the clerical concubine has changed surprisingly little throughout the centuries. They have come down to us as cooks, maidservants, and housewives. My findings, too, are based on a limited number of documents written by the women themselves, their children and other relatives, their priestly lovers, and the authorities. But even these sources allow fresh insights. For example, cooking, serving, and

---

[49] StAM, Fürstentum Münster, Landesarchiv, 2a Nr. 16 Bd. 10, date unknown.

[50] StAM, Fürstentum Münster, Landesarchiv, 2a Nr. 16 Bd. 8, 26 June 1614.

[51] Schafmeister, *Herzog Ferdinand*, 95.

housekeeping were just some of the roles fulfilled by concubines, who were also lovers and partners, nurses and carers, and in some cases mothers too, just like other women. Moreover, the authorities' depiction of these women as 'loose' conflicts with their profession of conventional aspirations and their strong personalities.

Even the report of the papal nuncio quoted earlier reveals the remarkable self-confidence many concubines exhibited in a hostile environment. 'The women call themselves prelatesses (*Pröpstinnen*) and abbesses, and make sure they are called thus on their gravestones and other public inscriptions.'[52] Another letter, this time addressed to Dr Johannes Hartmann, reveals the same self-confidence and willpower. Anna Nydders, whom the official who passed on the letter to the *heimgelassener Rat* referred to as a *professa* at the Winnenberg convent, turned to the vicar general in financial matters. Nydders had supported her former lover, the priest of Winnenberg, Hinderich Schulz, financially, though he 'brought me to fall and ruin of my body'. Now that their affair had ended she wrote to Hartmann to get her money back and every *Reichstaler* she had spent for Schulz on top. This included her expenses in childbed plus compensation, the size of which she wanted the council to assess, for the 'pains, damage of my honour and health of my body'.[53]

The letter shows someone fighting for her rights. Nydders did not excuse her past behaviour, nor did she adopt the male partner's strategy of eliciting compassion. The second page of the petition itemizes her expenses: 'half a *Thaler* when the child had been so ill for fourteen days, the burial of the child 3 *Thaler*, had a coat made for the child which cost me 3 *Thaler*', and so on. She demanded that 'Hinderich Schulten who stays in Harsewinckel at his sister's, or his guarantors, should repay the money he owes me . . . and that he recompense me according to the council's judgement for the pains and damage'.[54] The letter is all the more impressive because of its clear structure and precise wording. Although written in dialect, Nydders even used a few well-chosen Latin expressions. Anna Nydders did not place her trust in luck. She knew that her only chance was to argue her case as persuasively as possible. Her status as *professa* at the Winnenberg convent, which had strong ties to the aristocratic convent of Überwasser, and her apparent education suggests that Anna came from a well-off family. Some of the other concubines also came from families where education mattered, as is clear from their ability to read and write. It would be a mistake, though, to claim that many concubines

---

[52] Hüsing, *Der Kampf um die katholische Religion*, p. 351.
[53] StAM, Fürstentum Münster, Landesarchiv, 2a Nr. 16 Bd. 12, 6 Sept. 1617.
[54] Ibid.

came from the upper strata of society. We simply do not possess the material that would provide us with such information. All we can conclude is that concubines appear to have belonged to all strata of society, even the highest. This hypothesis is also supported by the case of a nun from Überwasser who, for many years, lived more or less undisturbed by the authorities with a canon of the cathedral chapter. When Bishop Ferdinand complained about this affair, the chapter defended its inactivity thus: 'no measure had been taken against the canon von Nagel, because the nun who does his housekeeping belongs to a noble family, and because the family would have been exposed had any procedures been taken against her.'[55]

Anna Nydder's letter reveals the two biggest dangers that a concubine faced. The first was lack of financial security. As long as the woman lived with her partner she might be well fed and comfortably off, but the end of the relationship might find her on the streets without the rights an abandoned wife could claim from her husband. Nor could she expect support from her local community. These financial considerations were serious, but the ethical dimensions of concubinage were of even greater significance. This is what lies behind Anna's reference to the 'pains, damage of my honour and health of my body'. Honour and health were probably the two single most precious attributes of a woman in the early modern period. A woman's honour was, as we know, intimately connected to her sexual behaviour.[56] It was her own duty and that of her husband to protect her honour. But could an unmarried woman in an illegal relationship meet this social standard? If we apply the common standards of the time, the answer is simply 'no', for Münster allowed neither concubines, whom it categorized as prostitutes, nor their children to gain citizenship.[57] The protocols concerning *Brüchten* from the end of the sixteenth century also stipulate that concubines should wear special clothes.[58] Officially, concubines were neither single nor married, but in reality they were both. Living in long-term relationships, they considered themselves to be matrons.[59] Their demands and general attitude indicate that they perceived themselves as quasi-wives (remember these were Ferdinand's

---

[55] This case also reveals that the introduction of enclosure at the Überwasser convent in the 1610s and 1620s was not as successful as hitherto believed. Unfortunately it is not possible to examine the sources on which Karl Schafmeister based his study because they were lost in WWII. Schafmeister, *Ferdinand von Bayern*, 95.

[56] Cf. Alfing, *Frauenalltag*, 38.

[57] Ibid., 130.

[58] StdAM, A VIII Vermögen der Stadt, Nr. 277 Brüchtenprotokolle (1591–1644), fol. 21v, 15 July 1596 and fol. 38, 12 Sept. 1625.

[59] Cf. StAM, Fürstentum Münster, Landesarchiv, 2a Nr. 16 Bd. 8, 26 June 1614.

words too!) and long-term companions.[60] In their opinion this also gave them some rights. A concubine from Oplte, for example, refused to move out of the priest's house after his death, though a qualified successor had long been chosen, because she insisted on the 'year of grace', the same privilege as was given to the widows of those holding civic positions.[61] This, she clearly assumed, would give her the time she needed to reorganize her life after the death of her partner. In their letters, most women did not excuse their behaviour or reveal any signs which would allow us to conclude that they felt their honour had been diminished by their relationships with clergymen. The example of the '*Pröpstinnen*, prelatesses, and abbesses' shows, on the contrary, that many women felt their honour and social status had been heightened through association with such respected men. The women's definition of honour clearly did not conform to official standards.

Society, nonetheless, could punish them for their nonconformist behaviour through social marginalization. Anna Nydders's demands reveal that she was aware she would not be able to reclaim her honour and acceptance in society. This was why she demanded compensation. Money was the only way to soften the consequences of her unorthodox lifestyle and deal with the consequences of her relationship with the priest. Since she probably considered it only fair that her lover should have to pay for his share in the relationship too, she was self-confident and firm about her requests. To her, a woman's honour was a commodity with a negotiable value.

Strong bonds and family affection shine through the letters sent to the authorities by the people involved in cases of concubinage. In July 1620, for example, Dietherich Wilkens wrote to the *heimgelassene Rat* to plead mercy for his mother Gertrud Löckmanns, who was sitting in prison 'despite her grave-heading age'.[62] Wilckens described how his mother had obediently followed the bishop's decrees and how she and his father, Dietherich Stephani Wilckens, the canon of Freckenhorst, had separated. Lately though:

---

[60] See also Wilhelm Kohl's judgement that '[i]n all cases with very few exceptions, concubinage meant marriage-like relationships which merely lacked public blessing. The canons and their "maids" always remained committed to their relationship and separated for a short time under pressure only to get back together once the attention of the authorities had diminished.' W. Kohl, 'Tridentinische Reform im Domkapitel zu Münster', in (ed.), Remigius Bäumer, *Reformation Ecclesiae: Beiträge zu kirchlichen Reformbemühungen von der Alten Kirche bis zur Neuzeit: Festgabe für Erwin Iserloh* (Paderborn, Munich, Vienna; Zürich, 1980), 741.

[61] StAM, Fürstentum Münster, Landesarchiv, 2a Nr. 16 Bd. 8, 3 Oct. 1614 and StAM, Fürstentum Münster, Landesarchiv, 2a Nr. 16 Bd. 8, 23 Oct. 1614.

[62] StAM, Fürstentum Münster, Landesarchiv, 2a Nr. 16 Bd. 16, 1 July 1620.

my mother has unfortunately heard and seen how pitiable and miserably my father has to lie because of his *podragischen*[63] limbs, that he needs the help of two people to be turned and moved around . . . full of pity she stepped into his house, her thoughts were without any carnal desire, as one would expect from such stone-old people, but only to give him a helping hand, according to her means, in his poverty and weakness . . . but last Friday she has been caught and imprisoned.[64]

This is a heartfelt lament at the inhuman behaviour of the authorities, about their attempt to inaugurate a new age of morality without recognizing that these relationships had existed for a long time and had thus acquired some legitimacy in their own right. The case of Elsabe von Horst and Heinrich Ledebur, a canon at the Münsteran cathedral chapter, leaves us with the same impression. In November 1613 he was questioned about his relationship, and without hesitation Ledebur admitted his weakness, though he refused to vow never to return to Elsabe, saying that he 'would rather lose his head or that a knife would be twisted in his heart'. In 1614 the two were forced to separate, but Ledebur was 'so inconsolable, that he wants to push a knife into his belly. He doesn't know why he was treated like that. If he was supposed to go to hell, he would prefer to do it himself sooner rather than later.' And when Elsabe had died in 1618 he had a tombstone erected for her, 'and this with much anger'.[65] Some, as in the case of Wilckens and Ledebur, had even started a family, though the secular authorities regarded the offspring of such unions as dishonourable. Even so, Sabine Alfing mentions the case of Anna Volmers, who was granted citizenship despite the fact that her four children were born in concubinage.[66] This, and the example of our earlier anonymous repentant concubine who had been granted citizenship by the city council of Dülmen, demonstrates that the demarcations of honour were not as clear as it might seem. The viewpoint of the Church on the offspring of these unions was clear:

That the memory of the incontinency of the fathers may be banished as far as possible from places consecrated to God, where purity and holiness are most especially becoming, it shall not be lawful for sons of clerics, not born in lawful wedlock, to hold in those churches in

---

[63] His father suffered from gout. See *podagel/Podagra* in Lübben, *Mittelniederdeutsches Handwörterbuch*, 281.

[64] StAM, Fürstentum Münster, Landesarchiv, 2a Nr. 16 Bd. 16, 1 July 1620.

[65] Kohl, *Tridentinische Reform*, 741.

[66] Alfing, *Frauenalltag*, 130.

which their fathers have or had some ecclesiastical benefice, any benefice whatsoever, even though a different one, or to minister in any way in those churches, or to have salaries from the revenues of the benefices which their fathers hold or formerly have held.[67]

The Council of Trent had ruled that illegitimate sons of clerics were to be excluded from any offices or benefices of the Church, but for the Münsteran clergy this rule existed only on paper. We know from Wilhelm Kohl's study of the Münsteran cathedral chapter during the sixteenth and seventeenth century that the higher echelons of the clergy used their connections to provide a place in the Church for their illegitimate sons.[68] Our *Officiant* Wilckens also saw no reason to conceal his son's existence: the son was even given his father's first and last name, thus making his parentage unmistakable.

Despite these emotional bonds, the concubines realized the peculiarity of their situation. They knew that their behaviour was judged as morally reprehensible by their lovers' superiors, and did not close their eyes to the possible consequences. The precariousness of their situation must have become absolutely clear when Trent knocked at their doors, causing some of them to take steps to protect their future. One way to build security for hard times was to open the doors of the clerical houses to their relatives. This proved useful when the concubine was forced to leave by the authorities. Her relatives, on the other hand, remained unaffected by the orders. This is what happened to Elsa Steinbickers and her family. Elsa had embarked on what we might call the typical career of a concubine, being 'in service and on duty' at Mr Wycks's house, the vicar of Freckenhorst.

> But she turned away from him following the orders of His Grace, obediently abstained from his presence and his conversation . . . and told her confessor about it . . . But now last Friday she went to Mr Wyck's home, not to visit him and without any indecent thoughts or deeds, only to see her sister and her daughters who live in his house and to get her clothes, which she had to leave behind because she had to move out in such a rush.[69]

As a consequence of the decree Steinbickers had to leave her life and belongings behind. At that point it was her family that offered help. Family and other relatives provided important safety networks in times of hardship through their material and practical assistance, by writing petitions, and

---

[67] Session XXV reform, ch. XV: 'From what benefices the illegitimate sons of clerics are excluded', in Schroeder, *Canons and Decrees*, 248.

[68] W. Kohl, *Tridentinische Reform*, 741.

[69] StAM, Fürstentum Münster, Landesarchiv, 2a Nr. 16 Bd. 16, July 1620.

through giving emotional support. Another way to achieve some security was to employ the same weapons as the ecclesiastical authorities. Hence, some concubines placed their trust in paper:

> The priest of Werne complains that the *Officiant* of Werne, Bernard Conradi, does not want to dismiss his concubine . . . He had dismissed her before, but after my departure she had instantly been allowed to return. Item likewise too; only a few days ago a person came to his house, who had been his concubine before this one and who has a child from him, who exhibited a paper, on which he declares his engagement to her, she demands support for the child.[70]

The concubine had shrewdly used the power of the written word to secure her future and that of her child by making the *Officiant* sign an 'engagement contract'. We do not know whether this was effective, but it reveals some clever thinking and shows the concubine not as a victim but as a determined woman. But why does this surprise us? Conventional thinking perhaps likes to characterize them as weak characters and loose women, but does it not take more strength and willpower to live an unconventional life, despite the disapproval of the majority? This is what these women did, without excusing themselves.

Conclusion

Just as the Church fathers at Trent had anticipated, one rebuke was not enough to end relationships between clerics and concubines. In most cases this could not be achieved with theological arguments, but only through threats and force. The evangelical Church had long ago allowed clergy to marry, sanctioning relationships which had already been very common amongst the clergy of the old faith. After all, even the Saviour Jesus Christ himself had acknowledged that celibacy was impossible without a special sign of God's Grace.[71]

Until the Council of Trent concluded in 1563, there was still hope amongst the Catholic clergy that this option could be possible for them too. The idea had some powerful supporters, including Emperor Ferdinand, who did not wish to follow the Protestants in condemning celibacy but wanted to adjust to the reality by officially allowing cohabitation.[72] Such opinions in

---

[70] Ibid., Bd. 8, 26 June 1614.
[71] Cf. Matt. 19: 12, quoted in Franzen, *Zölibat und Priesterehe*, 34.
[72] Ibid., 84.

the end failed to gain enough support within the Church, and the Church fathers rejected a more pragmatic approach to celibacy.

Initially, these questions were not of much consequence for the situation in Münster where, during the second half of the sixteenth century, Protestantism and Catholicism had silently coexisted. The general leniency in questions of faith and morality was, in the eyes of some Church superiors, a grave danger. The *Großinquisitor* Pius (1566–72) wrote to the then bishop of Münster that he worried 'day and night' about how the heresy which had spilled over from Germany could be fought. He saw the root of the evil as lying in the 'immoral and shameful lifestyle of the clergy who lived in their houses with their concubines just like legitimate wives. In the face of such public anger the heretics had a simple game with the people, because they only needed to point to the disgraceful life of the priests.'[73] Alarm was caused by the existence of heresy in the Dutch territories just across the borders of the bishopric and, nearer to home, amongst the people of the bishopric itself. Many of them followed a rough-and-ready mixture of Protestant and Catholic traditions. Reports from the town of Warendorf, for example, confirm that people sang German hymns in Mass and celebrated the Eucharist in both kinds. Although Warendorf was later won back to the Catholic Church, the deep alienation of some sections of the laity from Catholicism and its clergy was clear. During the 1610s and 1620s these were contested areas, where people were able to see alternative lifestyles and religious beliefs practised. As a result it was not quite so obvious which way religion would move. The election of two Wittelsbach bishops who were also serious proponents of the Counter-Reformation, Ernst of Bavaria and his nephew Ferdinand, brought change. Ferdinand certainly had no intention of tolerating this confessional muddle any longer, and chose concubinage as his starting point for reform.

The road to triumph, however, was rocky, and the officials had to be content with small victories. On the positive side the authorities could point to the establishment of a more formalized procedure in the dealings with concubinage. Some officials used notaries for their examinations.[74] Others even used witnesses in addition to the notary to confirm their statements.[75] The officials at least do not seem to have harboured any doubts as to the bishop's sincerity about ending concubinage, and his determination bore fruit as the news from the bailiff of Legden shows: 'as far as my territory is concerned

---

[73] Ibid.
[74] StAM, Fürstentum Münster, Landesarchiv, 2a Nr. 16 Bd. 7, 12 Aug. 1613.
[75] Ibid., Bd. 10, 17 Aug. 1615.

I have carried out the investigation with all the seriousness required . . . the clergy living in this territory (*Vogtei*) obediently follow the orders and have dismissed their concubines.'[76]

The real breakthrough against concubinage, however, only came with Ferdinand's successor, Christoph Bernhard of Galen (1650–72). Admittedly, his task was made easier by the growing popularity of the Jesuit schools in the bishopric and the existence of a proper seminary. This had a markedly positive influence on the younger generations, who quietly conformed to the norms laid down in the decrees of Trent. A chronicler described Christoph Bernhard's success in the following words: 'Amongst all the magnanimous deeds and praiseworthy decrees which he did, he was able right at the beginning of his government to end the concubinage of the clergy.' Yet it took almost one hundred years before concubinage finally disappeared. Westphalia thus in many respects lagged far behind southern Germany, where episcopal Catholic reform movements succeeded in the last quarter of the sixteenth century.[77]

At the heart of concubinage lay a complex web of dependence, personal friendship and animosities. This is why concubinage was essentially a matter of constant struggles between the bishop and the cathedral chapter, between the officials and the clergy in the city and in the localities. The fight required a good deal of strength and resolution as well as finesse and diplomacy. The significance of concubinage for the Tridentine cause sprang from the recognition that it was about more than sex and celibacy, that it was about everything Trent stood for: renewal of the clergy, improvement of its relationship to the laity, revival of traditional ideals of purity in the *imitatio Christi*. As long as concubines continued in their defiant immorality, the credibility of Catholic renewal was in doubt.

---

[76] Ibid., Bd. 7, 29 Aug. 1613.
[77] Kohl, *Tridentinische Reform*, 745–6.

A Confessor and His Spiritual Child: François de Sales, Jeanne de Chantal, and the Foundation of the Order of the Visitation

Ruth Manning

I have never understood that there was any bond between us which carried any obligation except that of charity and true Christian friendship, which St Paul calls *the bond of perfection*, and that is truly what it is, for it is indissoluble and never weakens. All other bonds are temporal . . . broken through death or other circumstances; but the bond of love grows and strengthens over time. It is exempt from the scythe of death . . . So there, dear sister (and permit me to call you by this name, which is the one by which the Apostles and the first Christians expressed the intimate love they had for one another), this is our bond, these are our chains, the more they are tightened and press against us, the more they bring us comfort and freedom. Their strength is sweetness; their violence is gentleness; nothing is more pliable; nothing is stronger.[1]

This was one of the earliest letters written by François de Sales to Jeanne de Chantal following their first meeting in 1604. After just a short period of acquaintance, a deeply emotional friendship had formed between them. De Sales's love and admiration for his spiritual daughter were unstinting, and these sentiments were reciprocated. Such a relationship between a director and his directed was not unique in the history of the Catholic Church. Confessional relationships were a common feature of the Catholic Reformation when the post-Tridentine Church placed greater emphasis on the sacrament of penance and launched a newly trained profession of directors of conscience and personal confessors.[2] As Olwen Hufton pointed out, this is also

---

[1] François de Sales [FdS] to Jeanne de Chantal [JdC], 24 June 1604. *Oeuvres de Saint François de Sales, édition complète*, 27 vols. (Annecy, 1892–1964) [henceforth referred to as *FdS*], xii. 285. All translations are my own unless otherwise stated.

[2] J. Bossy, *Christianity in the West 1400–1700* (Oxford, 1985), 127–8.

Past and Present (2006), Supplement 1

a story about women: women, elite widows in particular, demonstrated an enthusiasm for the confessional experience that far outstripped that of their male counterparts.[3] Thus a woman like Louise de Marillac sought the direction of Vincent de Paul after the death of her husband, while the baroness Jeanne de Lestonnac chose the guidance of the Jesuit Father Bordes. The confessional relationship between François de Sales and Jeanne de Chantal proved especially fruitful: together, they made the first major attempt to establish an active female apostolate on French soil: the Order of the Visitation. This chapter seeks to explore the unique dynamics of this relationship and the ways in which this historical collaboration contributed to the beginnings of a new type of social Catholicism, 'le catholicisme au féminin'.[4]

In 1640, eighteen years after François de Sales's death, his friend Jean-Pierre Camus, the bishop of Belley, published a biographical tribute to him.[5] He portrayed the life of the saint through the medium of re-created conversations, and devoted several chapters to what Camus recognized as de Sales's distinctive relationship with female parishioners.

> Once someone said rather unkindly to the bishop that he was continuously surrounded by women.
>
> 'It is not that I wish to make a presumptuous comparison,' François answered, 'but it was similar with our Lord . . .'
>
> His friend continued the matter by saying: 'Well, I certainly don't know why they gather around you so much, for it seems to me that you say very little to them.'
>
> 'Is it little to let them talk as much as they will to me?' asked François. '. . . Don't they talk enough for us both? I really think they come to me because I am a good listener . . .'
>
> But his friend, rather than drop the subject, pressed on to say that he always notices that the bishop's confessional was surrounded by many more women than men.

---

[3] O. Hufton, *The Prospect Before Her: A History of Women in Western Europe, 1500–1800* (London, 1995; 1997), 365.

[4] This phrase comes from C. Langlois, *Le Catholicisme au féminin: les congrégations françaises à supérieure générale au XIXe siècle* (Paris, 1984); O. Hufton and F. Tallett, 'Communities of Women, the Religious Life and Public Service in Eighteenth Century France', in M. J. Boxer and H. J. Quataert (eds.), *Connecting Spheres: Women in the Western World, 1500 to the Present* (New York, 1987), 77.

[5] J.-P. Camus, *L'Esprit du Bienheureux François de Sales*, 6 vols. (Paris, 1640). An accessible and readable edition of this biography is C. F. Kelly (ed.), *The Spirit of St François de Sales* (London, 1953).

'What would you have?' he replied. 'Are not women more devout than men? How I wish men were as much interested in penitence!'[6]

Whether or not this conversation ever took place, the author's point is clear; de Sales was noted for his direction of women. Camus went on to contrast de Sales's practices with those of other prelates of their time.

> I have been told of a certain prelate who was so determined that no women, regardless of class, should be admitted to his house that he built a little parlour with a grating adjacent to the chapel, where he saw them . . . since he was quite young, he thought he might be led astray . . . [François] laughed pleasantly over this.[7]

Contemporary attitudes towards women in seventeenth-century France have been the subject of many studies.[8] As Robin Briggs has astutely argued, although it is too simplistic to characterize this era as misogynist, one can certainly detect a sense of hostility towards women. Believed to be inferior to men, women were assumed to have little or no grasp of reason or control over their passions; they were thought to be ruled by the lower part of their nature and subject to fits of hysteria governed by the womb. This rendered them dangerous to society. Much theological, legal, social, and medical reasoning posited women as the progeny of Eve; frivolous, inconstant, and carnal. They were held to be primarily responsible for original sin, believed to be naturally disposed towards evil and corruption, and to be susceptible to the powers of the devil. The note of panic in some clerics' voices is unmistakable; and more than one warned from the pulpit that 'Women have been the door through which the Devil entered the world'.[9]

Camus pointedly positions de Sales as an exception to this rule, recounting times when contemporaries challenged him for lending an ear so readily to women. The most vicious attack came when he founded the Order of the Visitation.

---

[6] Kelly (ed.), *Spirit*, 225.

[7] Ibid., 226.

[8] The most recent is M. Bernos, *Femmes et gens d'église dans la France classique XVIIᵉ–XVIIIᵉ siècle* (Paris, 2003). See also R. Briggs, *Communities of Belief: Cultural and Social Tensions in Early Modern France* (Oxford, 1989), esp. ch. 6; E. Rapley, *Dévotes: Women and the Church in Seventeenth Century France* (Montreal, 1990); N. Z. Davis, *Society and Culture in Early Modern France* (Stanford, 1975); G. Fagniez, *La Femme et la société française dans la première moitié du XVII siècle* (Paris, 1929).

[9] Étienne Bertal, quoted in H. Mills, 'Negotiating the Divide', in F. Tallett and N. Atkin (eds.), *Religion, Society and Politics in France Since 1789* (London, 1991), 33.

One day someone said to the bishop concerning the Order: 'What do you plan to do with all these women? Of what use will they be to God's Church? . . . Would it not be better if you founded some college for the education of priests rather than spend your time with these women who have to be told a thing a hundred times before they can retain it?'[10]

The author is clearly making a hagiographic point here, but it is evident that de Sales's attitude to women was a subject of debate amongst contemporaries.

François de Sales was a Savoyard and a Gallican graduate. This distinct combination of Savoy experience and French education manifested itself throughout his life's work to reunify the Catholic Church, a mission forged in the struggle against the Calvinist threat; his episcopal seat was Geneva. Like the Jesuits, he envisaged a programme of preaching and persuading through the means of a better-taught body of clergy who could combat the spread of heresy. These were the means and methods being proposed and experimented with in France at this time, means that de Sales wished to introduce in Savoy.

But de Sales added something of his own personal vision to this programme of conversion. The policy of reform within the ranks of the clergy would be complemented by the participation of a community of 'devout souls' who would exemplify and live out the life of Christian perfection in a variety of states and vocations, a programme he codified in his publication *L'Introduction à la vie dévote*.[11] While recognizing that 'the practice of devotion must differ for the gentleman and the artisan, the servant and the prince, for widow, young girl, or wife',[12] he celebrated every member of society's ability to attain holiness without the necessity of entering a monastery.[13] The message of this publication gave it mass appeal: both men and women had scope to participate in the religious life. De Sales's *Introduction* was one of the most successful good-conduct books for women ever written.

Central to the thesis of the *Introduction* was, of course, the overarching role of spiritual direction. As Hufton has noted, understanding the role of

---

[10] Kelly (ed.), *Spirit*, 266.

[11] FdS, *L'Introduction à la vie dévote* (Lyon, 1609). The saint added to this work and republished it in 1619. For an examination of the evolution of different editions see R. Devos and A. Ravier (eds.), *Oeuvres de Saint François de Sales* (Paris, 1969), 16–18. This volume also contains a faithful reproduction of *L'Introduction*, 19–317.

[12] Devos and Ravier (eds.), *Oeuvres*, 36.

[13] H. Bremond, *Histoire littéraire du sentiment religieux en France depuis la fin des guerres de religion jusqu'à nos jours*, 12 vols. (Paris, 1967–71), i. 387.

the father confessor is 'critical to understanding how the Catholic Church sought to control the minds and behaviour of women, perhaps in particular women of some education and wealth whose energies and resources could be used by the Church'.[14] And who better to target than the upper-class widow? She had time, she had refinement, she had money.

De Sales displayed a special concern for widows, dedicating a section of his *Introduction* to advising them. He recommended that the best course of action, after the death of a husband, was to remain a widow rather than to remarry, 'in order to centre all her affections on God'.[15] Remarriage was a contentious theological issue. Taking a second spouse after the death of the first had always been permitted by the Papal See; however, Pope Alexander III (1159–81) began a movement preventing second marriages from being solemnized with the nuptial blessing, arguing that it could not be a sacrament twice over.[16] In the seventeenth-century ecclesiastical elites preached this preference from the pulpit in the context of a wider negative view of the marital state that many ecclesiastics held in stark contrast to the elevation of the state of celibacy.[17] There was also a more practical side to the argument for abstinence from remarriage. Some secular authorities preferred widows to remain as such, because it prevented the complications of dowries and inheritance incurred in a second marriage. In addition, some clerics were interested in keeping the widow's dotal resources free for Church use. For women themselves, the freedom that widowhood presented was often welcome, as Nicolas Causin wrote in his *Instructions pour les veuves*: 'Oh, how many times while you were tied down by marriage have you said that if God would only take away your husband, you would give yourself completely to Him.'[18] Many devout women vowed their widowhood to God, *even before they were widowed*, as de Sales commented: 'Origen . . . [advises] wives to vow themselves to a chaste widowhood in the event of their husband's death so that even while they enjoy the pleasures of marriage they may anticipate the merit of such widowhood.'[19] Thus the death of a husband was often taken as a divine prompt to reorder their lives.

In 1604, four years prior to the first draft of the *Introduction*, de Sales travelled to Dijon to preach a series of Lenten sermons. It was here that he met the

[14] Hufton, *Prospect*, 375.

[15] FdS, *L'Introduction*, in Devos and Ravier (eds.), *Oeuvres*, 244–6.

[16] J. A. Brundage, *Sex, Law and Marriage in the Middle Ages* (Aldershot, 1993), 68.

[17] FdS, *L'Introduction*, in Devos and Ravier (eds.), *Oeuvres*, 17–19.

[18] Dechene, 'La Veuve', in W. Leiner (ed.), *Onze études sur l'image de la femme dans la littérature française* (Tubingen, 1978), 165, quoted in Rapley, *Dévotes*, 18.

[19] FdS, *L'Introduction*, in Devos and Ravier (eds.), *Oeuvres*, 244–6.

widow who was to play the most significant role in his career, the baroness
Jeanne Françoise Frémyot de Chantal.[20] Daughter of a Dijonese lawyer, she
was the widow of Baron Christophe de Rautin-Chantal and the mother of four
children. She was the model widow that de Sales would write about in his chapter on 'Advice to Widows' four years later. She had no intention of remarrying,
sought spiritual direction for the course of her widowhood, wished to dedicate
herself to God, and yet was committed to her children as long as they were
dependent upon her. This was exactly the kind of spiritual charge de Sales
relished. He became Jeanne's director officially on 21 August 1604.

It is hagiographic strategy to portray women as subservient to their confessors, and Jeanne de Chantal often emerges in secondary literature as the
subordinate figure in her relationship with François.[21] Wendy Wright and
Joseph Power's work on the letters of spiritual direction from François to
Jeanne examined her traditional role as the subsidiary partner in the relationship, and only accorded her respect for her organizational and spiritual
independence in the day-to-day running of the Order. They positioned her
as a figure who came into her own from 1610 onwards, once the Order was
founded.[22] However, the question of Jeanne's participation in the conception of the Order has yet to be fully explored.

Historians of the Order of the Visitation see its conception as the work of
de Sales. They view it as a natural development of the saint's thoughts and
theology, the culmination of his concern with achieving Christian perfection
and with the service of the poor.[23] They also point out that he personally knew
of many women who had led active religious lives, such as St Francesca da
Romana in fifteenth-century Rome. Francesca, born into the Roman nobility,
combined her duties as wife and mother with the provision of services to the
poor, and went on to found a society of devout ladies under the rule of
St Benedict, without religious vows.[24] In a letter to Jeanne in 1608 François
recounted meeting André Valladier, who wrote the first *vie édifiante* of

---

[20] Unsurprisingly, there are fewer works of biographical scholarship for Jeanne de Chantal than
for de Sales. The most accessible (although now outdated) works are H. Bremond, *Sainte
Chantal* (Paris, 1912) and E. Stopp, *Madame de Chantal: Portrait of a Saint* (London, 1962).

[21] See M. Georges-Thomas, *Sainte Jeanne de Chantal et la spiritualité salésienne* (Paris, 1963).

[22] W. M. Wright and J. F. Power (eds.), *Francis de Sales, Jane de Chantal: Letters of Spiritual
Direction* (New York, 1988).

[23] ET.-J. Lajeunie, *Saint François de Sales. L'Homme, la pensée, l'action*, 2 vols. (Paris, 1966),
240–63; R. Devos, *Les Visitandines*, 26.

[24] For a good introduction to this saint see G. Boanas and L. Roper, 'Feminine Piety in
Fifteenth Century Rome: Santa Francesca Romana', in J. Obelkevich and L. Roper (eds.),
Disciplines of Faith: Studies in Religion, Politics and Patriarchy (London, 1987).

St Francesca da Romana: 'he told me that . . . he himself had written her Life in Latin . . . she had been married for forty years, and . . . in her lifetime she erected a Congregation of widows who lived together in a house, in which they observed a religious life and no one entered therein except those with great cause; they, nevertheless, went out to serve the poor and the sick.'[25] This was certainly a powerful example, especially as da Romana had just been recently added to the catalogue of saints, on 29 May 1608 by Pope Paul V, the only female saint that he created. The fact that de Sales chose to discuss this in a letter to Jeanne was not insignificant. François was certainly the 'push factor' in this partnership when it came to proposing the Order, but the idea may also have owed much to the dynamics of his relationship with Jeanne.

The friendship between the two saints was frequently played out over great distances, with François based in Annecy and often travelling on business, while Jeanne resided in Dijon. This meant that letter-writing was their main form of communication for long periods. This was not unusual. The most prominent men of the Church were sought as directors by women from far and wide, not just by locals, and these men were often stretched between their parish or diocese and other locations where they would be invited to preach or work in some capacity. Vincent de Paul and Louise de Marillac conducted their relationship through the medium of the letter for these very reasons.[26] Even when letters were not necessary because of distance, they still served a purpose in the business of spiritual direction. Throughout the history of the Catholic Church confessors had encouraged their spiritual charges to commit to paper material such as their prayers, meditations, religious experiences, and retreat notes. Such written exercises were a part of the confessional process which offered women a way to understand themselves, or to undergo a cathartic experience.[27] This written

---

[25] A. Valladier, *Speculum sapientia matronalis, ex vita Sancta Francisa Romana, fundatricis Sororum Turris Speculorum, panegyricus* (Paris, 1609). The same year an edition in French appeared under the title *Miroir de la sagesse matronale*. Letter from FdS to JdC, 29 Sept. 1608, *FdS* xiv. 69.

[26] This correspondence is found in P. Coste (ed.), *Saint Vincent de Paul, correspondance, entretiens, documents*, 14 vols. (Paris, 1920–5).

[27] Italian scholars have explored this facet of the feminine confessional experience: W. Boer, 'Notte sull'introduzionale, sopratutto in Italia', *Quaderni Storici*, 77: 91, 543–72; R. Guarnieri, ' "Nec domina nec ancilla, sed socia". Tre casi di direzione spirituale tra Cinque e Seicento', in E. Schulte van Kessel (ed.), *Women and Men in Spiritual Culture XIV–XVII Centuries* (The Hague, 1986), 111–32; G. Paolin, 'Confessione e confessori al femminile: monache e direttore spirituali in ambito veneto tra '600 e '700', in G. Zarri (ed.), *Finzione e santita tra medioevo ed eta moderna* (Turin, 1991), 366–411.

material also served another purpose in the construction of a *vie édifiante*. Confessors worked with their spiritual charges to develop this significant literary genre: the story of an individual man or woman's spiritual development. Such publications would serve as inspirational reading-matter for women in both lay and religious society, while also serving to enhance the confessors' own reputations as spiritual directors.

François de Sales invited Jeanne de Chantal to use letter-writing as a means to explore herself and her relationship with God. He instructed her to 'Write to me, I beg you, as often as you can and with total trust'.[28] However, their letter-based relationship also allowed the saints to develop and explore their own relationship. The style of their interaction ranged from the professional to the personal. Discussions of confessions, meditations, and spiritual development were interspersed with reflections of a private nature. They expressed sentiments of care and concern for one another and their immediate families. They reflected on the growth and development of their friendship and their mutual love, admiration, and respect. The distance between François and Jeanne certainly did not seem to impede their relationship. If anything, their reliance on the medium of the letter allowed them a greater freedom of personal expression. François often remarked that 'The further away I am from you, the closer I feel is our interior bond',[29] and it was through their letters that they forged this tie.

A close reading of both sides of the correspondence between François and Jeanne suggests that their relationship rapidly developed, from that of director and directed to one of friendship and intimacy.[30] Their first letters testify to the significance of the connection. On the very day that François left Dijon, after first meeting Jeanne in 1604, he sent a short note to her to express his feelings: 'God, it seems, has given me to you; I made increasingly sure of this as the hours go by.'[31] This was the first of many deeply introspective reflections on the bond that had formed between them so quickly. Just months later François wrote again to Jeanne to explain his earlier words: 'from the very beginning when you conferred with me about your

---

[28] FdS to JdC, 3 May 1604. *FdS* xii. 266.

[29] Ibid., 263.

[30] The best analysis of this relationship, although dated, is M. Muller, *Die Freundschaft des hl. Franz von Sales mit der hl. Johanna Franziska von Chantal* (Munich, 1924). A more recent and spiritually focused study is W. M. Wright, *Bond of Perfection: Jeanne de Chantal and François de Sales* (New Jersey, 1985). Although not many of Jeanne de Chantal's letters have survived, what little there are are contained in M. P. Burns (ed.), *Correspondance de Jeanne-Françoise Fréymot de Chantal*, 6 vols. (Paris, 1986–90).

[31] FdS to JdC, 26 Apr. 1604. *FdS* xii. 262.

interior, God gave me a great love for your spirit. As you become increasingly open with me, a tremendous obligation arose for my soul to cherish yours more and more, that is what made me write to tell you that God has given me to you.'[32]

This was a relationship that quickly became based on mutual love, trust, and frankness. François was not only Jeanne's confessor but also became her best friend and partner in the dealings of day-to-day life, to whom she confided all her spiritual and personal trials. His letters constantly offered her advice, comfort, and support. But François too came to rely on Jeanne, a form of reciprocal dependency unusual in a confessional relationship. He never hesitated to express his most inner thoughts, fear, and anxieties and was never concerned to maintain the front of authority or spiritual superiority that the role of confessor conferred. As he himself admitted: 'I allow you to see my heart such as it is and its various moods so that, as the Apostle said, you do not think more of me than what I am.'[33]

The bond between Jeanne and François was undoubtedly deeper than that which normally existed between a confessor and his spiritual child. We need only read François's words written when Jeanne's letters had been delayed in order to gauge the strength of his feelings for this woman and his dependence upon her:

> I have spent ten whole weeks without receiving a single word of your news, my dear, my very dear daughter . . . in my heart my good patience had almost given up, and I believe that it would have given up entirely, if I had not reminded myself that I must preserve it in order to be at liberty to preach it to others. But at last, my very dear daughter, yesterday a packet arrived for me . . . Oh how welcome it was and how I loved it![34]

This mutual spiritual passion quickly matured into a spiritual marriage. Jeanne emerges in their letters as a wife-like figure, expressing concern for François's well-being and concerning herself with his most intimate daily routines, constantly urging him to take care of himself; to which François responded: 'do you know what I am going to promise you? To take more care of my health . . . having absolutely cut out the late nights and the writing that I do at this hour and eating more sensibly too. But believe me, your wishes have their part in this resolution, these decisions are down to your wishes;

---

[32] FdS to JdC, 14 Oct. 1604. *FdS* xii. 354.
[33] FdS to JdC, 11 Feb. 1607. *FdS* xiii. 266.
[34] FdS to JdC, 11 Feb. 1607. *FdS* xiii. 260–1.

because I deeply care about what makes you happy.'[35] This form of human love was nurtured alongside their spiritual love. It enriched their lives, as François wrote: 'Each affection has its own particular difference . . . that which I have for you has a certain particularity which infinitely consoles me and, when all is said, is extremely good for me.'[36]

Not only did the saints enter each others' lives, but they were also accepted into their respective immediate families. François reported that 'my brother is most grateful for your remembrance . . . remembering you continually at his altar',[37] while 'my mother could not have been more taken with you'.[38] In return, François became a regular correspondent of both Jeanne's father and her brother, the archbishop of Bourges. He also assumed a more intimately husband-like role, watching over her finances and household budgets and involving himself in the raising of Jeanne's children. His correspondence on these subjects resembles that of an absent father sending paternal advice back to his wife: 'As for Celse-Bénigne [Jeanne's son] you will have to inspire him . . . as he grows up, with God's help, we shall think of specific ways of doing this . . . If Françoise wants to be a nun of her own accord, fine; otherwise I do not approve of her being influenced by any recommendations.'[39]

The correspondence is littered with evidence of an awareness that their relationship was not only unique, but might also have bordered on the improper. François's lengthy expressions of love and admiration for Jeanne frequently conclude with comments such as: 'That is too much said on a subject that I was not going to mention',[40] or 'I did not intend to say so much',[41] as if he was consciously stopping himself from expanding upon sentiments that should not really be mentioned. Jeanne, on the other hand, showed more prescience, which is remarkable considering that he was meant to be 'directing' their relationship. When she came to edit the first volume of François's letters following his death, she cut out (as was revealed when the letters were compared with the surviving manuscripts for the Annecy edition) sentiments that she thought might be judged too personal. She wrote: 'The world cannot grasp the incomparable purity of this saint's love . . . this kind of thing has to be taken very carefully.'[42] She was aware that they had

---

[35] FdS to JdC, 8 June 1606. *FdS* xiii. 182.

[36] FdS to JdC, 14 Oct. 1604. *FdS* xii. 354.

[37] François' brother was Canon Jean-François de Sales. FdS to JdC, 24 June 1604. *FdS* xii. 288.

[38] FdS to JdC, 14 Oct. 1604. *FdS* xii. 369.

[39] Ibid., 360–1.

[40] FdS to JdC, 8 June 1606. *FdS* xiii. 183.

[41] FdS to JdC, 14 Oct. 1604. *FdS* xii. 354.

[42] E. Stopp, 'Saint Francis de Sales: Attitudes to Friendship', *Downside Review*, 392 (July), 177.

shared a deeply emotional and intimate partnership, something that would not be judged typical of a confessional relationship, and she chose not to release the details of this to the public.

It was this intensity of emotion and the depth of their affection for one another that singled out their relationship as unique. De Sales did not lavish this degree of affection on all his spiritual charges.[43] For example, Madame Madeleine de la Fléchère was another of his 'spiritual widows' whom he held in high esteem. He had become familiar with the de la Fléchère family in 1608 when preaching the Lenten sermons in Rumilly, not far from Annecy. The correspondence between himself and Madeleine is the only one, certainly in terms of volume, comparable to that which passed between himself and Jeanne. He wrote of her: 'After Madam de Chantal, I do not know if I have ever encountered in a woman a stronger soul, a more reasonable mind, or a more sincere humility.'[44] Yet their relationship never approached the degree of intimacy that existed between him and Jeanne. In contrast, he described his first meeting with Madeleine as 'a good beginning', and always maintained a level of cool composure and authority in his letters to her.[45]

Jacques-Benigne Bossuet was also a self-styled confessor, and a follower of François de Sales.[46] Amongst his numerous spiritual charges he could count many prominent women of the day, including Mademoiselle Alix Clerginet,[47] Madame Cornuau,[48] and Madame d'Albert de Luynes.[49] While employing the standard salutation of 'my dear daughter', as used by other contemporary directors such as de Sales and Vincent de Paul, Bossuet never forged any relationship with a comparable degree of intensity or intimacy. He used the medium of letter-writing as any confessor might do, yet his correspondence

---

[43] A handy volume for the study of François de Sales' spiritual friendships is A. Ravier (ed.), *François de Sales. Correspondance: les lettres d'amitié spirituelle* (Paris, 1980).

[44] *FdS* xvii. 143. Quoted in Wright and Power (eds.), *Letters of Spiritual Direction*, 157.

[45] For the correspondence between FdS and Madeleine de la Fléchère, see *FdS* xiv. There is also a brief discussion and a few translated letters to be found in Wright and Power (eds.), *Letters of Spiritual Direction*, 157–62.

[46] A good edition of Bossuet's letters of spiritual direction is G. Webb and A. Walker (trans.), *Jacques-Benigne Bossuet: Letters of Spiritual Direction* (London, 2001).

[47] Foundress of the Maison de la Propagande de la Foi, for which Bossuet helped draw up the constitutions.

[48] A widow who first went into retirement with the 'Filles Charitables' and later with the Benedictines at Jouarre. She was the first to edit Bossuet's correspondence with herself and Madame d'Albert de Luynes.

[49] Madame Henriette-Thérèse d'Albert de Luynes. She was educated at Port-Royal under Angélique Arnauld. In her widowhood she became a nun at Jouarre.

clearly remained within the boundaries of acceptable confessional relations. The language of the letter never approached the degree of affection used so freely between François and Jeanne, and he always maintained his position as director.

The bond between François and Jeanne was one of substantial force, and its passion released tremendous energy, allowing them to talk freely, discussing topics with a frankness that encouraged comment and critique. It was with Jeanne that François could debate issues that preoccupied him such as devotion, charity, prayer, virtue, humility, friendship, and resisting temptation: themes which eventually formed the backbone of his *Introduction*.[50] As Ravier and Stopp have both remarked, the letters that flowed between François and Jeanne adopted an interactive style which was closer to the rhythm of speech.[51] De Sales developed the ideas that are expressed in the *Introduction* through these dialogues with Jeanne. While it is well known that the *Introduction* was based on the letters of spiritual direction written to his cousin, Madame de Charmoisy, it is not commonly known that it also derived from this correspondence with Jeanne de Chantal. So we find, in a letter that he wrote to Jeanne in 1609, a request that her letters be returned to him for the second edition of the book,[52] and it is also evident that he consulted her more than once in the process of writing.[53] In turn, much of what de Sales committed to paper for the *Introduction* ultimately found its way into the rules and constitutions of the Order of the Visitation. It was no coincidence that François met Jeanne de Chantal, conceived of the Visitation, and published his *Introduction* all within five years, and it is striking that whenever he discussed the Visitation in correspondence with her, he referred to it as 'ours'.

The first plans were made for the Order of the Visitation in June 1607. Jeanne had proved to be instrumental in focusing de Sales' vision of how 'good widows' could be utilized in his 'community of devout souls', and the energy of their relationship fired their mutual desire to found an active female apostolate. This was to be the first serious attempt at establishing such an apostolate on French soil, living in community, without the constraints of cloister or excessive physical mortification. It was inspired by and

---

[50] For examples of these discussions see *FdS* xii. 263–6, 352–70; xiii. 4–11, 74–7, 80–6, 161–4, 146–8, 199–201, 201–12, 305–9, 355–7, 392–4; xvi. 107–9.

[51] Ravier, *Un sage*, 127–9; E. Stopp, *St. Francis de Sales: Selected Letters* (New York, 1960) 35–9.

[52] FdS to JdC, mid-Feb. 1609. *FdS* xiv. 131. See also the comment in Stopp, 'Attitudes to Friendship', 175–92.

[53] FdS to JdC, 4 July 1608. *FdS* xiv. 44.

created for Jeanne de Chantal and others like her; widows with family commitments or frail health which prevented them from entering into existing religious orders, but who wished to dedicate themselves to God nonetheless.

Reducing physical mortification as a feature of the female devotional life was an idea that had also been explored by Angela Merici. In an age of reformed convents there were fewer options for women who wished to embrace a religious life but whose bodies could not withstand it. The practice of mortification was scrutinized by de Sales, who criticized it as unnecessary: mortification was best left as an activity of the heart. Only once an individual had reformed their 'interior' and achieved conformity with Jesus could the physical signs be seen. De Sales used the imagery of the almond tree to illustrate this argument:

> Men engaged in horticulture tell us that if a word is written on a sound almond seed and it is placed again in its shell, carefully wrapped up, and planted, whatever fruit the tree bears will have that same written word stamped on it . . . I cannot approve the methods of those who try to reform a person by beginning with external things, such as bearing, dress, or hair. On the contrary, it seems to me that we should begin inside.[54]

The 'open' structure of the Visitation Order allowed the sisters to dedicate themselves to a social mission: visiting the local poor and needy and providing education for girls. Here, de Sales was in line with a wider movement within the post-Tridentine Church, concentrated on education and social Catholicism. The poor and sick were in need of help, the vulnerable needed protection. Catholic reformers stressed that heresy could only be combatted if the ordinary Catholic worshipper was as well versed in Catholic spirit as the Protestants were in heresy. Young children needed to be educated in the Catholic manner if the next generation of believers was to be secured. But who would attend to this? And, in an age with little female education and low literacy rates, who would teach the girls? In short, elements in the Catholic Church were reluctantly coming round to the conclusion that they needed women to provide these critical social services for the female sex. However, this made it necessary to encourage qualities of activism in women, otherwise enjoined to domestic passivity.

Attempts to meet this social need had already been made in Italy in the sixteenth century. In 1535 Angela Merici formed a group of women intent

---

[54] Quoted in Wright and Power (eds.), *Letters of Spiritual Direction*, 54–5. For a discussion of this facet of Salesian spirituality see 54–61.

on dedicating themselves to the care of the sick and needy, and to the education of girls. They arrived in France in 1610, expecting to attract French women who would not seek enclosure, only to find that their new recruits had actually been hoping to join the newly reformed Carmelite mission to France. Demand from within met with pressure from without to enclose, and they opted for claustration in 1612. In Italy and Spain the Catholic Reformation exercised a powerful grip on the country through its male ecclesiastical hierarchy, and the lives and behaviour of women were heavily regulated. Yet, because of its Gallican tradition of independence from Rome, it was not until 1615 that the French Assembly of the Clergy actually accepted the authority of the Council of Trent, delaying implementing many of its principles. Challenged by the Protestant threat, France was in something of a religious vacuum, open to individual initiative. It was in this context that de Sales and de Chantal introduced the Order of the Visitation.

The process of founding such an order, committed to an external social mission, was no mean feat. De Sales himself, well versed in canon law, envisaged problems from the outset.[55] He therefore embarked upon a shrewd campaign of spreading the word about his order, and the right word at that. Seeking to ensure that the order would be well received and that those of consequence were fully informed as to its existence and purpose, he targeted those who were likely to be supportive, sympathetic, and helpful, in particular the Savoyard Jesuit Father Nicolas Polliens, and Monsieur Jean-François Ranzo, a *Gentilhomme* and *Conseiller* of His Highness, Charles-Emmanuel I of Savoy,[56] in a deliberate ploy to establish favour with the ruling house of Savoy.

On behalf of the Visitation, de Sales also built networks of women upon whom he called to support the order financially and socially. In 1608 he wrote to Jeanne: 'God wants to help our plans, he is preparing the souls of élites for us. Mademoiselle de Blonay[57] . . . has declared to me her desire to be a Religious. God has marked her for our congregation.'[58]. This is just one of the many women whom de Sales's letters mention as volunteering to staff and support the order. In 1609 he wrote to report his meeting with two widows, Jeanne de Requeleyne[59] and Marie de Mouxy,[60] and he even remarked

---

[55] FdS to JdC, 6 July 1608. *FdS* xiv. 44.

[56] FdS to M. Ranzo, 6 May 1610. *FdS* xiv. 299.

[57] Marie-Aimée de Blonay. The young girl had been known to the saint since childhood, during his missionary work in Chablais.

[58] FdS to JdC, late Dec. 1608. *FdS* xiv. 101–2.

[59] The widow of the noble Claude David, lawyer to the *parlement* of Bourgogne and *conseiller des états particuliers* of the Comté d'Auxonne.

[60] The widow of Louis de la Touvière, Seigneur d'Escrilles (or 'Crilles').

that in the end 'we will have too many people, that is to say more than we can receive'.[61]

He did not stop there. In late 1613, after the first official foundation had been opened at Annecy and the constitutions had been formulated and committed to paper,[62] de Sales turned his attention to ingratiating the order with the ruling house of Savoy fully. He did not address Charles Emmanuel I but turned to his daughter Marguerite de Savoy, the duchess of Mantua,[63] requesting that she become the Order's protectoress, 'to accept and receive this Congregation under her special protection . . . in the favour of her charity'.[64] As de Sales had anticipated, Marguerite was flattered to accept,[65] and with her power and position she secured favours for the new Order from her father and the senate of Savoy, which declared that the Order was always to be favoured and protected in their lands, and in accordance with practice, 'lettres patentes' were issued.

The love and support that Jeanne conferred on François underpinned the energy of this apostolate. She taught him the value of relationships in the business of survival in seventeenth-century French society, and she gave him the means by which to negotiate the necessary political, financial, and moral support needed for the Order. Under Jeanne's guiding influence, de Sales in turn ensured that the Visitation was an Order created by women, for women, in every possible sense of the word.

However, not everyone was in favour of such an experimental form of female religious life taking root in French soil. In 1616, when the Order expanded from Savoy to Lyon, the Visitandines crossed the path of the archbishop cardinal Denis-Simon de Marquemont, a representative of a Gallican Church deeply shaken by the religious wars. Marquemont's response to the Order reflects the underlying tensions of the Catholic Reformation:

> those who see a nun in the world . . . will be scandalized . . . the Monasteries which we are trying to enclose in obedience to the Council will

---

[61] FdS to JdC, 11 Dec. 1609. *FdS* xiv. 227.

[62] There are three manuscripts that survive today that show the evolution of the Visitation's constitutions. The first (*Manuscrit de Thonon, G*) dates from June–July 1610 and the second (*Manuscrit d'Annecy, H*) dates from July 1610. These are both incomplete writings, in the hand of François de Sales, which were ultimately written up into the final manuscript of 1613 (*Manuscript de Guingamp, K*). For a short discussion of these manuscripts see the note in *FdS* xxv. 203–10.

[63] Marguerite de Savoy was the daughter of Charles-Emmanuel and Catherine-Michelle d'Autriche. In 1608 she married François de Gonzague, the elder brother of Vincent, duke of Mantua.

[64] FdS to Duchess of Mantua, late Nov. 1613. *FdS* xvi. 104–9.

[65] Duchess of Mantua to JdC, 22 Dec. 1613. *FdS* xvi. 402.

have something to say . . . furthermore, Protestants and libertines will be able to criticise clausura in our Monasteries.[66]

And there was also the issue of the Visitandines' simple vows. The Papal Bull of 1566, *Circa Pastoralis*, had decreed that the only way for women to enter the Religious life was to take the three solemn vows of poverty, obedience, and chastity and submit to enclosure. Instead, the Visitandines proposed to live under simple vows, without enclosure, which did not bind them to the 'civil death' regulations of the religious state, under which they would have renounced their claims to worldly rights and worldly goods. As Marquemont saw it, the sisters could easily leave the Congregation, marry, and dishonour their families, and this would also place a question-mark over their inheritance. The parents:

> do not know if they are Religious or seculars . . . if they will share with their brothers and sisters or if they will remain content with the dowry that they will have been given . . . parents [in Lyon] are not well disposed towards consecrating their daughters to the service of God, but when they do there are a lot of temporal considerations.[67]

Marquemont was more concerned with potential criticism than with rejection of the good work that the Visitation could do. He gave them a choice: to remain as they were and be suppressed, or to accept enclosure under the rule of St Augustine. This was the obvious candidate since it was the least demanding rule, and it would allow the Congregation to continue to accept widows and girls of poor health. After much consideration and consultation between Jeanne and François, they agreed.[68] The circumstances under which the Visitation came to be enclosed demonstrated one vital lesson. The establishment of such an initiative relied on the support of two powers: the state, as embodied in a ruler, and the bishop or archbishop. In Savoy both forms of authority were obtained, but this was not to be the case in Lyon.

The historian of the active female apostolate might be tempted to leave the history of the Visitation at this juncture. Yet, despite having fallen foul of

---

[66] Marquemont to FdS. *FdS* xxv. 327.

[67] Ibid., 324.

[68] The scope of this article does not allow for a full discussion of the reasons behind Jeanne's and François' agreement, which are complex. For a summary of the debate surrounding this issue see Rapley, *Dévotes*, 39–40 and M. P. Burns, 'Aux origines de la Visitation. La Vraie Pensée de Saint François de Sales', in *Les Religieuses dans le Cloître et dans le Monde. Actes du Deuxième Colloque International du CERCOR* (Saint-Étienne, 1994).

the Cardinal, the Visitandines had still managed to dedicate six years to the demonstration of a new ideal of feminine piety at large in society. It was in France that the development of Counter-Reformation confessional culture was open to a degree of individual initiative, allowing directors such as François de Sales to experiment and innovate with the potential for collaboration with his female charges. In Jeanne de Chantal, de Sales found a unique match with a woman of intelligence, drive, and importantly, means. She showed great character, breaching gender norms, often challenging and guiding de Sales, and formulating an active apostolic role for herself, forbidden to women. Together Jeanne and François worked in practical terms towards the same end, inspired by the same drive, with mutual trust and affection, and giving shape to one of the most innovative works of charity in seventeenth-century France.

Although the Visitandines were ultimately suppressed in their apostolic form, the first six years of their establishment, 1610–16, set in motion a movement which, as Olwen Hufton described, eventually 'drove a coach and horses through the principle of enclosure'.[69] It was during these first experimental years that the dynamism between François de Sales and Jeanne de Chantal demonstrated what was possible with the help of networks of both male and female supporters that they forged strategically. These same networks crop up repeatedly in the record of their history, supporting later female apostolic initiatives, such as the Daughters of the Cross, until finally, in 1633, the active female apostolate was safely secured in France in the form of the Daughters of Charity.[70] At the root of this achievement lay the inspirational example of the Order of the Visitation, which constituted the horsepower of this 'coach and horses'.

---

[69] Hufton, *Prospect*, 381.

[70] My doctoral thesis, 'Breaking the Rules: The Emergence of the Active Female Apostolate in Seventeenth-century France', Oxford University (2006), is concerned with these wider issues of connection between the Order of the Visitation, the Daughters of the Cross, and the Daughters of Charity, and the ways in which they benefited from mutual networks of supporters first created by the Order of the Visitation.

Letters to Lucie: Spirituality, Friendship, and Politics During the Dreyfus Affair

Ruth Harris

The wellsprings of Dreyfusard activism are normally ascribed to rationality, secularism, even rabid anticlericalism. The Affair is conventionally seen as a key episode in the ideological construction of 'les deux Frances', in which the Left waged war against the Right, secularism opposed Catholicism, rationality triumphed over obscurantism, and the universalism of the French Revolutionary tradition vied with an increasingly exclusive and aggressive nationalism. This vision has remained so persistently attractive because it reinforced the myths of the protagonists on both sides of the political divide. They felt they represented two different value systems and two opposing views of French identity.

From the very beginning, Dreyfusard historiography upheld this dichotomy, seeing their advocacy as rationalist and civil-libertarian, keen to distinguish themselves from what was regarded as the monstrous fabrications and religious fanaticism of the Right.[1] They prided themselves on being 'intellectuals',[2]

---

[1] For the classic example of this kind of history by one of the leading campaigners see J. Reinach, *Histoire de l'Affaire Dreyfus* 7 vols. (Paris, 1901–8). In it he marshalled thousands of documents, established a chronology, and provided a narrative of verifiable facts that was a monument to 'positivist' history. The Dreyfusard editor Pierre-Victor Stock published 129 books on the Affair, 76 of which were documentary editions to provide the public with 'rational' evidence on which to make a better judgement. For his role see his *L'Affaire Dreyfus: mémorandum d'un éditeur* (Paris, 1994).

[2] See e.g. the compendious Jean-Denis Bredin, *The Affair: The Case of Alfred Dreyfus*, trans. Jeffrey Mehlman (London, 1987), 490–1, in which the author cites the disappointment caused by the loss of 'mystique' among leading Dreyfusards but without analysing this emotional element. At times such passionate emotions are given a secondary role when linked to the petitions of the Ligue des Droits de l'Homme and are hence analysed as part of *engagement*. See Pascal Ory and Jean-François Sirinelli, *Les Intellectuels en France de l'Affaire Dreyfus à nos jours* (Paris, 1986); this book, which examines the 'société intellectuelle et l'Affaire Dreyfus', is typical in underscoring the sociological and political dimensions of *engagement*, but is largely uninterested in its emotional bases.

Past and Present (2006), Supplement 1

a term of abuse hurled at them by right-wing opponents who saw the Dreyfusards' 'abstract' loyalties to truth and justice as injurious to the 'intuitive' cult of nationalism and anti-Semitism. Only Charles Péguy, who unusually combined socialism with Catholicism, countered this prevailing myth with an emphasis on Dreyfusard 'spirituality'.[3] He argued that, in the early days of the struggle, the Dreyfusards embodied a 'mystique' that encompassed the primordial Christian virtue of charity, evinced in a passionate commitment to truth and justice that went beyond the temporal power of the Church. His interpretation was unusual in that it placed this epochal 'modern' moment in political history squarely within the tradition of religious aspirations and ideals.[4]

By examining two sets of letters, first from hundreds of strangers (largely women) to Lucie, Alfred Dreyfus' wife, and secondly from leading Dreyfusards, this chapter will show the importance of legacies of spiritual engagement normally associated with earlier historical eras. These feelings were not anachronistic hangovers from some dying past. They were indeed 'survivals', but not in the sense of being Weberian residues battling against

---

For more on particular forms, see Jean-François Sirinelli, *Intellectuels et passions françaises* (Fayard, 1990), esp. 21–32, and its discussion of the 'petition'; see also the pioneering article by Jean and Monica Charlot, 'Un rassemblement d'intellectuels: La Ligue des Droits de l'Homme', *Revue Française de Science Politique*, 9 (1959), 995–1019; for more classic statements of the role of the intellectuals in the Dreyfus camp (as well as their opponents) see Christophe Charles, 'Champ littéraire et champ du pouvoir: les écrivains et l'Affaire Dreyfus', *Annales, ESC*, 32 (1997), 240–64, and Madeleine Réberioux, 'Histoire, historiens et dreyfusisme', *Revue historique*, 255 (1976), 407–32 as well as the articles in Géraldi Leroy (ed.), *Les écrivains et l'Affaire Dreyfus*, Actes du Colloque, Centre Charles Péguy et Université d'Orleans (1981). For modifications on the stereotypes of *engagement* see Michel Winock, *Le Siècle des intellectuels* (Paris, 1997), 11–65. There are two general ways in which the Affair has been analysed. The first concentrates on the 'spy' story and on the events between the major political actors; these are generally narrative accounts. For the classic expositions in this vein, see Douglas Johnson, *France and the Dreyfus Affair* (London, 1966), and Bredin, *The Affair*, 245–85, in which he traces the fault-lines among intellectuals and accepts the Dreyfusard self-characterization. The second concentrates more on unearthing the world of the intellectuals and the nature of their commitment.

[3] Charles Péguy, *Notre jeunesse* (Paris, 1957), esp. 58–132.

[4] In examining the role of emotion, I am in the same terrain as William Reddy, *The Navigation of Feeling: A Framework for the History of the Emotions* (Cambridge, 2001). Although I am not using his conceptual framework, I applaud his attempt to understand 'sentimentality' and its relationship to the violence of the French Revolution.

prevailing currents of 'modernity'; rather, they were the traditions upon which correspondents built a crusading idealism in the new political climate of Republican mass politics.

The first group of more than 400 letters reveals a compassionate, religious sensibility that pervaded the Dreyfusard movement.[5] The letters reflect the high-water mark of the epistolary mode in Western society, before the widespread use of the telephone, and when mass literacy made it possible for even the most humble to write to a stranger and offer moral support and spiritual advice. They prayed for Alfred and Lucie and likened them to Christ and Mary, seeking through biblical quotation and religious precepts to find meaning in the couple's joint 'martyrdom'. Their spiritual concerns and tireless ecumenicism sat uncomfortably with the leading anticlericals of the movement, who increasingly supported an intolerant vision of secular society (laïcité). For these women correspondents, religion was at the heart of Dreyfusard politics, and demonstrates how, in their case, the conventional divide between the religious and secular simply did not apply.

The second set of letters came from close associates who had staked their emotional and political identity on Captain Dreyfus's release and exoneration. Wives of leading Dreyfusards, as well as leading male activists, discussed politics and tactics with Lucie—and vented their Republican anticlericalism.[6] They were dedicated to extending the cause of rationalism, but invested their advocacy with an almost quasi-religious dedication. They fused intellect and passion, as they sacrificed themselves in a manner which confirmed Péguy's vision of a pure, saintly 'mystique'.[7] These letters, in the wake of Dreyfus's pardon in September 1899—when the captain was released but was still not exonerated—show the difficulty of maintaining the 'mystique' in the face of a debate over tactics that entailed personal disenchantment and latent anti-Semitism. The darker, absolutist nature of their engagement

---

[5] Dreyfusards acknowledged the presence of such 'emotional' (women) campaigners when describing those who 'pleurant sur le martyr'. Despite the antifeminism of this remark, it somehow captured the essence of many women's activities. See *Regards sur l'Affaire Dreyfus; textes réunis et présentés par Jean-Pierre Halévy* (Paris, 1994), 204. For more on this remarkable Jewish 'dynasty' see Henri Loyrette, *Entre le théâtre et l'histoire. La famille Halévy (1790–1960)* (Paris, 1996).

[6] The Dreyfusard family papers are in now at the Musée d'Art et d'Histoire du Judaïsme (hereafter MAHJ); see Olympe Havet (in 97.17.51.26, Paris 1899. 12. 06) and Noémie Pschiari (in 97.17.042.85, Paris 1900. 03.13), who both expressed anticlerical sentiments. They were the wives of leading Dreyfusards, and their remarks were rare among Lucie's female correspondants.

[7] Alas, we do not have always have Lucie's response to these letters.

when it slipped into fear and disgruntlement demonstrates how such campaigners embodied a religious zealotry that mirrored the destructive passions of their opponents.

The nature of this emotional ebb and flow is inexplicable without a bare account of the story of the Affair. At the end of September 1894 French Intelligence stole an undated and unsigned letter received by the German military attaché in Paris, General Schwarzkoppen. Torn to pieces and retrieved from a wastepaper bin by a charlady, this document—forever after known as the *bordereau*, or memorandum—contained French military secrets. By the middle of October a Jewish captain of Alsatian origin was accused of being its author. Few questioned the verdict of the subsequent court martial, nor the punishment of solitary confinement for life on Devil's Island in the Caribbean. Alfred Dreyfus's public degradation in the courtyard of the École militaire on 5 January 1895 testified to the horror in which the crime was held. He was led out before a crowd screaming 'Death to Judas, Death to the Jew', and was ritually stripped of his military rank; his epaulettes were torn from his shoulders, even the red military stripes on his trousers were ripped off and thrown onto the ground. His sabre was taken from him and broken in two. Now dressed in rags, he was paraded around the courtyard so he could be abused by the crowd once more. Then he was led away to captivity.

The ceremony seemed a fitting, even cathartic, end to a straightforward case of high treason—'more exciting than the guillotine' as the author Maurice Barrès remarked at the time. So complete was the belief in Dreyfus's guilt that no one had any inkling that the verdict would even be queried, let alone that the case would become the most famous *cause célèbre* in French history, changing the political course of the nation and transforming the way the country itself was viewed.

Dreyfus was illegally condemned on the basis of secret documents that remained hidden from public scrutiny because they were deemed to jeopardize national security. This concerned almost no one. His conviction confirmed the need for ruthless vigilance against traitors who sought to weaken France against Germany, which had defeated her in 1870–1 and continued to threaten with its economic and military strength. In an age of great-power rivalry, when European nations sought global imperial dominion, Dreyfus—with his German accent and Jewish background—incarnated the dangerous subversive, the enemy within.

Dreyfus and his family struggled hopelessly against this perception. Rather than wishing to undermine France, he had joined the army because of a desire to regain his beloved Alsace for his country. Indeed, this patriotism overrode narrrow family considerations. His father, an impoverished pedlar, had made a fortune from a textile business in Mulhouse, but after 1871 the family moved the factory to French Belfort, exiling themselves from Alsace to take up French patriality.

Such family patriotism mattered little. They lived in shamed isolation, with Alfred's elder brother, Mathieu, working tirelessly, but aimlessly, in search of new evidence.[8] They knew nothing of Georges Picquart, a brilliant career officer and head of the Statistical Section in 1896, who, in attempting to confirm Dreyfus's conviction, inadvertently stumbled upon the real culprit, Walsin Esterhazy. Unlike Dreyfus, who was rich, devoted to his career, and happily married, Esterhazy hated the French, was in debt, and was a notorious womanizer, providing both psychological and economic motives for treason.[9] It was his handwriting, rather than that of Dreyfus, that Picquart recognized on the infamous *bordereau*.

Picquart was the 'second' hero of the Affair; when he sought to alert his superiors of the miscarriage of justice, he was first removed from his post and sent abroad and later imprisoned.[10] It was only in November 1897 that Mathieu Dreyfus independently uncovered Esterhazy's guilt by distributing widely a facsimile of the *bordereau* and being contacted by a stockbroker who recognized the handwriting. A military tribunal, however, subsequently exonerated Esterhazy in the beginning of 1898, and at that point the Dreyfusards threw over their discreet tactics within the political establishment and replaced them with a more robust public campaign.

The Dreyfus Case turned into an Affair when, in early 1898, the novelist Émile Zola intervened with his public letter, 'J'accuse', accusing the military hierarchy of complicity in the cover-up. Zola was condemned for libel and fled to London, having endured the riots and execrations of anti-Semitic and nationalist mobs. It was at this moment that violence against Jews and their property erupted in French cities and in Algeria. New pressure-groups like the Ligue des Droits de l'Homme emerged to plead for Dreyfus and for a wider programme of Republican humanitarianism, with the Right riposting with the Ligue de la Patrie Française, an even larger organization, which opposed the revision of the verdict against Dreyfus. Public rallies on both sides of the political divide often ended in violence, with right-wing leagues blending anti-Semitism and anti-parliamentarianism in a bid to undermine the regime.

---

[8] See this moving series of family letters at MAHJ series 97.17.30.

[9] Marcel Thomas, *Esterhazy ou l'envers de l'Affaire Dreyfus* (Paris, 1989).

[10] See Francis de Pressensé, *Un Héros: Le Colonel Picquart* (Paris, 1898); Picquart was imprisoned in the military fortress of Mt Valérian in January 1898; for the details of the charges against him see Bredin, *The Affair*, 318–19.

The Affair thus revealed deep-seated political rivalries and hatreds at the same time that it gave birth to new nationalist and anti-Semitic movements. Only at the very end of August 1898 did public opinion begin to sway in favour of the Dreyfusards, when Lieutenant-Colonel Henry, also of the Statistical Section, committed suicide after admitting that he had forged evidence to incriminate Dreyfus as early as 1896. After these dramatic events the judicial wheels began to turn, and Dreyfus finally returned from Devil's Island to face a second court martial in Rennes in August 1899. He came back to France disoriented and ill, so emaciated that he needed cotton wadding to fill out the uniform that hung from his stick-like frame. The rejoicing among the Dreyfusards proved short-lived, however. He was again found guilty in September 1899—albeit in a split decision—and condemned to ten years imprisonment. Although pardoned almost immediately, he was not fully rehabilitated until 1906.[11]

Understanding the tone of the letters to Lucie requires an analysis of her image which evoked the messages of sympathy and solidarity. Normally veiled behind the public activism of her brother-in-law, Mathieu,[12] whose unwavering devotion was central to the campaign, Lucie became famous for her heroism in the face of adversity. From the moment of Alfred's arrest on 15 October 1894, she endured the searches, harangues, and innuendoes of abusive officers, persisted in proclaiming her husband's innocence, and fought to visit him.[13]

When the Case turned into an Affair towards the end of 1897, Lucie became an even greater focus for idealization and identification. The famous 'reporteresses' of *La Fronde*, the feminist newspaper founded in December 1897, marvelled at her courage in trying to join her husband in his captivity, knowing that the torrid heat and contaminated food might kill them both.[14] They recorded the way she defied witnesses who claimed that her husband had

---

[11] There are many books which tell this story, but a good brief account of chronology is Denis Bon, *L'Affaire Dreyfus* (Paris, 1999).

[12] M. Burns, *Dreyfus: A Family Affair* (London, 1992), 171–94. The letters of Mathieu to Alfred during his stay in Devil's Island testify to an extraordinary love, see MAHJ series 97.17.30.

[13] BN NAF 24895, Lucie Dreyfus to Joseph Reinach, pieces 2–3, n.d. and Bredin, *The Affair*, 70.

[14] See C. Crosnier, 'Les "reporteresses" de *La Fronde*', in *Les Représentations de l'Affaire Dreyfus dans la presse en France et à l'étranger*, Actes du colloque de Saint-Cyr-sur-Loire November 1994, Tours, pp. 73–81.

confessed,[15] applauded her struggle against ministerial inhumanity,[16] and endorsed the way she furthered his legal cause. They admired her iron will in hiding their father's dishonour from her innocent children. *Le Figaro* explained how 'maternal love' had confined the children in such 'a prison so gentle' that they were prevented from having friends and learnt their lessons at home.[17] They published Dreyfus' letters, which Lucie must have released to them, in which he credited her with his survival, recognizing her quiet strength and resolve as the crucial inspirations enabling him to fight against intolerable odds.

> All that I can say to you is that, night and day, at all hours, at every minute, my heart, my thoughts, everything that is alive in me is for you, for our children.[18]

So unimpeachable was Lucie's character that one journalist remarked at Rennes that 'She does not at all have the air of asking for justice. One would say that she is justice herself.'[19] *La Constitution* commented on her remarkable willingness to knock at every door: 'She, the wife of the Jew, has sustained the Republican press, encouraged Zola and Picquart, invoked the impartial intervention of the judges of the Cour de Cassation.'[20] Her refusal at Rennes to accept the magnificent bouquets that so many well-wishers sought to bestow upon her was seen as dignity personified.[21] By calling her 'the wife of the Jew', *La Constitution* had evoked not only the status of Jews in Christian society—those who were persecuted and tormented—but had associated her with a certain image of 'la juive', a woman of active virtue. *La Fronde* explicitly paid homage to this 'type' when it asserted that Lucie differed from Catholic women—all too willing to submit to the will of God—because of her inexorable determination to see Dreyfus returned to her.

---

[15] Anon., 'Autour de la revision', *La Fronde*, 18 Nov. 1898.

[16] 'Bradamante'(pseudonym), 'Dupuy, Roi Nègre', *La Fronde*, 14 Nov. 1898.

[17] Charles Chincholle, 'Avant le retour de Dreyfus à Rennes', *Le Figaro*, 19 June 1899; this discussion of her determination to hide the dishonour from her children was common across the Dreyfusard press. Pierre Dreyfus maintained that he had absolutely no sense of his father's plight until Alfred returned to his family in Carpentras after his pardon in September 1899. See Burns, *Dreyfus: A Family Affair*, 275–6; this policy was not shared by all the major protagonists. Mathieu Dreyfus and Joseph Reinach told their children about events from early on; see ibid., 344.

[18] Anon., 'Chronique, "L'Affaire Dreyfus" ', *La Fronde*, 6 Sept. 1898.

[19] Charles Chincholle, 'Avant le retour de Dreyfus à Rennes', *Le Figaro*, 29 June 1899.

[20] Anon., 'Madame Dreyfus', *La Constitution*, 30 June 1899.

[21] Anon., 'Avant le retour de Dreyfus à Rennes', *Le Figaro*, 30 June 1899.

It is no longer the Christian woman who, resigned, offers her sufferings to God and keeps her intimate pains with a sublime renunciation; it is the Jewish wife, for whom the absent husband, the new family are the new *patrie* and gods. . . . Her weakness finds infinite treasures of initiative and tenacity.[22]

We can only guess whether these associations drew on literary tradition, embodied in Rebecca, Sir Walter Scott's heroine in *Ivanhoe* (1819), who was one of the most widely loved characters of Romantic genre fiction and painting in France.[23] Rebecca tends to the wounded knight and never abjures her faith, showing both her virtue and intellectual prowess throughout the novel. Such ideas once again took shape in *La Juive*, an opera by Meyerbeer that was performed endlessly in the nineteenth century, featuring the martyrdom of a virtuous Rachel who refused to convert after falling in love with a Christian nobleman.[24]

Activism, martyrdom, and victimhood all came together in painting Lucie's portrait. And yet there were other moments when the 'Jewish' dimension of her character evaporated in language that associated her more with the Virgin and the 'Christian' model of suffering that *La Fronde* had alluded to. She was portrayed as a 'silent' sufferer, a model of 'abnegation', as supporting 'the most appalling martyrdom that the annals of Pain have recorded'.[25] By invoking 'douleur' with a capital 'D', *La Fronde* suggested the torments of Jesus's Mother who was *Notre-Dame des Douleurs*, obliged to watch the death of her son crucified on the cross.

This elision was not surprising, as New Testament images of suffering pervaded the Affair. Dreyfus was regularly portrayed as a Christ-figure, an attempt to counter the widespread anti-Dreyfusard association of the Jewish captain with Judas.[26] Théodore Reinach, the brother of Joseph, published a

---

[22] 'Osmont', 'Leurs Femmes', *La Fronde*, 21 Mar. 1899.

[23] Jon Whitely, of the Ashmolean Museum, first alerted me to the signficance of this art-historical theme; see Beth Wright, 'Scott's Historical Novels and French History Painting', *Art Bulletin*, 63 (1981), 258–87; 'Walter Scott et la gravure française', *Nouvelles de l'Estampe*, 93 (1987), 6–10; and esp. (with Paul Joannides), 'Les Romans historiques de Walter Scott et la peinture française', *Bulletin de la Société de l'Histoire de l'Art*, 1982 (1984), 119–32, and 1983 (1985), 95–115.

[24] Ronald Schechter of William and Mary College is currently working on perceptions of the Jewess in nineteenth-century France; I am grateful to him for conveying this material. See his unpublished 'The Jewish Syndrome: Gender, Sexuality and the Jewish Question in Modern Europe'.

[25] 'Jeanne Brémontier, 'Chez Madame Dreyfus', *La Fronde*, 1 Sept. 1898.

[26] C. Forth, *The Dreyfus Affair and the Crisis of French Manhood*, 67–70.

short story entitled 'Gonse-Pilate' in *Le Siècle*, in which he associated General Gonse, one of the central figures in the military conspiracy, with Christ's treacherous betrayer.[27] In an open letter to Lucie in *Aurore*, after the captain's pardon in 1899, Zola described Dreyfus as a 'martyr un-nailed from his cross', obliged during his trial to hear witnesses who 'covered him with spittle, inflicted numerous stabs, pouring on his wounds bile and vinegar'.[28]

The letters which Lucie received were very much in step with this public exploration of the couple's joint martyrdom. Indeed, her correspondents' willingness to write about their own problems and to offer advice on hers rested on their conviction that they already 'knew' her from the press reports. Often they justified their approach to her by remarking on her heroic qualities: 'You have given to women in all countries, and particularly to French women, such a noble example of conjugal fidelity and courage in adversity.'[29] She was the 'model of the true wife'[30] and the 'veritable heroine of modern times';[31] she was the essence of active virtue, 'the strong woman, loyal, energetic, the intangible wife, who defends, with a superhuman courage and at the price of all trials and sacrifices, your martyr husband . . .'.[32] One woman assured her that 'the cross of the Légion d'Honneur' would compensate her for her 'sufferings'.[33]

Letters awaiting Dreyfus's return during June 1899 were full of celebratory anticipation. One officer's wife wrote: 'yesterday again I was crying with joy in thinking about the emotion you would experience in seeing your dear husband again!'[34] Another could barely contain her emotion: 'for months, I have not stopped thinking of you, and I suffered, really suffered, all your moral tortures.' She was so overcome that she kept on going to Lucie's house on the rue Chateaudun, 'with a mad desire' to introduce herself, and only stopped herself for fear of being taken 'as an indiscreet or extravagant person'.[35]

Similar compassionate outpourings focused on Alfred's health, especially his ailing digestion after his ordeal on Devil's Island. Who could not be

[27] Ibid., 95–9.

[28] Emile Zola, 'Lettre à Madame Alfred Dreyfus' *L'Aurore*, 22 Sept. 1899.

[29] MHAJ 97.17.032.01, Clémence Dally, 1899. 09. 16.

[30] MHAJ 97.17.032. 138, Marie Duhaut, Hungary, 1899. 07. 07.

[31] MHAJ 97.17.032. 148, Louise Dupont, England, 1899. 09. 14, Frenchwoman living in England.

[32] MHAJ 97.17.033.75, J. Rivoire, Lyons, 1899. 08. 05.

[33] MHAJ 97.17.033. 91, Clara Darcey Roche, Paris 1899. 06. 07.

[34] MHAJ 97.17.032.42, Eugénie Defaux, Grenoble 1899. 06. 30.

[35] MHAJ 97.17.032.44, Gabrielle Degois, Versailles 1899. 07. 02.

moved by the tale of his suffering, reported in detail in the Dreyfusard press, of the time when a palisade was constructed to obscure his view of the sea, or when his hands were manacled to his bed while he slept? One woman who had worked with Siberian exiles warned Lucie not to worry if her husband was unable to 'express emotions of happiness or hope', to remember that it might take as long as four to six years 'of family life . . . to make minds which have suffered too much function morally'.[36] Women fussed over Dreyfus's digestive disorder, identifying with Lucie's wifely concerns to bring him back to health. Often, in the same letter, they would switch their identification from her to her husband. One correspondent recounted how her 'nerves had been tested by fatigue, trials, disappointment, the work of anguish', and recommended a patented flour that would take away 'nausea and bitterness', physical sensations that referred, perhaps, to the same emotional states.[37] Such missives demonstrated how letter-writers sought to relate their own stories to Lucie and Alfred as much as to offer the couple support.

Repeatedly, correspondents wrote of Lucie's trials in a Catholic idiom, with a widow from Lorraine of a military background telling how she and her mother followed 'with a painful and deep sympathy the last stages of your Calvary'.[38] This metaphor of her Calvary was reiterated in several letters, and thus consciously associated Lucie with Christ's travails. At other times she was Mary who 'consoles' 'the poor martyr', becoming the 'most noble . . . woman'.[39] They also took up the association between Dreyfus and Christ, with one woman asking Lucie to send a photograph of her husband so that she could give it a 'place of honour next to our Christ!' on her mantelpiece.[40] Another assured her that 'the resurrection of your Husband is as assured as that of Christ',[41] while yet another suggested that Alfred 'incarnated . . . all of human pain'.[42]

Devout Catholics were keen to show their support for the cause through ecumenism, with one woman proclaiming that she and her friends did not admit 'divisions in the struggle of the "only God" for all religions'; they had 'no other objective in life than these two primordial principles: Charity and

---

[36] MHAJ 97.17.032.165, Thyn Catherine Alberdingk, 1899. 06. 11.

[37] MHAJ 97.17.032.141, Marie Dumas, n.d.

[38] MHAJ 97.17.032.69, Marie Derevogue, Chalons, 1899. 07. 20.

[39] MHAJ 97.15.032, Marianne Dale, London, 1899. 09. 12.

[40] MHAJ 97.17.032.128. Marie Dubois, 1899. 09. 20.

[41] MHAJ 97.17.033.75, J. Rivoire, Lyons, 1898. 08. 05.

[42] MHAJ 97.17. 032.16, Henriette Dans, Neuilly, 1899. 09.

Justice',[43] a remark which suggests that Péguy's conception of Dreyfusard activism was widely felt.

Other letters show the range of religious, regional, and national interests that came together, a shifting coalition in which Lucie served as a screen for a myriad of projections. While these adherents were welcome, they often represented minority or 'foreign' interests which confirmed anti-Dreyfusard fantasies of internal subversion linked with external threat. Protestants, for example, identified with Jews as a persecuted minority,[44] and evoked their own history; they spoke of the late seventeenth-century Revocation of the Edict of Nantes, which withdrew their rights to limited toleration, and referred to the Calas Affair as evidence of Catholicism's long history of persecution.

This Affair concerned a Huguenot textile merchant who was accused in 1761 of murdering his eldest son to stop him converting to Catholicism; Calas was broken on the wheel and his son buried as a Catholic martyr. The case became a *cause célèbre* when Voltaire intervened, triggering a public inquiry that led to Calas's rehabilitation and the promulgation of an Edict of Toleration.[45] The Calas case inspired Dreyfusards like Joseph Reinach, who, in August 1897, sought to convert Auguste Scheurer-Kestner—vice-president of the Senate, Alsatian and Protestant[46]—to the Dreyfusard cause by addressing him as Arouet, Voltaire's real name. He repeatedly made the link between Scheurer's would-be activism and the *philosophe*'s prominent role in defending the Protestants of the eighteenth century. For Reinach, both the past and the present were a time for heroes: 'I give you only one piece of advice: it is to reread the Calas Affair. It is always exactly the same obstacles, the same difficulties, the same arguments. Only the names have changed . . .'[47]

---

[43] MHAJ 97.17.034.66, Louise Villiers, Paris, 1899. 06. 27.

[44] André Encrevé, 'La Petite Musique huguenote', in Pierre Birnbaum, *La France et l'Affaire Dreyfus* (Paris, 1984), 451–504; Pierre Pierrard, *Les Chrétiens et l'Affaire Dreyfus* (Paris,), 111–18.

[45] For the relations between the two 'Affairs' see Raoul Allier, *Voltaire et Calas: une affaire judiciaire au XVIIIème siècle* (Paris, 1898), and Edgar Sanderson, *Historic Parallels to l'Affaire Dreyfus* (London, 1900); see also Voltaire, *L'Affaire Calas* (Paris, 1975), and André Castelot, *L'Affaire Calas* (Paris, 1965).

[46] See Sylvie Aprile, 'L'Engagement dreyfusard d'Auguste Scheurer-Kestner: un combat pour l'honneur de la République et de l'Alsace', *La Société de l'Histoire du Protestantisme et son Bulletin* (1996), 55–79.

[47] Quoted in André Roumieux, editor of Auguste Scheurer-Kestner, *Mémoires d'un sénateur dreyfusard*, (Strasbourg, 1988), 4l.

Others also picked up the parallel: one Protestant from Castres wrote to Lucie after the Rennes trial that, 'your husband undergoes martyrdom as my co-religionists, Calas and Sirven, underwent it with the same innocence in 1762'.[48] They referred repeatedly to a common Jewish-Protestant commitment to the Old Testament, especially the prophets, with their emphasis on inner conviction and godly behaviour rather than outward displays and ritual.[49] Their sense of a shared God was evoked by one Protestant wife of a cavalry officer who wrote to Lucie: 'Let me tell you that the small herd of Protestant Christians in Laôn . . . call out cries of appeal towards your God, who is our own.'[50]

Even though small in number, Jews too wrote to Lucie and reflected a range of positions in their missives. Letters from the chief rabbi of France, Zadoc Kahn, and his wife suggest that the Affair was at the forefront of their preoccupations,[51] while the letters of a demoted official who shared Dreyfus's name show remarkable solidarity, despite his suffering. These men and women shared the language of martyrdom and victimhood that inspired their Christian counterparts, interpreting the Affair as a religious trial. But the angry, critical tone of other correspondents reveals a more troubled dimension of Jewish feeling. Until the Affair, French Jews had perceived themselves as privileged inhabitants in the 'land of liberty'.[52] But the violence of the Affair[53]—in France itself, and especially in Algeria—threatened such optimistic beliefs,[54] with some arguing that assimilation had brought God's just chastisement.

---

[48] MHAJ 97.17.033.007, Camille Rabaud, Castres 1899. 09. 10.

[49] One Alsatian theologian, Louis Leblois, the father of the eminent Dreyfusard, was important in elaborating these ideas. See his *Les Bibles et les initiateurs religieux de l'humanité* (Paris,), 72–272. For the importance of this tendency in biblical and religious studies see Perrine Simon-Nahum, *La Cité investie: la 'Science du Judaïsme' français et la République* (Paris, 1991), 237–9.

[50] MHAJ 97.12.032.143, Paul Dunal, Laôn 1899. 09. 12. In the original French: 'Ah: tu es un Dieu qui te caches. Dieu d'Israël' (Isa. 45: 15).

[51] MHAJ 97.17.043.96, Zadoc Kahn, Interlaken, 1899. 11. 02 and Ernestine Zadoc-Kahan, 1899. 11. 02.

[52] See Paula Hyman, *The Jews of Modern France* (Berkeley, 1998), 53–76, in which she describes the difficulties of acculturation but also the desire to be good French citizens. For a survey of Russian persecution see Hans Rogger, *Jewish Policies and Right-Wing Politics in Imperial Russia* (Basingstoke, 1986).

[53] Pierre Birnbaum, *Le Moment antisémite: un tour de la France en 1898* (Paris, 1998).

[54] Steven Wilson, *Ideology and Experience*, passim; for a more interpretive account see Michel Winock, *Nationalism, Anti-Semitism and Fascism in France*, trans. Jane Marie Todd (Stanford, 1998); for more on the reaction of Jews to the Affair see the classic interpretation of Michael R. Marrus, *The Politics of Assimilation: The French Jewish*

Rather than feeling solidarity with Dreyfus, some blamed him for his plight, and offered a bleak vision of withdrawal from an anti-Semitic world.

While Catholics, Protestants, and Jews all had their various agendas, other letters from abroad demonstrated how important the Affair was to the world at large. People wrote from North and South America, and from all over Europe, but especially from Switzerland, the Low Countries, and above all England. A woman from Basel recounted the moment when the citizens gathered in front of a newspaper's offices to await the Rennes verdict. 'We Swiss . . . we are not very . . . theatrical people; I did not hear exclamations, but I saw men paling when they read the fatal bulletin.' For her the Dreyfusard cause evoked the struggle for the Swiss confederation in the early fourteenth century, the group of cantons which thwarted the ambitions of the German empire for more direct rule.[55] The writer recalled the victorious battles which were seen as proof of divine election: 'At the battle of St Jacques, the Swiss confederates, in struggling against an army ten times more numerous than their own, pulled out the arrows from their breasts to refire them against the enemy. It is necessary to return to the charge, it is necessary to reconquer the honour of your husband and that of your children.'[56]

This woman's solidarity was grounded in an unblemished, mythological vision of Swiss history. The English, who wrote in the largest numbers, used the same strategy, but were nonetheless ambivalent. Great-power rivalry informed their response when, at the height of the controversy surrounding revision in 1898, the British and French tussled over dominance in the Upper Nile at Fashoda.[57] Such imperial rivalry intensified the long-standing ambivalence towards the French and their culture, a split appreciation that was revealed in the letters accompanying the 150,000 signatures sent to Lucie by the *Daily Chronicle* after Rennes.

Community at the Time of the Dreyfus Affair (Oxford, 1971), and a revisionist account which underscores the extent of Jewish activism, Pierre Birnbaum 'La Citoyenneté en péril: les juifs entre intégration et résistance', in id. (ed.), *La France et l'Affaire Dreyfus* (Paris, 1994), 505–42.

[55] Olivier Zimmer, *A Contested Nation: History, Memory and Nationalism in Switzerland, 1761–1891* (Cambridge, 2003), 21–31.

[56] MHAJ 97.12.32.157, Mina Durr, Basel 1899. 09. 10.

[57] E. Malcolm Carrol, *French Public Opinion and Foreign Affairs, 1870–1914* (Hamden, Conn., 1964), 162–82, and Thomas M. Iiams, Jr, *Dreyfus, Diplomatists and the Dual Alliance: Gabriel Hanotaux at the Quai d'Orsay (1894–1898)* (Geneva, 1962), 45–63.

While the petition assured the Dreyfuses that the signatories were 'firm friends and deep admirers of the French people and their institutions',[58] letter-writers often scarcely hid their pleasure at what they perceived as Gallic shame. One suggested that the 'poor', 'victimized' children of Alfred and Lucie would find educational salvation in a British public school,[59] while another attempted to organize a phalanx of British cyclists to protect Dreyfus from the insults of a hostile French crowd when he arrived in Rennes.[60] While a touching—if eccentric—offer, the letter also displayed a desire to contrast manly British moral courage with French perfidy.

Both in personal missives and in letters to the editors of the *Daily Chronicle*, British men and woman saw Lucie and Alfred in the same martyrological terms as their French counterparts, with the Protestant theme emerging even more strongly. One woman from Tunbridge Wells wrote a prayer: 'may our God, who hears the sorrowful singing of the poor prisoner, still help and support both him and you, and restore him to you and to his children again.'[61] Above all, English evangelicals hated Catholicism:

> Until the sacrilegious verdict was delivered under the Holy Crucifix(!) [sic] at Rennes on Saturday last, I was even charitable towards Roman Catholicism and Ritualism.
>
> When, however, I observe the guilty silence of the Roman Catholic priesthood throughout the world towards such a blasphemous outrage of truth, perpetuated under the very image of Him who is the ever living Truth[sic] I pray the God of Truth to save England and the whole world from a form of religion which is more cruel and injurious than irreligion.[62]

The writer had correctly identified the strange alliance that brought fierce Protestants together with irreligious anticlericals. Reinach famously excoriated Jesuitry and all priestcraft, but he was a proud rationalist, who would have found this letter-writer's Protestant piety difficult to comprehend. In this distinction lay the great difference in political and religious sensibility between England and France. Whereas in English evangelism, the language of conscience and liberal reformism intermingled, among French Republicans issues of conscience were often explicitly severed from Catholicism. By

[58] MAHJ 97.17.035.021

[59] MAHJ 97.17.035. 051, M. B. Ferguson, Mainz, 1899. 09. 13.

[60] MAHJ 97.03.86, F. H. Dodd, Paris, 1899. 09. 19.

[61] MHAJ 97.17.032. 059, Rose Delves, Tunbridge Wells, n.d.

[62] MHAJ 97.12.035.12, G. G. Blackwood, 1899. 09. 13.

its perceived link to hierarchy and the confessional, Catholicism was portrayed as wedded to unquestioning authority and oppression.

These unknown supporters' relationship with Lucie was based on an idealization, while her relationship with leading players in the Dreyfusard struggle reveals a more complicated dynamic. The man to whom she owed most was Joseph Reinach, the son of a German Jewish banker[63] and disciple of the early Third Republican premier, Léon Gambetta.[64] Reinach held a vision of French Republicanism that was meritocratic, populist, anti-socialist, and anti-German, despite his German origins and the impact of his brothers, Théodore and Solomon, in bringing German scholarly techniques and ideas to the French study of antiquity.[65]

At the heart of his vision was a belief in the Voltairean strand of Enlightenment tolerance that he saw as central to ensuring continued equality for Jews.[66] This conscious investment in rational politics based on secular moral outrage was typical of leading Dreyfusards. But such an ideology scarcely veiled a phantasmagoric fear of, and obsession with, the Jesuits, whom Reinach believed were responsible for the plot against Dreyfus.[67] Reinach's conviction demonstrates the role of 'irrationality' in shaping his Dreyfusard activism, despite his rational conscious beliefs.[68]

---

[63] For this remarkable family saga, reminiscent of the social ascent of the Rothschilds, see Jean-Yves Mollier, *Le Scandale de Panama* (Paris, 1991), 209–38.

[64] Reinach first worked for Gambetta's newspaper, *La République française*, as a German translator, and was later given the honour of compiling Gambetta's *Discours et plaidoyers*; during his political career he gravitated naturally to other Gambettists, who formed an important generation within the Dreyfusard ranks.

[65] For more on the brothers see the excellent analysis by Perrine Simon-Nahum, *La Cité investie*, 222–9; the author also describes their centrality to the creation of a current of 'reform' Judaism inside France, reminiscent of its counterpart in Germany.

[66] Corinne Touchelay, 'Joseph Reinach avant l'affaire Dreyfus: un exemple de l'assimilation politique des juifs en France au début de la Troisième République', Thèse de l'école de Chartes (1982).

[67] Reinach, *Histoire de l'Affaire Dreyfus*, vol. 1, p. 216.

[68] See also Geoffrey Cubitt, *The Jesuit Myth: Conspiracy Theory and Politics in Nineteenth-Century France* (Oxford, 1993); Joseph Reinach was the quintessential example of a 'juif d'état', who associated the Republic and its values with the fate of his co-religionists, even though his identity was entirely secular. It was for this reason that throughout the Affair he laid emphasis on preserving and extending Republican values rather than defending Dreyfus as a Jew. When, after 1892, anti-Semitism exploded in reaction to the role of a few Jewish financiers in the Panama scandal (including his father-in-law), he equated the rise of anti-Semitism with anti-Republicanism. He dedicated himself

Lucie cherished Reinach's advice and indefatigable energy in letters that demonstrate an aching gratitude that overwhelmed her natural reserve.[69] One cannot help but be struck by the depth of her political inexperience in contrast to his enormous fund of worldly savvy and social contacts. His letters mix virtual orders with a genuine appreciation of her importance and moral courage which, he believed, had secured a place for her 'in history'.[70] On several occasions he actually produced model letters that she recopied in her own hand. He listed those who required photographs of Alfred to thank them for their support, told her when to install a telephone to make communication more rapid, and insisted that she write to Madame Waldeck-Rousseau, the wife of the premier, who—through his mediation—had enabled Lucie to see her husband without a guard when he returned from Devil's Island.

This dedicated officiousness was exemplified by a conversation that Reinach had with Marguerite Durand, the editor of *La Fronde*, which in mid-1899 inexplicably stopped its campaign in favour of Dreyfus. Reinach discovered that Durand was irritated that Lucie had never thanked her for the paper's support. In an effort to smooth the ruffled feathers of this 'disinterested' but very 'sensitive' woman, he explained to Durand that Lucie's 'excessive reserve' and 'exaggerated timidity' had prevented her from expressing her gratitude. He then urged Lucie to go straight to the newspaper's offices, or to visit Durand at home.[71]

She did as she was bid, but not without protest, explaining that she had thought of writing, but had renounced the idea in case the letter ended up printed in the newspaper, offending the other journalists who had also aided the campaign.[72] She also refused his request for a press photograph to send to an English woman, remarking coyly that she would happily send *him* one when it included her husband, a statement which both underlined her wifely modesty and made clear her hatred of publicity.[73]

Lucie leaned on Reinach and believed rightly that he was a key figure in her husband's liberation. But other friends within the movement were even closer to her. Their complicated emotional history reveals both the 'mystique'

---

to combating both simultaneously, and was convinced that only through Englightenment universalism and secularism could the Republic and the Jews be saved.

[69] BN NAF 24895, Lucie Dreyfus to Joseph Reinach, n.d., pieces 10–12.

[70] MAHJ 97.17.053.016, J. Reinach, Paris, 1899. 07. JJ.

[71] MAHJ 97.17.053.06, J. Reinach to L. Dreyfus, Paris, 1899. 06. 16.

[72] BN NAF 24898, Lucie Dreyfus to J. Reinach, n.d., pieces 36–7.

[73] Ibid., Lucie Dreyfus to J. Reinach, n.d., pieces 45–6.

and the 'politique' of Péguy's analysis, the mobilizing passion of the Dreyfusards, and the subsequent emotional pain in the midst of the movement's
disintegration after Dreyfus's pardon in September 1899.

Among Lucie's most devoted correspondents were Olympe and Louis
Havet, a philologist and professor at the Collège de France. While Louis often
figures in histories of the Affair, Olympe is generally absent; yet her correspondence shows how, for years, the Affair was the crucible out of which her
political vision was moulded and the emotional centre of her marriage. While
Louis wrote to the male elite of the cause, Olympe dedicated herself to Lucie,
although she, too, had close relations with men, especially Georges Picquart.
Picquart was never her lover, but she clearly loved him, and it was Lucie's
unwillingness to convince Alfred to follow Picquart's tactical line after the
Rennes verdict that brought about the breach in their relations.

But before these days of disillusion the Havets embraced their supportive
role as a kind of moral pilgrimage: 'whatever happens to us . . . you have
changed the orientation of our life, you have raised us above ourselves; we
are better than we would have been.'[74] Their missives reveal an almost mes-
sianic fervour, as well as the emotional roller-coaster ride that was the lot of
active Dreyfusards. When Zola was condemned in early 1898, Olympe was
convinced that, despite the perfidy of the judges and military men, Alfred
would eventually go free. She recounted a dinner conversation with Picquart
who, with 'simplicity, serenity', had affirmed that revision would take
place.[75] She described moments of paralysed stupor when things went
wrong, and gave vent to feelings of bitterness and rage, especially in the wake
of Henry's suicide.[76]

Olympe's involvement was not confined to outrage and sympathy, however.
She aided her husband's campaign by detailing the brutal conditions on Devil's
Island,[77] visited Picquart in prison,[78] and managed to contact someone who
had seen Dreyfus and could give some account of his health.[79] We can only
imagine what this must have meant to Lucie, who thirsted after such news.

Although furious at the Rennes verdict, the Dreyfuses and the Havets
knew a rare moment of joy when, after his pardon, Louis received a letter from
Alfred:

---

[74] MAHJ 97.17.51.14, Olympe Havet to L. Dreyfus, 1899. 07. 11.

[75] MAHJ 97.17.51.01, Olympe Havet to L. Dreyfus, Paris, 1898. 03. 18.

[76] MAHJ 97.17.51.08, Olympe Havet to L. Dreyfus, Paris, 1898. 07. 08 and 1898. 09. 01.

[77] MAHJ 97.17.51.15, Olympe Havet to L. Dreyfus, Rochecorbon (Indre-et-Loire) 1899.
07. 13

[78] MAHJ 97.17.51.05, Olympe Havet to L. Dreyfus, Paris, 1898. 7. 23.

[79] MAHJ 97.17.51.03, Olympe Havet to L. Dreyfus, Paris, 1898. 06. 30.

I cannot tell you of the emotion of my dear husband when he recognized the handwriting of the Captain on the envelope. He said to me: 'A year ago, he knew nothing of what we were doing for him, and today he is with his wife and his children.' And the letter illuminated him with joy for several days; he related it to some friends in order to make them understand your husband's character, and those that read it were first penetrated by emotion, and they were duly conscious of the grandeur of the cause of Dreyfus.[80]

They became a kind of foursome, with Havet writing to Dreyfus, and Olympe writing to Lucie. But the joint love affair, and the pleasure of absolute accord, soon dissolved. The ambiguity of the pardon—which liberated Alfred but did not resolve the moral and political debate—threw up divisive issues. Nor was their experience unique, as many erstwhile allies within the Dreyfusard camp broke with each other after ugly disputes.[81]

Olympe urged Lucie and Alfred to take a more active role in condemning the amnesty that the government issued after the Rennes trial which not only shielded the culprits but also prevented Picquart, Zola, and Reinach from proving their innocence in other legal actions. At the end of 1900 she scolded the Dreyfuses for their 'exile' in Switzerland: '*you must return to France—it is your absolute duty*—and to Paris, *even if there were danger.*' For the first time she relayed to Lucie the growing perception that Dreyfus *was* a coward, and transmitted to her Picquart's belief that the Dreyfuses were looking after themselves rather than furthering the 'cause'.[82]

At this stage Alfred and Lucie heeded her advice, and the Dreyfuses returned, responding also to Mathieu's reports that their Swiss 'exile' was being misinterpreted.[83] But by 1901 more serious matters were at stake. The real traitor, Esterhazy, had admitted his guilt in London, and a large contingent of Dreyfusards wanted to renew the campaign for rehabilitation. There was no disagreement over the ultimate aim, but Dreyfus's legal advisors informed Mathieu that Esterhazy's confession would not ensure final victory. But for Havet, who wrote to Alfred, the choice was clear: 'It is your right,

---

[80] MAHJ 97.17.51.22. Olympe Havet, 1899. 3. 10.

[81] For these sorry tales of distrust and resentment between Labori (one of Alfred's lawyers at the Rennes trial and the hero of Zola's first trial) and the Dreyfuses, Havet and the Dreyfuses, and Picquart and the Dreyfuses see Alfred Dreyfus, *Carnets, passim*. Philippe Oriol's discussion in the footnotes provides an invaluable aide to understanding the reasons behind their disputes.

[82] MAHJ 97.17.051.29, Olympe and Louis Havet to L. Dreyfus, Paris, 1900. 11. 03.

[83] Burns, *Dreyfus: A Family Affair*, 288–9; while he reported the general consternation among the Dreyfusards, Mathieu remained worried about Alfred's security.

and, I dare to say it, your duty. With or without hope of immediate success . . .
I believe that the moment has come when you must demand revision.'[84]

When the Dreyfuses rejected this plan, relations between the two couples
never really recovered. It seemed as if the Havets required sacrificial, martyred figures at the centre of the campaign. When Alfred and Lucie refused
their allotted roles, the Havets felt that their 'mystique' was mortally threatened. The spiritual underpinnings of the movement, despite its secular aims,
had a narrative and moral logic that was increasingly absolutist, and Alfred's
and Lucie's mutual decision to reject the Havets' vision of the Dreyfusard
'mystique' utterly destabilized them.

The Havets' disappointment was matched by their deepening friendship
with the soldierly Picquart, whose letters—both in prison and out—shone
with wit and cultivation. The Havets were ever solicitous of his intellectual and
physical comfort,[85] which he appreciated in letters peppered with thanks for
the food their servant Annette prepared for his delectation. Indeed, so extraordinary was the culinary largesse of 'terrines',[86] 'rillettes'[87] a 'superb spiny lob-
ster',[88] and a 'galantine of pigeon'[89] that he once exclaimed: 'I am becoming
the most difficult and the most gluttonous of men by your fault.'[90]

It was not just gratitude that he offered, though, but a community of taste
and intellectual interests. He mused from prison on the magnificence and
barbarity of Rome,[91] spoke of his love of Wagner,[92] and waited eagerly for
their reports of a new exhibition of Rembrandt in Amsterdam. It was in the
last letter that his latent anti-Semitism emerged. He had the misguided
impression that Rembrandt was Jewish, and admitted to experiencing 'an
instinctive feeling of resentment, moreover immediately repressed'. While
he acknowledged the shameful depth of his prejudice, he ascribed to
Rembrandt's art 'Jewish' characteristics which he had hitherto not compre-
hended: 'this ostentation, this sort of showiness that he likes to deploy on
certain occasions; those feathers, those strange turbans; all of that which is
from the Orient that this Dutchmen knew in the latent state.'[93] By focusing

[84] MAHJ 97.17.051.29, Louis Havet, Paris, 1901. 05. 16.

[85] BN NAF, 24503 (1) Georges Picquart, 138–9, Paris, 1 Sept. 1898.

[86] BN NAF, 24503 (1) Georges Picquart, 153–4, Paris, 12 Nov. 1898.

[87] BN NAF, 24503 (1) Georges Picquart, 142–3, Paris, 11 Oct. 1898.

[88] BN NAF, 24503 (1) George Picquart, 168–9, Paris, 29 Mar. 1899.

[89] BN NAF, 24503 (1) Georges Picquart, 170–1, Paris, 10 Apr. 1899.

[90] BN NAF, 24503 (1) Georges Picquart, 145, Paris, 10 Dec. 1898.

[91] BN NAF, 24503 (1) Georges Picquart, 168–9, Paris, 29 Mar. 1899.

[92] BN NAF, 24503 (1) Georges Picquart, 142–3, Paris, 11 Sept. 1898.

[93] BN NAF, 24503 (1) Georges Picquart, 149–50, Paris, 6 Nov. 1898.

on the sumptuousness and 'orientalism' of Rembrandt's painting, Picquart believed he had found its Jewish essence.

Such artistic commentary, however, was only the beginning of an anti-Semitic outpouring. In a letter of 1901 he remarked bitterly that the same government that had pardoned right-wing extremists like Paul Déroulède had pardoned Dreyfus, leaving the unwanted impression that the two men could be equated. With exasperation he proclaimed: 'Here is where the pusillanimity of the Jews has brought us.'[94] Whatever their views on such explosions, there is no doubt that, for the Havets, Picquart became a 'truer' hero than Dreyfus. This judgement was integral to their disagreement over tactical and political differences, and their anger at Dreyfus's caution.

No doubt at the heart of these reflections was hurt and a heartfelt, if irrational, feeling of betrayal. Despite their joy at Dreyfus's release, the Jewish captain was not, in real life, what they had wished him to be. Endless were the commentaries in the press about the monotonous quality of Dreyfus's testimony during the trial, his apparent lack of passion, his inability to inspire that sympathetic ardour that the French expected from their heroes. While the Havets were less small-minded, their complaints nonetheless manifested the same reserve; somehow Dreyfus was unworthy of the righteous passion that they and Picquart had invested in the cause. Louis continued to write, albeit in a cooler tone, while Olympe fell silent altogether and even became ill with migraines. She admitted later to Lucie that 'I almost became sick with emotion because of our differences of opinion'.[95]

Indeed, relations became so bad at one point that there were open and heated quarrels between Alfred and Louis, wounds that stopped bleeding but that nonetheless left scars. When Dreyfus retired from the army after his rehabilitation in 1906, disillusioned yet again because he had been denied the full promotion that Picquart had won, Olympe disapproved of this decision too, and told Lucie so. It seemed that their disagreements would never end. It is a testimony to the attempt to cherish those moments of past endeavour and shared idealism that, despite the pain of these later years, Olympe was able to sign her last letter, 'Your loyal friend for life'.[96]

Causes célèbres are predicated on the need for passionate involvement, an engagement central to political mobilization and effective intervention, even if later recriminations show how hard it is to sustain such a campaign. The

[94] BN NAF, 24503 (1)Georges Picquart, 199–200, n.d.

[95] MAHJ, 97.17.51,31, Olympe Havet, Paris, n.d.

[96] MAHJ, 97.17.51.42, Olympe Havet, Rochecorbon (Indre-et-Loire), n.d.

Dreyfusards' conscious commitment to rationalism, as well as the subsequent historiography, obscured the spiritual substratum that supported their political convictions. They were ambivalent about the relationship between emotion and intellect, and distrustful of a Christian religious language that they used tactically but did not formally endorse. The images of a suffering Mary and a martyred Jesus, of ecumenical renewal, of a just God who would redeem Dreyfus, were all central to those who wrote to Lucie, but disturbed their secular 'mystique'. The religious politics of the letter-writers tapped into a ubiquitous language of martyrology and prayer that had little in common with the leadership's vehement anticlericalism.

However, even if they eschewed the self-conscious religious models of the strangers who wrote to, leading Dreyfusards also expressed their commitment in quasi-religious terms. Their vibrant eloquence in defence of Enlightenment values and a Republic purged of 'superstition' contained a strong missionizing element. But this positive idealism was often shadowed by irrational feelings of threat. Reinach's conjuring up of the Jesuitical conspiracy testifies to the occult dimension of their political psychology. The disenchantment between the Havets and the Dreyfuses emerged from Alfred's refusal to continue in the role of martyr. Their vision of the Affair became as absolutist in its zealotry as the 'fanaticism' it opposed. When he accepted the pardon and refused any new judicial adventures in order to protect himself and his family, he lost his heroic stature. When he was diminished, they too felt slighted, and so they turned to one more worthy.

It is through understanding these various *fin-de-siècle* emotional resonances—both the idealism and the fear—that the Dreyfus Affair comes alive again, not merely as a struggle between Right and Left, but as a spiritual and psychological journey, the roots of which grew out of imagery, psychological identifications, and visions of suffering that owed much to the religious legacies of the past.

Witchcraft, Nostalgia, and the Rural Idyll in Eighteenth-Century Germany

Lyndal Roper

In 1747, over a hundred years after the witch craze had ended, Magdalena Bollmann found herself accused of witchcraft. Bollmann came from the village of Alleshausen in what is now part of Württemberg, high on the plateau by Lake Federsee, a flat, brooding landscape dotted with pilgrimage churches and ruled by the Praemonstratensian monks of the Abbey of Obermarchtal. Bollmann was not the first to be accused of witchcraft in this particular outbreak of witchcraft trials. By the time the accusations against her were heard, four women had already been burnt as witches, and three more would meet their deaths before the episode was over, seven women in a population of barely 500 people.[1] It was extraordinary for such a large outbreak of witch-hunting to occur so late: this was the period of the first stirrings of the Enlightenment. Even the executions did not put an end to it. Just nine years later, three more women in the neighbouring village of Brasenberg were tried for witchcraft, escaping burning only because the village mayor and the advisory jurist declared the evidence inadmissable and so brought the trials to a halt.[2]

At about the same time as these horrific trials, a young monk from the monastery of Obermarchtal was enjoying his early literary successes. Sebastian Sailer (1714–71) is hardly a name to conjure with outside Swabia. But Sailer played a not-insignificant role in the development of German literature that reached its apogee in the late eighteenth century: he knew the Enlightenment poet and translator of Shakespeare Christoph Martin Wieland (1733–1813), who hailed from nearby Biberach and who lived there between 1760 and

---

[1] A census of 1719 lists 52 *Lehenleute* and 13 *Beisitzer*. These were heads of household. In 1746 there were 59 and 8 respectively; in 1769, 55 and 15. In 1719 there were also 29 unmarried sons, in 1746, 66, and in 1769, 52. A census from 1833 lists 68 families, giving a total of 482 souls. *Kreisbeschreibungen des Landes Baden-Württemberg. Der Landkreis Biberach*, 2 vols. (Sigmaringen, 1987, 1990), i. 403.

[2] For more on this series of cases, see Lyndal Roper, *Witch Craze: Terror and Fantasy in Baroque Germany* (London 2004), 222–46.

1765; and his literary works were read by the likes of Johann Wolfgang von Goethe. Sailer was the first Swabian dialect poet, producing wonderfully idiosyncratic religious plays where Eve makes the speciality of the Swabian kitchen, *Spätzle*, and God watches the weather like a shrewd Swabian peasant, and other comic dramas based on village life. At first his dialect dramas circulated only in performance, while the devotional works which he also composed—and for which he was well known during his lifetime—were printed. But the texts of the plays were soon copied in manuscript form and passed from hand to hand; and from at least the late eighteenth century his plays began to be printed, not only by local presses in tiny townlets like Riedlingen, but by major printers. In 1783 a version of one of his plays was published—suitably rendered into the local dialect—in Vienna.[3]

Sailer's work was part of the early Enlightenment discovery and creation of folk culture that was to find its full flowering in the nineteenth century, as academics created dialect dictionaries, scoured peasant households for fairy tales, and documented the marriage customs and costumes of the local peasantry. In his poems and dramas Sailer immortalized the world of the peasants in rural Swabia, mocking their pretensions and narrow-mindedness with affectionate humour. Like so many local scholars at this time, working far from metropolitan centres but influenced by the new intellectual currents, Sailer was fascinated by language and determined to preserve local culture. We also know that he had an early posting as an assistant priest in the village of Seekirch, Alleshausen's parish church, at just the time when these trials were beginning. How did these two very different mid-eighteenth-century worlds connect, Sailer's satirical version of coarse but cosy village life, animated by Enlightened curiosity, and the relentless cruelty that characterizes the trials?[4]

---

[3] See Hans Albrecht Oehler's revised edn. of Sixt Bachmann (ed.), *Sebastian Sailers Schriften im schwäbischen Dialekte* (Weissenhorn, 2000), (hereafter cited as Oehler, *Sebastian Sailer*: all quotations from Sailer's works will be taken from this edition), 10–11 (*Vorrede* by Sixt Bachmann to the edition of 1819). Bachmann was a member of the Order in Marchtal and had known Sailer. He compiled the first collected edition of Sailer's works, based on copies of the works he was able to find. Bachmann's preface to this volume is our main source for Sailer's biography. In it, Bachmann alludes to printed copies of various plays from presses in Kreuznach, Riedlingen, and Ulm, all with many transcription mistakes. See also *Nachwort*, by Hans Albrecht Oehler, pp. 274–5.

[4] On Sailer and on Marchtal, see Andrea Polonyi, 'Die Übertragung des heiligsten Kreuzpartikels von Rom nach Marchtal. Zum Erscheinungsbild barocker Reliquienverehrung'; Ludwig Walter, 'Pater Sebastian Sailer—Der schwäbische Mundartdichter aus Marchtal'; Konstantin Maier, 'Der schwäbische Meister der "geistlichen Wohlredenheit". Chorherr Sebastian Sailer (1714–1777) von Marchtal'; Karl Butscher, 'Das Leben eines

The case against Magdalena Bollmann began with apparently trivial incidents. Conrad Citterel was leading his little 2-year-old son by the hand as they walked by her house and Bollmann, hearing the toddler pass, leaned out of her window to give him a bit of warm rissole to eat. His father, however, told the child to keep it in his fist, and when they reached Bartle Brugger's house he gave it to the cat, who promptly vomited it up. A few days later the little boy went to Bollmann's house for an hour or so, and that evening he was taken ill. He vomited strange white material, was distant and alienated from his parents, as they noted, and he threw his food about wildly. Finally he fell into a sweat and lay quietly in his father's arms. Conrad Citterel's son never recovered and eventually died in agony.[5] Several village women also appeared to testify, alleging that Bollmann had attended their births, or had visited them during the period of lying-in. Then their babies had died, or they themselves had suffered terrible illnesses and pain. But it was not just the community of matrons whose support Bollmann had apparently lost: her own husband repeatedly nagged the mayor, demanding that his wife be taken for trial, because it was 'impossible' for him to continue living with her in the current atmosphere of suspicion.[6]

The village mayor duly assembled the accounts of six witnesses and sent the case to the central court at Obermarchtal, barely half a day's journey away in this tiny territory. There, Bollmann was interrogated and imprisoned. The questioning went on for over six months without any confession from

---

Chorherrn auf einer inkorporierten Pfarrei der Abtei Marchtal'; Winfried Nuber, 'Abtei Marchtal und seine Pfarrei in der Stadt Munderkingen': in Max Müller, Rudolf Reinhardt, and Wilfried Schöntag (eds.), *Marchtal Prämonstratenserabtei, Fürstliches Schloß, Kirchliche Akademie* (Ulm, 1992); Franz Georg Brustgi (ed.), *Sebastian Sailers Schriften im schwäbischen Dialekte. Gesammelt und mit einer Vorrede versehen von Sixt Bachmann*, facsimile of Bachmann edition (Reutlingen, 1976), 'Ergänzungen der Vorrede Sixt Bachmanns' and Bachmann, 'Vorrede'. Sailer worked as an assistant priest in Seekirch from 1745 until 1747 (Brustgi, 'Ergänzungen', p. vi), and then worked for many periods in nearby Reutlingendorf and Dieterskirch.

[5] SAS, Dep. 30, Marchtaler Hexenprozesse, Pak. 255, Magdalena Bollmann, 27 Apr. 1747, testimony of Conrad Citterel, p. 1 ff.

[6] Ibid., pp. 15 and 19, 19 and 20 May 1747. He mentioned the 'cross' all this uncertainty meant he had been forced to bear. His allegiance became even clearer later, when he went to the authorities in Obermarchtal to allege that his wife must have realized through occult means that he was outside her cell, and had called out to him: ibid., p. 106, June 1747. And he had undertaken a visit to his stepdaughter Barbara's girlfriend, to quiz her about Barbara's behaviour: now, he reported the tell-tale details he had learnt that suggested his step-daughter was a witch too, ibid., p. 107.

Bollmann, and the authorities' patience snapped. They began to bully her in questioning, saying that if she refused to confess she was a witch then she was accusing those women who testified against her of perjury and dishonour. Then they moved to torture, applying thumbscrews not only to her thumbs but to her toes, and they had her bound to a bench and whipped for a quarter of an hour. In following sessions they resorted regularly to whipping on the bench, one of the more severe forms of torture. When she collapsed onto the floor, the executioners redoubled their efforts, whipping her on her arms and back as she lay there. By this point Bollmann began to fall unconscious during interrogation, and so, to wake her, the interrogators ordered that the soles of her feet should be burnt with blessed candles and that candles should be put under her nose. The next day, when she again fell insensible, they attempted to rouse her by whipping the black and blistered soles of her feet, but to no avail. Three times during her trial Bollmann was made to suffer the indignity of being strip-searched by the executioners, who secretly 'pricked' her witches' marks and investigated her privy parts. Finally, Bollmann was dragged unconscious by a rope down the stairs to her cell, where she was found dead a few hours later. In its meticulous recording of all the torture and its duration, there are few documents from the European witch hunt to match this case for sheer brutality.[7]

Magdalena Bollmann came from the same village in which Sebastian Sailer began his career as a priest, and this was the region which was to inspire his creative work as a writer for the next thirty years. Following the model of Counter-Reformation best practice, the Obermarchtal monastery sent its own brothers to act as parish clergy for the villages it ruled, where they came to know their parishioners intimately, keeping the written registers of births, marriages, and deaths and writing chronicles of village life. The monks themselves were mostly locals from near Marchtal or from wider Swabia, the sons of peasants or small-town burghers, and they had learnt High German and Latin as well as the dialect with which they grew up. The monastery library was poor, but the monks' horizons extended to the other monastic foundations dotted about the lake, and to the Order. It was in one of these neighbouring monasteries, the Praemonstratensian house at Schussenried, that Sailer first performed his comedy *The Creation*, playing all the parts and accompanying himself on the violin.[8] The monks heard, through Sailer's brilliantly meticulous literate transcription, the rough, broad vowels and coarse speech their education had been designed to make them unlearn,

---

[7] Ibid., pp. 144 ff., 26 Sept. 1747 and following.
[8] Walter, 'Pater Sebastian Sailer'; Oehler, *Sebastian Sailer*, 10 (Bachmann, 'Vorrede').

sharing the joke with others who understood only too well the vexations of ministering to Swabian bumpkins.[9]

Sailer first wrote the religious plays in the Swabian idiom for which he is famous, and then, during the 1750s, 1760s, and 1770s, he produced a series of village plays in which he caricatured all the stock figures of the rural landscape. There is the hamlet mayor, rolling drunk in the village inn,[10] the minor local official who is paralysed with fear at the sight of a hare, the tavern-keeper who is only too candid about how he and the mayor are in cahoots with each other, and the district official, who speaks High German and has only contempt for the peasants. All have their parallels in the trials. Catharina Schmid, executed for witchcraft in 1747, was firmly convinced that she was the victim of a plot hatched between the publican and the mayor in their drinking bouts together. The anxieties of a man like Josef Cadus, the barely literate village mayor, evident in his crabbed handwriting as he tries to compile a dossier of witness statements that will impress the legal authorities in Obermarchtal, find their fictional counterpart in the worries the mayor expresses in the *Die sieben Schwaben (The Seven Swabians)* about whether he is up to the job. Sailer's mayor is not too hot on bureaucratic exactitude, and neither was the real-life mayor of Alleshausen: when Cadus put his list of witnesses together, he forgot to correct it, and one of the women he proudly lists never appeared in the case and had to be replaced by a 15-year-old youth, too young even to give sworn evidence.

Sailer was also well aware of the growing class nature of village society, and reflects this in his plays. From the late sixteenth century on, throughout southern Germany, village society had become increasingly divided, as small groups in each village of five or six families crystallized who owned substantially more land than their fellows, and who monopolized political offices. These families pursued calculated marriage and inheritance strategies, consolidating land and family power, and by the eighteenth century their grip on village politics was secure, often deliberately supported by landlords and rulers who assigned leases accordingly.[11] In Alleshausen the monastery was

---

[9] It used to be thought that the plays were performed by Sailer himself at various local gatherings; however, it has recently been argued by Monika Küble that the audience would have been an educated, bourgeois public, not peasants themselves.

[10] As the mayor puts it, 'jetz sey ih selig scho, weil ih bi woara Schtaatsperso', Oehler, *Sebastian Sailer*, 148 (*Die sieben Schwaben*).

[11] See David Sabean, *Property, Production and Family in Neckarhausen 1700–1870* (Cambridge, 1990), and *Kinship in Neckarhausen 1700–1870* (Cambridge, 1998); Thomas Robisheaux, *Rural Society and the Search for Order in Early Modern Germany* (Cambridge, 1989); Govind Sreenivasan, *The Peasants of Ottobeuren 1487–1723: A Rural*

the main landlord as well as the political authority, and by the eighteenth century it had named each farm after a saint, creating a religious topography of status—every peasant would have known what 'St Sigismund' or 'St Sales' was worth. Inequalities of wealth were clearly part of the background to the witch hunts: the same families of Cadus and Engler held the large farms and recur in the lists of mayors and jurors; while those accused of witchcraft did not come from their group. As in witch hunts all over Europe, those accused of witchcraft tended to be slightly poorer, on the whole, than those who accused them, but the social distance was not great. The Bollmanns were apparently a new family, but they had intermarried with the well-established Stroms; Magdalena's first husband had belonged to the large Weyler clan. Those who went to court against Magdalena were her neighbours and roughly her social equals.[12] The same village hierarchies are reproduced in Sailer's plays: we soon get to know that Veit Balger is the village bounder, or that the tavern-keeper thinks he is a cut above the others, or that Lizelnuss is going to vote for his brother-in-law.[13] Everyone knew what everyone else was worth—after all, the monastery knew the value of each of its farms, and the peasants knew just how much tax everyone should pay. But, though church and layfolk worked the same system of social ranking, Sailer's own ambivalence about it is clear in the character of Florian Simpel, the upright and modest farmer who is his ideal mayor though he is poorer than his neighbours.

Yet for all his mockery, Sailer's picture of village life is good-humoured. His target is the small compass of the peasants' world: in *Sonn- und Mondfang (Sun and Moon Hunt)*, the villagers think they can catch the sun and the moon, which they are convinced rise and set behind their own local hill, the Aisterberg. If, as the educated student character tells them, the earth moves, then why hasn't their village passed through France and Spain yet? Sailer laughs, too, at village politics: in *The Mayoral Election at Limmelsdorf* the town mayor is voting for the publican, his drinking pal, because 'they get on with each other' and that's the key, even though, as he says, they haven't the least idea how you run a village; while in the *The Seven Swabians* the drunken sot of a mayor tries to teach his simpleton beadle how to treat him

---

Society in Early Modern Europe (Cambridge, 2004); and on agriculture and village dynamics, Rainer Beck, *Unterfinning. Ländliche Welt vor Anbruch der Moderne* (Munich, 1993).

[12] SAS, Dep. 30, Kloster Marchtal, Bd. 1951, Beschreibung of 1646; Bd. 1961, Specification of 1733.

[13] Oehler, *Sebastian Sailer*, 198–219 (*Schultheißenwahl zu Limmelsdorf*).

with respect, French-style, by raising his hat. The mayor's idea of bold leadership is to launch a crusade against the hare who he is sure is terrorizing the village, but he flees in terror once he sees the animal itself, with its pointy ears, twitching nose, and rolling eyes. Just occasionally, Sailer authorializes. He intervenes in the character of the student in *Sun and Moon Hunt*, son of the village official, to praise reason, *Vernunft*, and to advocate doing what educated men tell them.[14] In *The Mayoral Election* the message is the same: Florian Simpel refuses to cast a vote for mayor because he's happy to leave it all to the authorities, who will be the best judges of who should do the job.[15] Both the student and the district official speak High German, unlike all the other characters except the priest. But Sailer is too good a writer not to undercut his own moral: it is the anarchic energy of characters like Veit Balg in the elections at Limmelsdorf, pig-headedly refusing to vote as they should, that actually gives the plays interest and drama.[16]

Just how ambivalent Sailer's attitude to village life was can be seen in his treatment of religion, which, perhaps strangely for a long-standing cleric and preacher, does not escape his satirical eye. When the mayor is trying to persuade the *Bannwarth* (watchman) to undertake the dangerous job of spying on the sun and the moon, he reasures him that since he always bows to every single saint every matins (that is, failing to grasp the point of the calendar, which is to honour each individual saint on their own day), they are surely guaranteed to protect him now. And *The Seven Swabians* ends with a mock religious procession, where Blitzschwab is so stupid he doesn't even realize he has landed the plum job of carrying the banner, while the chorus sing: 'they tell us all about eternal life, but even more about how we should pay taxes.'[17] Sailer also criticizes the priest in Limmelsdorf for spending too much time in the inn.

---

[14] Ibid., 194–6 (*Schwäbischer Sonn- und Mondfang*).

[15] 'Ih gieb koi Vautum ih, ih laß dar Herrschaft über. / Maitweaga Schultas sey dar Otter oder Biber. / Denn sui woißt wohl, wear daugt', ibid., 211 (*Schultheißenwahl zu Limmelsdorf*), and see p. 176.

[16] And Balg gets the last word, even though the district official locks him up for insolence. The play finishes as Balg says 'That's how it goes in the world; now the fun's over' ('So goaht as in dar Wealt; jetz hoat dar G'schpaß a End'), ibid., 219 (*Schultheißenwahl zu Limmelsdorf*). Sailer has a predilection for this kind of pragmatic moral, and the proverbs and sayings he mints often run along these lines: 'Zua g'scheahne Sacha muaß ma s'Bescht reda', ibid., 196.

[17] 'Ma sait is viel vom ebiga Leaba, / Hodiho, Alleluia. / Und noh viel maih vom Stuira geaba / Hodi Hodiho, Alleluia', ibid., 171 (*Die sieben Schwaben*).

Yet Sailer's rustic paradise, where God is in his Swabian heaven, is a very partial vision. For a start, there are no women in the village plays. In part this is for reasons of propriety. Female absence, however, has a deeper logic. Women do not form part of Sailer's view of village politics because they do not vote, cannot stand for office, and cannot write down their opinions as their menfolk do. But it is apparent from the witchcraft trials that women were very actively involved in the village court, bringing cases and bearing witness against those whom they suspected. Time and again women's statements described what had happened in the birthing chamber or in the lying-in room amongst the womenfolk: Magdalena Bollmann had held one woman's legs and supported her back as she laboured in the birthing chair, and afterwards the new mother had felt terrible pains in those places, never recovering; or she had allegedly cradled a newborn infant in her arms, and soon it had died. The role of women, and their emotional anchoring of these communities, is utterly erased from Sailer's plays, along with their murderous enmities. Women feature only offstage, as foolish females hankering after the prize seat at feasts and processions that comes with being the mayor's wife.

Indeed, Magdalena Bollmann was as pious and obedient a Swabian peasant as Sailer could have wished for. Putting her trust in the impartiality of the authorities, she demanded to be investigated for signs of witchcraft by the district official, the *Oberamtman*, and attempted to confide in him alone. When that failed, she asked to be tested by the Capuchin clergy. Throughout her trial she called steadfastly on Jesus, Mary, and the saints to witness her innocence. This was a woman who travelled to Biberach for special devotions, who went on pilgrimage, and was trusted to sew up the shrouds of the dead. It was second nature to her to appeal to the authorities for protection, for it was to the mayor she had turned seven years before when she was first branded a witch, and she had then received a formal apology from the woman who had insulted her. The case which ended in her death began when she and her husband brought Conrad Citterel and his wife to court for calling her a witch.[18] This time, her trust in the law was misplaced.

There is a pattern in the accusations. Most of those women who bore witness against Bollmann were younger than she, still fertile in their twenties or

---

[18] SAS, Dep 30, Marchtaler Hexenprozesse, Pak. 255, Magdalena Bollmann, 27 Apr. 1747. The same pattern was also evident in other cases: Maria Bingasser had brought a defamation suit which turned into a witchcraft trial against her, SAS, Dep. 30, Marchtaler Hexenprozesse, Gutachten von Sättelin, 28 Feb. 1747; and Catharina Schmid's case had also started with an insult, SAS, Dep. 30 Marchtaler Hexenprozesse, Catharina Schmid, 1745.

thirties, whereas Bollmann was at the end of her childbearing years. The key accusations against Bollmann involved her behaviour during other women's labour or her giving food to children, and this was connected: Bollmann seemed to be intervening in the fundamental functions of motherhood to do things better than other mothers. In the murky series of possession and obsession cases which surrounded the witch trials, no men seem to have fallen prey to the Devil: women appear to have been more susceptible to dramatizing their sufferings and emotions through physical paroxysms.[19] And the interrogators seem to be simply re-enacting the dramas of female village life when they confronted Magdalena Bollmann with the implications of her refusal to confess: if she did not admit she was a witch, then she was branding the other women as liars, perjurers, and women of no repute. In the female world of gossip, reputation was all; failing to fight an insult to one's honour was to lose one's good name, and a witch was a woman who was 'no use', as Bollmann herself repeatedly put it. Once one became 'useless', one was excluded entirely from the society of upright, honourable women. This is what effectively happened to Magdalena Bollmann.

There is a grisly pattern, too, in the fact that mothers and daughters were frequently targeted in these cases. Catharina Schmid and her daughter were both executed, as were Maria Bingasser and her daughter Anna; and during the trial of Magdalena Bollmann the interrogators intervened to warn Jakob Bollmann that he ought to keep an eye on his stepdaughter Barbara, because it was likely that she was a witch as well.[20] This was virtually inviting the villagers to bring yet another case of witchcraft. And yet the interrogators were only picking up here on a remark which had been made by Conrad Citterel in his first statement, when he deliberately mentioned that it was Magdalena's daughter Barbara who had returned his child from her house, implying that the two women were in it together, scheming to kill his little son. Something in the intensity of the relationship between mothers and daughters, the perceived complicity between them, seems to have excited the anxiety and aggression of their communities, and to have roused the hostility of women as much as it did of men.

---

[19] Catharina Schmid had been accused of causing the possession of 'the Holl girl', and Maria Bingasser was accused of causing Veronica Traub to become possessed; Magdalena Bollmann was blamed for the possession of Anna Kunisslin; while Barbara Getschler was also accused of causing Münst's possession. All these cases involved dramatic physical sufferings of the victim, while their kin made repeated efforts to get them cured, consulting religious specialists like the Capuchins.

[20] SAS, Dep 30, Marchtaler Hexenprozesse, Pak. 255, Magdalena Bollmann, p. 106, June 1747; p. 106, June 1747.

This dynamic found its most poignant expression when Maria Bingasser denounced her own daughter as a witch, in response to pressure from the interrogators. She told them she had corrupted her daughter, taking her to witches' sabbaths. But she loved her child, and if she were there she would say to her face: 'Annele! We have always loved each other, now let us go together to Eternity as well, and make sure we go to Heaven.' The interrogators promptly confronted Bingasser with her daughter, who was also in prison, and when she stoutly denied she was a witch, the two women now concurred that the whole thing had been a diabolic delusion, and were so adamant in their denials that the interrogators had to release them. Shortly after, when Anna began saying in public that she was a witch, they were both imprisoned again and the authorities at last got what they wanted: Anna confessed that her mother had seduced her into witchcraft. She said she never wanted to see her mother again, and 'that she was her enemy, because she had brought her into such a miserable state'. In this investigation, the interrogators' obsession with the intense relationship between the two women formed the emotional core of the case, and it ended only when they had made the daughter forswear their bond.[21]

Sailer can give us no notion of the constraints within which a woman like Magdalena Bollmann had to survive in Alleshausen, dependent on the web of relations with other, younger men and women, and on her second husband's kin. Bollmann had given birth to twelve children, only five of whom were still living by the time of her trial, when she herself was aged, as she said, '42 or 43'. She knew all about being in labour and bringing up children, so it is small wonder that she was summoned to attend when women felt the first birth-pangs. It is often argued that women accused of witchcraft were marginals, outsiders to the village, but in this case the witnesses against Bollmann all had close ties to her. After she had supposedly attempted to poison Conrad Citterel's son, the toddler spent an hour alone with her in her house; when, the previous autumn, she had supposedly caused the whole family terrible illness by giving them some of the *Saath hanen* (seed cock) she had baked; Citterel's pregnant wife was still happy to visit Bollmann in her house and delouse her; and on the Easter Saturday shortly before the accusation was made she, her husband, and Bollmann had gone to Seekirch together to be bled, and had then stopped at a pub where the two women had shared a beer, drinking from the same glass.[22] Anna Maria Münst might have been

---

[21] Ibid., Pak. 255, Urgicht of Anna Oberländer, 1747, Urgicht of Maria Bingasser, 1747.

[22] Ibid., Pak. 255, Magdalena Bollmann, pp. 1–10, 27 Apr. 1747, testimony of Conrad Citterel; 20 May 1747, testimony of Conrad Citterel, pp. 32–3.

convinced that Bollmann had caused the abdominal pains from which she had suffered since giving birth, but this did not stop her begging Bollmann for apples from her garden.[23] When it was Bollmann's sister-in-law who added her voice to those telling stories about her behaviour in the birthing chamber, Bollmann forfeited her husband's support. In a small village like Alleshausen, where most of the inhabitants shared the same half-dozen surnames, kinship did not always unite. The intersection of neighbourhood bonds with kinship meant reliance on others. It also permitted physical intimacy, but the closeness of touch in sharing a drink, holding a woman during the pain of childbirth, or delousing appears to have been deeply ambivalent. Witnesses traced back the calamities they suffered to that moment of physical closeness, and retrospectively interpreted Bollmann's intentions as malicious.[24]

When Sailer got rid of women from his village plays, he also got rid of witchcraft. The all-male monastic environment which was his intellectual retreat whenever he tired of peasant society allowed him to escape from women in real life as well. But witchcraft only appeared to be women's business because the rigid sexual codes of eighteenth-century society identified women with emotionality and physicality: the men who testified on their wives' behalf, who passed on rumours, and who tried out witch-finding techniques, were just as implicated in witch-hunting as women were. Eighteenth-century rural society offered women scant possibilities for independence, excluding them from political and economic power. Life was hard for women who lacked menfolk to protect them, and there were few options for older women outside the village either: none of those accused of witchcraft tried to flee. Gender divisions were hardening in lay culture too, and by the eighteenth century in Marchtal it was only ever women who were accused of witchcraft. This was new, for even at the height of the witch craze in the sixteenth and seventeenth centuries the identification of the witch with women had never been complete, and men too had been executed for witchcraft in significant numbers. But when Marchtal's rulers ordered that Bollmann's corpse should be publicly burnt under the gallows, they explicitly did so 'as a shocking example to the female sex'.

---

[23] Ibid., pp. 86–7, 3 June 1747, testimony of Anna Maria Münst.

[24] In all the trials, witnesses mention a lot of fairly aggressive physical contact, hitting, striking, slapping, and so on on the part of the witches and their victims. This may be because it was believed that if you hit a witch she could not harm you. The witch harmed her victims by touch, and witnesses recall even apparently glancing physical contact: Ibid., p. 40, 20 May 1747, testimony of Francisca Jos; and see Urgicht of Anna Oberländer.

It is striking how many of the allegations apparently dated back many years. The insult that Bollmann was a witch had been levelled at her seven years before by Anna Maria Münst, but it is far from clear that others shared her suspicions at the time: Bollmann certainly thought she had shrugged it off, and though she may have been naive to think the slur could be so easily disposed of, there is no indication that anyone avoided her or feared her touch. Rather, once Citterel made his allegation, the suspicions of others seem to have crystallized as they went back through what might have caused their own past tragedies. This was probably not a matter of chance: we know that the village mayor, Josef Cadus, had to put his file of accusations together for the authorities in Obermarchtal, and it is likely that he actively solicited testimony. Bollmann insisted that Citterell's wife had blamed Catharina Schmid, the executed witch, for her child's death; for whatever reason, her suspicions had now shifted to Bollmann. All these allegations were being formulated when four women from the village had already been burnt at the stake, and when terror and guilt seem to have plunged the community into a fevered state, convincing everyone that witches were harming those they loved. When Bollmann expressed her astonishment that people she knew well could think she was a witch, or that ailments everyone had attributed to natural causes could now be ascribed to her evil spells, she was probably not protesting mock ignorance as the authorities believed.[25] The accusations were most likely formulated only in the atmosphere of witch-hunting, during the heightened sense of the struggle between good and evil which it fostered.

This atmosphere was closely connected with the kind of religiosity the village was experiencing. Its drama could not be more distant from the kind of folksy piety that breathes through Sailer's plays. Sailer's is a picture of rough but heartfelt devotion, from peasants whose emotional responses to religion are warmly sincere even if their ignorance of the Bible is shocking. It seems at one with the glorious Baroque pilgrimage churches that were being built all over the region in this period, at nearby Steinhausen and Obermarchtal itself, with their fleshy putti and imitation marble and gilt.[26] By contrast, the

---

[25] She had allegedly said two years before: 'No one apart from Schmidin says that I'm a witch and I don't care about her'; since Münst, known as the Schmidin, was probably a strange woman, this may have been the general view: ibid., p. 88, 3 June 1747, testimony of Anna Maria Münst. So also, while Francisca Jos had said to Bollmann, after she had touched her on her left arm in front of the Capuchin church door, that if Bollmann were a witch, as people said, she'd be anxious: since Münst had journeyed with Bollmann to Biberach, Bollmann may very well have thought this was only a jokey confidence: ibid., p. 97, 3 June 1747.

[26] On the religious culture of Counter-Reformation southern Germany, see Marc Forster, *Catholic Revival in the Age of the Baroque: Religious Identity in Southwest Germany,*

religiosity that emerges in the witchcraft cases is all centred on possession and exorcism. The first witchcraft case involving Catharina Schmid revolved around a possessed girl, who had blamed first Schmid and then her daughter for causing her convulsions; while one of the witnesses against Bollmann was obsessed by a demon who made it impossible for her even to deliver her statement to the officials. When Anna Maria Münst came to testify against Bollmann, there was high drama, for the very mention of Bollmann's name caused both Münst and the obsessed woman to suffer terrible pains. Despite her physical agony, Münst was willing to undergo the ordeal of confronting Bollmann in person, and repeating her testimony to her face (the so-called 'confrontation' of witch and witness that often resulted in confession). When she had finished, she was nearly overwhelmed with the pain, as the protocols of the case note. All this would have been powerful proof to the authorities in the interrogation chamber of the viciousness of the accused witch who confronted them.[27]

Behind these dramas of possession lay the shadowy presence of the Capuchin friars. Conrad Citterel's little son had been taken to the Capuchins at Biberach for blessing when he fell ill. Magdalena Bollmann herself had been to visit the Capuchin house in Biberach too, and when Anna Maria Münst fell ill she had resorted to blessings from the Capuchins, who had told her that her illness was most likely caused by 'evil people'. Peter Strobel had been given a piece of paper by the friars—if you burnt it, it made such a terrible smoke that no witch could abide it, an oracle he tested on Catharina Schmid. In 1756, when yet another witchcraft case developed in nearby Brasenberg, it revolved around a possessed girl who had sought help from the Capuchin friars. So far from helping people to deal with witchcraft through religious means, the Capuchin response encouraged people to look for witches amongst those they knew. Nor were such beliefs confined to peasants. The court in Obermarchtal called in a Capuchin friar from Riedlingen to undertake exorcisms before each session of questioning and to bless the whip with which Bollmann was tortured. This was becoming established practice in Obermarchtal: Father Theobald of the Capuchin house in Biberach

---

1550–1750 (Cambridge, 2001); and on pilgrimages in the sixteenth century in Bavaria, Philip Soergel, *Wondrous in His Saints: Counter-Reformation Propaganda in Bavaria* (Berkeley and Los Angeles, 1993); on art, Jeffrey Chipps Smith, *Sensuous Worship: Jesuits and the Art of the Early Catholic Reformation in Germany* (Princeton, 2002), and see David Lederer, *Spiritual Physic: A Bavarian Beacon* (Cambridge, forthcoming).

[27] SAS, Dep 30, Marchtaler Hexenprozesse, Pak. 255, Magdalena Bollmann, p. 90, 3 June 1747, testimony of Anna Maria Münst; and pp. 120, 127.

had been called in earlier to exorcise Catharina Schmid when she was tried for witchcraft, and during the trial he undertook a journey to Alleshausen, where he reported on the 'miserable conditions' of the peasants there, plagued by possessions and demonic attacks. And it was Father Theobald whom Magdalena Bollmann wanted to summon to prove she was not a witch: diagnosing witchcraft was becoming a Capuchin specialism. When Maria Bingasser first accused her daughter Anna of witchcraft and then withdrew her allegations, the Capuchins at Biberach seem to have been behind what the court termed a 'miracle': after a visit to Biberach, Anna was moved to confess freely that she herself as well as her mother were witches.[28]

It was not that Sailer was unaware of the Devil, or that he did not share the villagers' belief in witchcraft. As late as 1771 he was still persuaded that the authorities had been right to execute the witches.[29] But the Devil that features in his plays is more like a figure of fun. The hare in *The Seven Swabians* looks like a terrifying demon, and it is part of the joke of the play that the peasants can celebrate their hunt for this harmless animal with a processional triumph over the powers of Hell; while the *Fall of Lucifer*, written around 1747, the year of the trial, features a Devil who promises his henchmen he'll make them mayor and district official if they beat up the Archangel Michael for him: St Michael gets revenge by locking Lucifer in the privy while he is shitting. Sailer probably did not share the kind of extravagant religious passions which the Capuchins were able to mobilize, and it is noteworthy that the Order of Praemonstratensians, to whom he belonged and who ruled the territory and acted as parish priests, barely features in the trials at all.

The Capuchins were an order of reformed Franciscans established during the Counter-Reformation, whose influence became increasingly powerful in southern Germany after the Thirty Years War. Between 1650 and 1770 their numbers rose in the region, as they gained a firm foothold in rural communities by acting as assistants to hard-pressed rural priests, hearing Easter confessions and administering the sacraments. By the second half of the seventeenth century they were more numerous than the Jesuits, fulfilling the kind of inspirational role in devotional life in small towns and hamlets that the Jesuits played in cities, but their emphasis was always populist rather than elitist, supporting pilgrimage and popular religious practice: in 1806 reforming Catholics building the Church structures of the new kingdom of Württemberg blamed the Capuchins for 'bigotry and superstition'.[30] A house had been

---

[28] Ibid., Pak. 255, Urgicht of Anna Oberländer, 1747.

[29] Nuber, 'Abtei Marchtal und seine Pfarrei in der Stadt Munderkingen', 142.

[30] Forster, *Catholic Revival*, 220–8.

established outside the walls of the nearby imperial town of Biberach in 1618, and rebuilt after the Thirty Years War in 1661, while at Riedlingen, to the west of Marchtal, a monastery had been erected in the mid-seventeenth-century.

The Capuchins certainly contributed much to the reinvigoration of rural Catholicism, a genuinely popular religion by the eighteenth century; but as their role in these witchcraft cases suggests, their success may have owed more than a little to their intuitive grasp of suffering, especially of women's travails, and their ability to exploit their flock's fear of the Devil. All this, of course, flowed seamlessly into the world of the glorious Baroque churches, for the other way to gain protection for one's loved ones or to deal with ill-ness was to go on pilgrimage. Blessings and pilgrimage, however, were not alternatives to belief in witchcraft, but were part of the same religious economy. After all, blessings were a form of exorcism, and when villagers stockpiled pilgrimages, visiting all the churches in the region, or had their animals repeatedly blessed, they did so to insure themselves against the assaults of the Devil, trying to ward off the calamities they feared would follow.

Sailer's plays also lack any sense of psychological complexity or interiority, of the kind that Lessing would provide for his characters barely a generation later. Lessing gave individuality to Jews and to servants whose social position might be thought to make them little more than stock characters. Sailer was no Lessing, and he drew on a different, much older tradition of the comic peasant for his inspiration, where the crafty peasant tricks the Devil, or where woodcuts show him parading a giant phallic nose. The sixteenth-century figure of the boorish peasant was a literary creation for educated townsfolk, who could laugh at the rustic world they had left behind. By contrast, Sailer seeks, but ultimately fails, to bridge the gap between himself and the peasants. His observation of peasant life is shrewd and penetrating, and his great accomplishment is to have recorded Swabian as a complete language with its distinctive intonation and sounds, capable of sustaining its own written liter-ature. Sailer himself, when he intervenes to moralize, speaks in the High German of the student and district official whose culture he shares. It is no accident that the axis of power in *The Mayoral Election at Limmelsdorf* is between the priest and the district official: Sailer would have known this only too well. There is a part of Sailer, certainly, who sympathizes with the trucu-lent Veit Balg who has no time for village niceties, and the hero of *The Seven Swabians* is the lowly *Bannwarth*. But perhaps, in Sailer's case, the price of reaching an accommodation between the peasant culture that surrounded him and the monastic, small-town world to which he owed his education, was to turn the peasants into buffoons. As he did so, he turned their murder-ous hatreds into village squabbles, and laughed at their pettiness instead of seeing apocalyptic significance in possessions and diabolic onslaughts.

Sailer's plays and the account of Bollmann's trial are two near-contemporary documents drawn from the same village world, both imbued with the same claustrophobia, the same iron sense of order, hierarchy, and reputation, and the same pervasive sense of religion; and yet they could hardly be more different. For the monk Sebastian Sailer, at once a local and outsider, there was always an escape from the village; for Bollmann there was none. There was no alternative to the network of relationships between neighbours and kinsfolk that could go so comprehensively wrong, leaving the accused woman devoid of any support. It would be too much, perhaps, to expect a man like Sailer to comprehend the agony of a woman like Magdalena Bollmann, or even to enter into the sufferings of his possessed female parishioners and their frenzied appeals for help against the attacks of witches.[31] More puzzling is the question of whether Sailer's vision of a lovable but boorish peasantry could only be maintained by removing women from its landscape altogether.

It is hard to find any historical explanation of why Magdalena Bollmann should have been accused of witchcraft and tried with such brutality. Part of the explanation may lie in the landscape around the Federsee lake, with its flat, brooding climate, where the cold chilled the bones and people suffered from rheumatism and fever, and where it was only too easy to imagine that witches caused the storms that skidded from one side of the lake to the other, or made the fish die in the weir.[32] After all, Alleshausen was highly unusual in hunting witches at so late a date,[33] long after the debates amongst theologians in southern Germany seemed to have settled the question of the reality of witches once and for all; and the village had a long tradition of hunting witches, having experienced a major witch hunt in the 1580s and another outbreak in the 1620s.

---

[31] Though we do know that he supported the protection of the lying-in period of four weeks, the scene of so many witchcraft accusations. Butscher, 'Das Leben eines Chorherrn', 290; and on lying-in and witchcraft, see Roper, *Witch Craze*.

[32] Johann Evangelista Schöttle, *Geschichte von Stadt und Stift Buchau samt dem stiftischen Dorfe Kappel. Beschreibung und Geschichte der Pfarrei Seekirch mit ihren Filialen Alleshausen, Brasenberg und Tiefenbach* (Bad Buchau, 1977; repr. of 1884 edn.).

[33] It was not, however, unique. See Wolfgang Behringer, *Witchcraft Persecutions in Bavaria: Popular Magic, Religious Zealotry and Reason of State in Early Modern Europe*, trans. J. Grayson and David Lederer (Cambridge, 1997), 347 ff.: witch-burnings were held in 1740, 1749, and 1751 at Burghausen, 1750 in Straubing, and 1749, 1752, 1754, and 1756 at Landshut; there was also a trial for witchcraft at Kempten in 1775, but there is no record of an execution. For a brilliant study of eighteenth-century witch-hunting in a village near Zürich, see David Meili, 'Hexen in Wasterkingen. Magie und Lebensform in einem Dorf des frühen 18. Jahrhunderts', Ph.D diss, Zürich (1979).

The grim religiosity of the eighteenth-century Capuchins also played its part in sparking such a late outbreak of witch-hunting. Part of the explanation for its viciousness may lie in the twisted psychology of individuals, people like Anna Maria Münst, who not only accused Bollmann but went on to denounce two other women for witchcraft as well, blaming them all for her own undoubted sufferings.[34] Or we might seek the reason in the claustrophobic intimacy of the women's culture, and in their tendency to dramatize their sufferings somatically, blaming others for mental and physical illness.

To blame the women for the episode of witch-hunting, however, would be to overlook the central actors in the court, the local jurors and the mayor, the secular administration of the monastery, and their legal adviser from the nearby imperial town of Biberach. If Josef Cadus had not set out to rid his village of witches, sending first the dossier on Catharina Schmid and then that on Bollmann to Obermarchtal, it is unlikely that the witnesses would have got very far. Just a decade later, in the neighbouring village of Brasenberg, similar accusations were made but the local mayor indicated that these were all about events which had happened too long ago. With this observation, Mayor Engler cut through the central dynamic of the cases, for once evidence from incidents lying in the past was deemed inadmissible, this put a stop to the process of going back through past miseries to look for the witch culprit, so often the way witch accusations mounted. He cast aspersions on the accusers: nearly all the allegations, he noted, could be traced back to two individuals who were possessed. By stigmatizing them as unreliable, Engler severed the link to the atmosphere of religious enthusiasm which had nourished the fears of witchcraft.

However, even that might not have put paid to the allegations had not the legal authorities at Obermarchtal sought the advice of a different jurist this time. Sebastian Sättelin of Biberach had proved a very compliant lawyer, approving the torture of Catharina Schmid retrospectively, after having voiced initial reservations. He turned in memorials justifying the execution of one woman after another, complete with citations from legal authorities to back up the arguments, and his memorials supported the burnings of all seven women.[35] Konrad Frey, also of Biberach, took a very different view. He agreed

---

[34] Peter Strobel is also to be found making accusations in several of the cases. He testified against Catharina Schmid and against Magdalena Bollmann, and is even to be found in 1756 amongst the accusers of a witch whose trial was halted.

[35] Amongst the authorities Sättelin cited were the Protestant jurist Carpzov, and such witchcraft classics as Bodin, Grillandus, and del Rio. See e.g. SAS, Dep. 30, Marchtaler Hexenprozesse, Gutachten von Sättelin, 13 Oct. 1746 (Bingasser), 28 Feb. 1747 (Bingasser, Schmid), 7 Sept. 1747 (Bollmann, Getschler, Muhl).

with the local mayor that the alleged incidents of witchcraft lay too far back in the past, and refused to countenance any further interrogation of the suspects.

But it is the brutality of the trial itself which remains so shocking in the case of Magdalena Bollmann, and which eludes explanation. Four members of the monastic administration conducted the interrogations with extraordinary savagery. They did not carry out the torture themselves: the two executioners, Bartholomeus Vollmar and his brother Veit from nearby Munderkingen, did so, as was always the practice in criminal trials. The Vollmar family had been the local executioners for generations, and we encounter the name of Vollmar as the executioner who dealt with the fifty-five women executed for witchcraft in Marchtal in the sixteenth century. Dynasties of executioners monopolized posts all over southern Germany, because, as dishonourable people, they could only intermarry with members of other dishonourable trades, such as knackers. In Bollmann's case, they used their professional technique of witch-pricking to 'prove' she was a witch: they identified suspicious marks, and reported systematically on her reactions as they managed to prick those marks without her knowledge. During interrogation, they applied torture with extraordinary severity from the outset. There was clearly a salacious element, too, in their investigation of Bollmann's privy parts, which they reported were swollen and well used like those of a much younger woman, indicating she had a diabolic lover. As part of the searches that preceded interrogation, they stripped her body naked, and shaved it.

This was behaviour that can only be termed sadistic, and it overstepped every limit that was meant to apply to torture at the time. But it cannot just be ascribed to the perversions of Bartholomeus Vollmar and his assistant. Every application of torture was minuted by the scribe and ordered by the interroga-tors, and at the first and second sessions of interrogation under torture four jurors from Alleshausen and Seekirch were especially summoned to attend. Each application of torture was surrounded with a religious ritual: Bollmann was left on the bench 'for six or seven Our Fathers', the whip and all instru-ments of torture were blessed, and Bollmann herself was repeatedly exorcised, as if the interrogators were engaged in a religious mission. As the months of interrogation passed without result, the tone of the questioning becomes noticeably more partisan: they begin exasperatedly: 'Since she has such an evil reputation in practically the whole village, the authorities must, in all fairness, suppose and believe, that she must be an evil person [that is, a witch].'[36] The

---

[36] '. . . da aber fast im ganzen dorff ein so übler ruef über sie ergehe, so müesse von Obrigkeits wegen allgemach billich gemuthmaßet, und geglaubet werden, Sie ein böses mensch seyn müesse', ibid. Pak. 255, Magdalena Bollmann, p. 114, 6 June 1747.

conviction on the part of villagers and of the authorities that they were fighting unseen and powerful cosmic enemies, that their loved ones were under threat of harm and death, and that only pain could be used to prise information out of the suspect, led them to feel justified in resorting to the most brutal kinds of torture, even showing no compunction about recording its use.

This was a collective psychosis. In reality, Bollmann was no death-dealing witch but was viciously killed by those who were responsible for protecting her. What is less clear is why her own community and the district officials should have been gripped by such fears, long after witch-hunting had largely ceased elsewhere, and when there was no obvious reason—poor harvests, sudden widespread illness, or internecine religious division—why the emotional life of the village should have imploded in a series of judicial murders.[37] Perhaps, as Catharina Schmid said, and as the sceptical Mayor Frey also argued, it all stemmed from the fact that people did not mind their own animals and farm their crops themselves but entrusted the work to others. Their explanation sounds risibly trite, but both were trying to find words for a profound change in village society, as social stratification increased and richer peasants began to pay others to do agricultural tasks they now felt were beneath them.

Whatever fomented accusations of witchcraft, a trial was possible only with the active involvement of the local mayor, the village jurors, and the officials at district level; in short, all the characters who feature in Sailer's plays. We might speculate that it was only possible for Sailer to create his rural idyll, and with it to help lay the foundations of the German folk-culture revival, by obliterating everything that had to do with the violent history of the actual exercise of power in just such communities. Sailer's unwillingness to see peasant men as anything more than jovial incompetents was a refusal to recognize their roles as persecutors and power-brokers.

What can the conjunction of Sailer's life story with the episode of witch-hunting in Alleshausen tell us? Sailer's relationship to the Enlightenment was ambivalent: a conservative, he opposed even the Catholic Enlightenment, vigorously defending the role of the religious orders; and though he read

---

[37] There had been a major fire in which much of the village burnt to the ground in 1714, but no one apparently linked this to witchcraft and it lay too far in the past to explain the outbreak of witch-hunting. In his *Das Jubilierende Marchtall* of 1771, which is a history of all the reigns of the abbots of Marchtal, Sailer mentions poor harvests during the period of office of Edmund Sartor (1746–68), but it is not clear exactly when these occurred or their relation to witch-hunting: Sebastian Sailer, *Das Jubilierende Marchtall*, facsimile edn., ed. Wolfgang Schürle with *Nachwort* by Hans Pörnbacher (Weissenhorn, 1995).

French and Italian, his shelves were crammed with sermons and devotional works in these languages, not with the works of the *philosophes*. But in his fascination with language and its relation to character, Sailer was was certainly exploring an Enlightenment problematic. He greatly admired the Enlightenment poet, critic, and stylist Johann Christoph Gottsched (1700–66), and avowedly took him as a model, even though Gottsched was a Saxon Protestant.[38]

Like many other scholars, Sailer wanted to improve his local peasantry, whom he saw as ignorant; while his idealization of the village was part of the Enlightenment creation of the bucolic, not just a throwback to sixteenth-century carnival and burlesque. His connection to popular religiosity and his endorsement of witch-hunting remind us how much of the old world still survived in the new, disenchanted world of the eighteenth century. There remains something disturbing in Sailer's determinedly jolly plays. The price of creating his comic peasants was that the universal, cosmic dramas of witch-hunting could have no place, and his rural folk could never be more than caricatures. Sailer meticulously preserved rural culture and Swabian dialect, but the comedies may also be his attempt to forget the realities of village life he witnessed.

---

[38] Maier, 'Der schwäbische Meister'.

The 'Religious Sense' in a Post-War Secular Age

Alex Owen

'There is a great deal of mystic religion about', Virginia Woolf wrote to the husband of her old friend Gwen Darwin, in March 1923. 'I've been asked to advise a woman as to the souls of the dead—can they come back? As I'm never quite sure which is which—spirit, matter, truth, falsehood and so on—I can't speak out as roundly as a Darwin should.'[1] Although Virginia Woolf apparently hesitated to pronounce definitively on the question of returning 'souls', she was nevertheless confirmed in her faith in the Darwin family when she heard that 'Gwen [Darwin] is a militant atheist: the world renews itself: there is solid ground beneath my feet'.[2] The boundaries between spirit and matter, truth and falsehood, might be insecure, but Woolf had little time for orthodox religion. As she stated towards the end of her life, 'emphatically there is no God'.[3]

In early 1923, however, 'mystic religion' was on her mind. The carnage and suffering wreaked during the Great War had caused thousands to turn to mediums and seances in an attempt to contact the fallen, and spiritualism enjoyed a boom during the war and its aftermath that was reminiscent of its Victorian heyday. Ordinary people sought relief and consolation in seances, but so, too, did the bereaved of the middle and upper classes. Sir Oliver Lodge, the eminent physicist, emerged as a champion of the spiritualist movement, as did the famous writer Sir Arthur Conan Doyle, who travelled the globe as

I would like to thank the Alice Berline Kaplan Center for the Humanities, Northwestern University, for a senior fellowship which enabled me to begin work on this topic, as well as audiences at Oxford University and Columbia University and the editors of this volume for their insightful and helpful comments.

[1] Virginia Woolf to Jacques Raverat, 30 Mar. 1923, in *A Change of Perspective: The Letters of Virginia Woolf*, ed. Nigel Nicolson and Joanne Trautmann, vol. 3 (London, 1977), 24.

[2] Virginia Woolf to Jacques Raverat, 30 July 1923, ibid., 59.

[3] Virginia Woolf, 'A Sketch of the Past', in *Moments of Being*, ed. Jeanne Schulkind (London, 1976), 72.

its international spokesman.[4] Indeed, while the war further weakened the social and political purchase of ecclesiastical authority, and hastened the decline of organized Christianity in its traditional stronghold of the middle class, spiritualism and different manifestations of spirituality were everywhere evident. Furthermore, although it was during the 1920s that agnosticism became the publicly articulated and accepted currency of intellectual life, those years also saw a renewed engagement with an unconventional religiosity that harked back to the pre-war period and bore little relation to anything the churches had to offer.

Virginia Woolf was commenting on a cultural phenomenon with which many of her more immediate contemporaries were familiar. Many of those at the centre of intellectual life in Britain—indeed, some of those in the vanguard of literary modernism—were caught up with 'mystic religion'. It filtered in its different aspects through the loose-knit group that gathered at Lady Ottoline Morrell's influential literary salons and famous 'weekends' at Garsington Manor, affected those on the outer reaches of Woolf's Bloomsbury networks, and permeated circles with which Woolf and her friends had only a nodding acquaintance—or, indeed, no acquaintance at all. This was not the Anglo- or Roman Catholicism that was still winning notable converts in the 1920s, but a different, less orthodox type of spirituality which implicitly questioned the designation 'religion' and explicitly challenged received wisdom on precisely that separation of spirit and matter (or, more conventionally, body and soul) that Woolf herself found so problematic. Here, in the post-war modern age, and among some of the most modern of individuals, mysticism was 'a household word'.[5]

This chapter considers the question of what happened to spirituality in the seemingly irredeemably secularized culture of post-war Britain by focusing on a particular moment in the intersecting lives of key members of the literary intelligentsia during the early 1920s. It takes as a point of departure the death of the young modernist writer Katherine Mansfield, but deals less with Mansfield herself than with what she represents in terms of the search for what we might think of as a secularized spirituality, or what her husband,

---

[4] Both men became public exponents of spiritualism in 1916, although it appears that the war was the occasion for, rather than the cause of, their support. For a recent discussion of inter-war spiritualism, see Jenny Hazelgrove, *Spiritualism and British Society Between the Wars* (Manchester, 2000). Jay Winter, *Sites of Memory, Sites of Mourning: The Great War in European Cultural History* (Cambridge, 1995), 54–77, considers spiritualism and the 'lost generation'.

[5] Isabelle de Steiger, *Memorabilia: Reminiscences of a Woman Artist and Scholar* (London, 1927), 154.

John Middleton Murry, came to call the 'religious sense'. One of the major themes of the chapter is the difficulty experienced after the war by those who sought some kind of meaningful spiritual life but could no longer relate in any way to organized religion or institutionalized belief system; and, conversely, the palpable irony of a professed agnosticism (even atheism) that nevertheless shaded into a deeply felt personal spirituality. This might be summed up as the problematic status of irreligion in a modern age. The context for the chapter is the much broader issue of long-term patterns of Western secularization, not least the secularization of consciousness. It seeks to make a small contribution to our understanding of these important developments while continuing to question long-held assumptions about secularization as an unproblematic decline of a religious sensibility—itself too often equated with the formalized conventions of organized Christianity.[6] The purpose here is to present an illustration of the pervasiveness of a religious sensibility in the midst of the decline of orthodox Christianity, and to argue for the importance of an immanentist spirituality for shaping certain aspects of intellectual and cultural life in Britain during the 1920s.

When Virginia Woolf wrote in 1923 that '[t]here is a great deal of mystic religion about', she knew that John Middleton Murry, a notable journalist and literary critic, had undergone some kind of mystical experience within two months of the death of his wife. As Woolf expressed it, 'Poor Middleton Murry has had a conversion'.[7] John Middleton Murry was the bereaved husband of Katherine Mansfield, the gifted New Zealand-born writer who had died of tuberculosis in January 1923 at the age of only 34. Woolf was grudgingly admiring of Mansfield, whom she saw as a literary rival, but Middleton Murry, a member of the interrelated circles in which many of the post-war literati moved, was decidedly not a favourite. 'Poor Middleton Murry' was not meant to be kind. Middleton Murry, for his part, wrote unashamedly about his so-called conversion with all the enthusiasm of the newly enlightened. The despair and confusion that he had felt following his wife's death were lifted in one momentous and life-changing spiritual epiphany.

Murry spoke of this event in terms of a 'great wave' of warmth and light that swept 'over the shores and frontiers of my self', a movement from darkness and a sense of hopeless abandonment into the light of personal

---

[6] For my sustained treatment of this theme in relation to pre-war occultism, see Alex Owen, *The Place of Enchantment: British Occultism and the Culture of the Modern* (Chicago, 2004).

[7] Virginia Woolf to Jacques Raverat, 30 July 1923, *Letters of Virginia Woolf*, iii. 59.

transformation. His account is rendered in the language of mysticism: 'the room was filled with a presence, and I knew I was not alone—that I never could be alone any more, that the universe beyond held no menace, for I was part of it . . . I was no longer I, but something different.'[8] This total and overwhelming sense of the dissolution of the 'frontiers' of self, and the certain knowledge, emerging from such an experience, that 'I was no longer I', are the classic hallmarks of mystical experience. Here, in one ecstatic moment, is the dissolution of the personality and the subsequent rebirth of the self as fundamentally and forever altered. 'I was no longer I.'[9] This was one of the defining moments of Middleton Murry's life.

He spent the next three decades trying to express his convictions in a series of books and articles dedicated to spiritual themes. T. S. Eliot, who converted to Anglo-Catholicism in 1927, would later argue with Middleton Murry over whether or not the latter was promulgating Christianity. In the end it hardly mattered to Middleton Murry, who saw himself as 'a sort of Christian mystic' confounded 'by the need of uttering the unutterable'.[10] For the moment, at this critical juncture so shortly after Katherine Mansfield's death, his experience taught him that 'the love I had lost was still mine, but now more durable, being knit into the very substance of the universe I had feared'.[11] In fact, Middleton Murry was later to admit that the 'presence' he had felt in the room 'was definitely connected with the person of Katherine Mansfield . . . In so far as the "presence" was connected with her it had a moral quality, or a moral effect: I was immediately and deeply convinced that "all was well with her".'[12] Katherine Mansfield was not lost to him; he was bound to her and others 'for ever';[13] he was at one with a beneficent universe. Middleton Murry was convinced that he had received a revelation for modern times: the universe is a loving and harmonious whole; we are all part of that whole; there is nothing to fear. This was summed up in his maxim, 'Faith in Life'.[14]

---

[8] John Middleton Murry, *To the Unknown God: Essays Towards a Religion* (London, 1924), 43. All the essays but one in this collection first appeared in the *Adelphi*, the magazine edited by Middleton Murry. This piece was published in the June 1923 issue.

[9] For a discussion of just such a sense of personal dissolution, involving the very different example of Aleister Crowley in 1909, see Owen, *The Place of Enchantment*, ch. 6.

[10] John Middleton Murry to T. S. Eliot, 8 Apr. 1948; cited in F. A. Lea, *The Life of John Middleton Murry* (London, 1959), 321.

[11] Murry, *To the Unknown God*, 43–4.

[12] John Middleton Murry, *God* (New York and London, 1929), 30–1.

[13] Murry, *To the Unknown God*, 44.

[14] See Murry, *God*, 34.

In the immediate wake of this experience John Middleton Murry turned to the business of conveying his message of hope and renewal to the broad British public. Together with D. H. Lawrence, then travelling in Mexico, and with the financial backing of other friends, Middleton Murry began to make plans for a new monthly magazine that would spread the word. Thus the *Adelphi* was born. Apart from a loosely spiritual agenda, the new magazine was dedicated to a particular vision of literature and culture that ran against the grain of all that literary Bloomsbury might be assumed to stand for. It supported the idea of 'conviction' literature, and stated categorically that it did not aim to be 'high-brow'. Instead, the *Adelphi* sought to be as 'comprehensible and interesting to as many people as possible'.[15] Middleton Murry expected to hold the fort as editor until D. H. Lawrence returned to England, and meanwhile proclaimed that the 'standard by which the contents of the *Adelphi* will be decided is "significance for life" '.[16]

Virginia and Leonard Woolf's Bloomsbury circle was possessed of a confident irreverence and scepticism (often manifested as class arrogance) that Middleton Murry conspicuously lacked. Murry came from a humble background, a clever London Board School boy who had won highly prized scholarships to Christ's Hospital (a venerable school) and Oxford University. Both Virginia and Leonard Woolf found him personally distasteful. Although he liked Katherine Mansfield, Leonard Woolf 'never liked Murry; there was a strong Pecksniffian vein in him which irritated and revolted me. He was always ready to weep loudly and generously over the woes of the world, but the eyes reminded me of the crocodile's.'[17] He recalled that in once reviewing one of Murry's books in the *Nation* he had mixed the author's words with those of Charles Dickens's Mr Pecksniff, and no one could distinguish between them. Virginia Woolf now stormed against the new *Adelphi* and its editor. She hit out at the very middlebrow character of the magazine that Middleton Murry sought to cultivate. The tone of her attack is symptomatic of a sense of class as well as intellectual superiority, and implicit disdain for anything deemed to be Low Church.

The same letter that referred to Middleton Murry's 'conversion' also notes that this event 'has had an odious Bantam—the Adelphi'. Woolf continues:

> As literature, it seems to me worthless—(only strong words are out of place): it seems to me mediocre then. The spirit that inspires it, with

---

[15] Prospectus of the *Adelphi*; cited in Lea, *The Life of John Middleton Murry*, 107.

[16] Prospectus of the *Adelphi*; ibid., 106.

[17] Leonard Woolf, *Beginning Again: An Autobiography of the Years 1911–1918* (London, 1964), 203–4. Pecksniff is a model of hypocrisy in Dickens's *Martin Chuzzlewit*.

its unction and hyprocrisy [*sic*], and God is love, which still leaves room for flea bites, pin pricks, and advertising astuteness, would enrage, were it not that there's something so mild and wobbly about that too that I can't waste good wrath. Most of my friends find it deplorable.[18]

Most of her friends undoubtedly did find it 'deplorable'. In a diary entry for the same period Woolf recorded a teatime conversation during which Desmond MacCarthy, an old family friend and literary editor of the *New Statesman*, asked: 'Have you read the second number of the Adelphi? Have you read Murry "I have been a miserable sinner . . . I have lied, I have swindled. I have laughed at what I love; but *now* I am speaking the truth." He's like a revivalist preacher.'[19] Virginia Woolf recorded herself as retorting, 'I dont [*sic*] object to opening the heart, but I do object to finding it empty. Murry has nothing whatever to reveal.'[20]

Thousands of people failed to agree. The kind of writers that Bloomsbury abhorred but the public enjoyed—Galsworthy, Bennett, Wells—supported and contributed to the *Adelphi*. Similarly, Middleton Murry wrote about his new spiritual philosophy in terms both general and urgent enough to appeal to a broad swathe of those who aspired to spiritual renewal in the wake of the Great War. His message was simple: 'I believe in the existence of God and of my own soul'; this belief emanates from within and bears no relation to the 'formulated creeds of the Christian Church'; 'the luminous certainty with which it is possible to apprehend the interdependent existence of God and one's self' lies at the heart of a life-affirming spirituality; to have faith in life is to begin to live again.[21] Within a week the *Adelphi*'s first edition of some 4,000 copies sold out; within two weeks it had been reprinted three times; 15,000 copies were printed and failed to satiate demand. It was one of the most successful launches of a new magazine in recent times.[22] For Middleton Murry, the initial success of the *Adelphi* augured just that great

---

[18] Virginia Woolf to Jacques Raverat, 30 July 1923, *Letters of Virginia Woolf*, iii. 59.

[19] Entry of 8 July 1923, in *The Diary of Virginia Woolf*, ed. Anne Olivier Bell and Andrew McNeillie, vol. 2 (London, 1978), 252 [original emphasis]. This is a loose paraphrase (with a good deal of artistic licence) of Middleton Murry's words in the June 1923 issue of the *Adelphi*. Desmond MacCarthy and Leonard Woolf were friendly rivals during this period. The latter had recently been appointed the literary editor at the *Nation* after John Maynard Keynes, the economist and another close Bloomsbury friend, became chairman of the paper's new board.

[20] 8 July 1923, *The Diary of Virginia Woolf*, ii. 253.

[21] Murry, *To the Unknown God*, 194.

[22] See Lea, *The Life of John Middleton Murry*, 109.

spiritual renaissance and transformation of society that so many had associated with the new century prior to the Great War. Now ordinary people were buying the magazine in huge numbers. Notably, many in the North of England, where a religious ethic born of Nonconformity and Roman Catholicism was still relatively strong, found Middleton Murry's magazine appealing. One Durham industrial worker recalled how 'All kinds of people were attracted to his work . . . Many shared my enthusiasm'.[23] It seemed to Middleton Murry that his message of hope and spiritual rebirth had struck a great chord.

What he did not anticipate was that his spiritual philosophy, so ardently expressed but resistant to systematization and somewhat vague on specifics, would prove incapable of sustaining a reading public. Additionally, Middleton Murry came to realize that the combination he had envisaged, of the *Adelphi* as both 'a good literary review' and 'the organ for exploring the possibility of a new religion', was unworkable.[24] Within a few short months he discovered that his readers were shocked by some of D. H. Lawrence's contributions, 'and that the contributors for the most part disapproved of each other and all disapproved of me'.[25] This was hardly a recipe for long-term success. Lawrence, the anticipated fellow-traveller, found the *Adelphi* tame and bland. Furthermore, his assessment of Jesus as a 'failure' managed to alienate readers and cut the *Adelphi*'s circulation by half. Equally, those Christian readers who might have remained loyal were troubled by Middleton Murry's increasingly egocentric and isolationist stance on religious matters. As Murry put it, 'I am not a Christian, I am not anything, but I have been forced to the conclusion that I am religious'.[26] Middleton Murry was trying to expound a 'religious' message founded on a deeply personal mystical experience but shorn of any orthodox Christian context. As a result, more-conventional Christian readers faded away.

On top of this, Middleton Murry used the pages of the *Adelphi* to promote the work and memory of his dead wife, Katherine Mansfield. For more than two years Mansfield made an appearance in every issue. Whatever the motivation for this, readers found it inappropriate and discomforting. Leonard Woolf thought it appalling that Middleton Murry should write about Mansfield's death, Virginia Woolf that he should profit by it.[27] The fastidious were repelled by Middleton Murry's confessional style. In later years

[23] J. H. Watson, *London Magazine* (May 1959), in ibid., 111.

[24] Murry, *God*, 35–6.

[25] Ibid., 35.

[26] Murry, *To the Unknown God*, 60.

[27] 8 July 1923, *The Diary of Virginia Woolf*, ii. 253.

Middleton Murry came to recognize his mistake, referring to himself in terms reminiscent of Virginia Woolf's account of Desmond MacCarthy's remarks: 'I was completely upset, *bouleversé*, by my mystical experience. I was like a newly converted revivalist preacher, and in my order, committed the same offences against "good taste" as they in theirs.'[28] The *Adelphi* was already faltering within a year of its launch.

As many in John Middleton Murry's circle were aware, Katherine Mansfield had died of a pulmonary haemorrhage at the Gurdjieff Institute for the Harmonious Development of Man located near Fontainebleau, some forty miles from Paris. For Mansfield, the Gurdjieff Institute was a last-ditch attempt to find meaning and peace towards the end of her young life. When a new X-ray treatment for her tuberculosis failed to yield improvement, she turned to an unorthodox alternative. The decision was triggered by reading *Cosmic Anatomy*, a book sent to Middleton Murry at the end of 1921 by A. R. Orage, an old friend of both Murry and Mansfield and editor of the respected periodical the *New Age*.[29] By the summer of 1922 Katherine Mansfield was following her own spiritual path, and along the way she and Middleton Murry agreed to separate. Some viewed this as the abandonment of a desperately ill wife by a self-absorbed (and worse) husband. Middleton Murry said that he 'acquiesced' to Mansfield's wishes, 'a poor ending to all that we had endured and hoped together; but it was at least honest'.[30] Whatever the story, Katherine Mansfield entered the Gurdjieff Institute in October 1922 and died there three months later.

Georgei Ivanovitch Gurdjieff was a charismatic spiritual teacher with a mysterious pedigree. Probably born in the 1870s, Gurdjieff had a Greek father, an Armenian mother, and grew up in Caucasia—an area over which Turkey, Russia, and Persia had disputed claims. There were persistent rumours that Gurdjieff had been a Tsarist agent in Tibet, and the refusal of the authorities to grant him and his extensive (mainly Russian) entourage entry to Britain in the early 1920s defeated plans for a British Institute. Gurdjieff was certainly widely travelled and knowledgeable about Eastern mystical traditions, as well as those of Central Asia. He lacked social polish but was possessed of a powerful persona and great personal magnetism.

[28] John Middleton Murry, Journal, 6 August 1932; cited in Lea, *The Life of John Middleton Murry*, 114.

[29] The book was *Cosmic Anatomy and the Structure of the Ego*, by 'M. B. Oxon.' (London, 1921). Its author was Lewis Alexander Richard Wallace, one of the original financiers of the *New Age* (the other was George Bernard Shaw).

[30] Murry, *God*, 17.

Gurdjieff accepted patients in his claimed capacity as a physician-hypnotist, and many thought that he possessed psychic powers, but his message was centrally concerned with the potentialities of human consciousness. In particular, he taught that human beings conventionally operate in a condition akin to the sleeping state, and that in order to realize our full potential we must, in effect, wake up. As expressed by his early Russian exponent Pyötr Demianovitch Ouspensky, Gurdjieff taught a 'psychology of man's possible evolution' which stressed the limitations of our mechanical everyday selves and the significance of the 'I' of complete realization.[31]

The 1922–3 prospectus for Gurdjieff's Institute for the Harmonious Development of Man at Fontainebleau spoke of the 'conditions of modern life' as alienating 'contemporary man', and detrimental to full self-realization. His 'psychological system', for which he also used the term '*psycho-analysis*', was designed '*to develop new faculties which are not given to man in life and which cannot be developed in him by general methods*'. These 'new faculties' might be understood by Gurdjieff's followers in either spiritual or secular terms, or a mixture of both. The point was that the emphasis lay on inner exploration, personal development, and 'the perfecting of the *I* according to the theories of European science and Oriental schools'.[32] Gurdjieff's 'system' was designed to break down the barriers that prevent full disclosure of the self in all its dimensions. In a tough regime dominated by hard physical work, elaborate sacred dances and exercises, and individualized programmes of study, Gurdjieff sought to break habitual patterns of thought and life and bring the intellectual, emotional, and instinctual aspects of the self into harmony. Equally, the harmonious self, the perfected 'I', was a self at peace and at one with the world.

This 'perfecting of the I' had been a goal of sophisticated pre-war occultists. Indeed, both the occultists and Gurdjieff's followers referred to this project as the Work. Gurdjieff and Ouspensky were influenced by Victorian and Edwardian occultism, but they extrapolated some of its central insights to formulate what their interpreters thought of as a new approach to self-realization.

---

[31] See P. D. Ouspensky, *The Psychology of Man's Possible Evolution* (London, 1947). This introduction to Gurdjieff's ideas was initially written as a series of lectures in 1934. P. D. Ouspensky, *Tertium Organum: The Third Canon of Thought. A Key to the Enigmas of the World*, trans. from the Russian by Nicholas Bessaraboff and Claude Bragdon (Rochester, NY, 1920), is the book that made his name. It was first published in St Petersburg in 1912.

[32] Prospectus for the Institute for the Harmonious Development of Man, Fontainebleau; cited in James Webb, *The Harmonious Circle: The Lives and Work of G. I. Gurdjieff, P. D. Ouspensky, and Their Followers* (New York, 1980), 234–5 [original emphasis]. According to Webb, the Fontainebleau prospectus was largely written by Ouspensky.

In particular, Gurdjieff and Ouspensky developed and taught a systematic 'psychology' which sought to address the dilemmas of modern existence— most significantly, perhaps, a sense of fragmentation, alienation, and meaninglessness—while drawing on the wisdom traditions of the past. This so-called new psychology offered a structured and disciplined blueprint for life as it is lived in a world without God, and addressed familiar issues of meaning and existence in a language partially stripped of arcane reference. But while Ouspensky's ideas as expressed in his books had a metaphysical or recognizably occult dimension, Gurdjieff's stated aims increasingly did not. His was a secularized message with spiritual affect.

This was a message that found immediate resonance after the devastations of the war. Middleton Murry summed up the feelings of many of his post-war generation in his 1919 essay 'The Republic of the Spirit': we are shamed by four years of barbarous inhumanity; we are maimed in ways that we do not comprehend; materialism has failed us; we must turn instead to the cultivation of the inner 'man' and a new 'aristocracy of the spirit'.[33] By *spirit*, Middleton Murry meant that strength and purity of the 'inner' self that can survive and stand in moral opposition to the base human impulse towards temporal supremacy, whether pursued in the name of civilization, justice, or democracy. But during the post-war period the message of his essay—we must cultivate the 'inner' self and all it represents—was equally appealing to those for whom *spirit* denoted that 'inner' wellspring and source of personal renewal that is a requirement of human life (what Katherine Mansfield called the 'spring of life'[34]); and that transcendent aspect of the 'I' or 'inner' self that apprehends, or touches, or is at some level synonymous with the divine, however divinity might be conceived.

The idea of spirit in each of these applications appealed to the post-war circles surrounding A. R. Orage. Orage, who had done so much to build the *New Age* into an intellectually cutting-edge periodical before the war, was typical of those who were drawn to the ideas of Ouspensky and Gurdjieff. Prior to 1914 he had been seriously interested in occultism, Theosophy, and a range of social issues including Guild Socialism, and had championed the work of Friedrich Nietzsche and Henri Bergson. He had also been the first to publish the young John Middleton Murry and Katherine Mansfield, among

---

[33] John Middleton Murry, 'The Republic of the Spirit', in *The Evolution of an Intellectual* (London, 1927), 222. The essays in this book were written during and after the war, and were first published in 1920. 'The Republic of the Spirit' is dated April 1919.

[34] 10 Oct. 1922, *Journal of Katherine Mansfield*, ed. John Middleton Murry (New York, 1927), 252.

many others. Orage's post-war *New Age* reflected his growing interest in psychoanalysis, and at the beginning of the 1920s he brought together some of the intellectuals and writers of his circle in a 'psycho-synthesis' group formed to develop a new kind of spiritualized psychology. In Britain after the war this dual concern with unorthodox spirituality and psychoanalysis was not unusual, and some of those who had been involved with occultism over a decade earlier were among the earliest Freudian enthusiasts. G. R. S. Mead, once Madame Blavatsky's private secretary and a leading figure in the Theosophical Society, had become interested in psychoanalysis, and a working relationship developed between participants in Orage's psychosynthesis group and Mead's Quest Society. Among those who participated in Orage's group were the sexologist Havelock Ellis, David Eder (a physician and one of the first British psychoanalysts), Maurice Nicoll, who had Theosophical connections, and James C. Young. Both Nicoll and Young were physicians and psychoanalysts who had studied with Carl Jung. Within a few short years of the armistice, then, the intellectual ground had been prepared for a new phase in the development of a psychology of self-realization. This is precisely what Ouspensky and Gurdjieff delivered.

A. R. Orage had met Ouspensky briefly before the war, and maintained contact with him during the chaotic aftermath of the revolution in Russia.[35] When Ouspensky arrived in London in the summer of 1921, ready to propound Gurdjieff's ideas, he found a ready audience among Orage's circle, Theosophists, and erstwhile occultists. He also found an early influential patron in Lady Rothermere, wife of the press baron. Orage set out from the start to promote the ideas of both Ouspensky and Gurdjieff, and by October 1922 had himself severed contact with his London life and made the journey to the Institute at Fontainebleau. For Orage, the quest for the perfected 'I' was equally the search for God—a God conceived as that spark of divinity within. For psychoanalytically trained members of the psychosynthesis group like James Young, Gurdjieff's ideas represented another dimension to his scientific inquiry into the self. Maurice Nicoll regarded the 'system' as a further exploration of a spiritual dimension to the Freudian self—something which Jung also seemed to promise. Some patients of both Young and Nicoll followed them to the Institute, as did others of Orage's London circle. In all, the Institute attracted some sixty or seventy people at a time, many from Eastern Europe and pre-war Russia, and all seeking self-realization.

---

[35] A. R. Orage published in the *New Age* a series of Ouspensky's letters written in Russia during the summer and autumn of 1919, and these have since been published as *Letters From Russia 1919* (London, 1978).

Katherine Mansfield, ill as she was when she arrived at the Institute, and unable to fully participate in the Spartan regime, felt at one with Gurdjieff's method and its message. As she wrote to Middleton Murry in December 1922: 'You see, my love, the question is always: "*Who am I?*" and until that is answered I don't see how one can really direct anything in oneself.'[36] For Mansfield, close to death, this question was perhaps inevitably (although not explicitly) linked to the possibility of both finding the 'I' and at some level transcending its annihilation. But Mansfield was also deeply attracted to Gurdjieff's emphasis on the importance of creating a harmonious relationship between the perfected self and the natural world. She longed 'to become a conscious direct human being', in harmony with 'the earth and the wonders thereof'.[37] At the Institute the emphasis was not on the spiritual, and yet, at one level, everything was dedicated to achieving a harmony that was often perceived in spiritual terms. Katherine Mansfield was aware of this and embraced it, telling Middleton Murry that 'the strangeness of all that happens here has a meaning; and by strangeness I don't mean obvious strangeness—there's little of it—I mean spiritual'.[38]

John Middleton Murry, ambivalent about his wife's attraction to Gurdjieff, sure that Gurdjieff's 'system' was not for him, nevertheless came close to Gurdjieff's rendition of self-realization in his own idealized formulation of the 'unity of man, the true Self'.[39] For Murry, 'the true Self' is one which acknowledges and exists in harmonious and connected relationship with an animistic and unified universe. Equally, for Murry, *God* is simply a convenient linguistic convention used to signify this unified universe. At one level, the self in its highest manifestation could be equated with God—a position that Jung approached but ultimately fought shy of ratifying. The self conceived as the source and repository of spirit eliminated the need for any external deity, even when the 'integrated Self' of a Middleton Murry acknowledged the reality of what *God* might be taken to represent. In this preeminently modern move, the self acquired supreme importance. What now became crucial was the full realization of this self.

This is what many sought in Gurdjieff's teachings and proposed agenda: '*to develop new faculties which are not given to man in life and which cannot be*

---

[36] Katherine Mansfield to John Middleton Murry, 26 Dec. 1922 [original emphasis], in *Katherine Mansfield's Letters to John Middleton Murry, 1913–1922*, ed. John Middleton Murry (New York, 1951), 697.

[37] 10 Oct. 1922, *Journal of Katherine Mansfield*, 254.

[38] Katherine Mansfield to John Middleton Murry, [no day] Nov. 1922, *Katherine Mansfield's Letters to John Middleton Murry, 1913–1922*, 689.

[39] Murry, *God*, 166.

developed in him by general methods.' It was the promise of pre-war occultism, and now, in its secularized manifestation, attracted increasing numbers of seekers. As Gurdjieff's teachings travelled across the Atlantic and permeated avant-garde circles in New York and beyond, an American audience began to take notice. A. R. Orage, who became a leading exponent of Gurdjieff's ideas in the United States during the 1920s, brought Jane Heap, co-editor of *The Little Review*, and the novelist Jean Toomer into the fold. Both Heap and Toomer became serious students of Gurdjieff, and, through Toomer, Gurdjieff's ideas filtered into the group of writers and artists central to what was to become known as the Harlem Renaissance.[40] D. H. Lawrence's American patron, Mabel Dodge Luhan, became so interested in Jean Toomer that by the mid-1920s she was offering Gurdjieff her ranch in New Mexico as a site for a new Institute. Although this offer was declined, she tried hard (but unsuccessfully) to convince Lawrence that Gurdjieff had something important to say. Lawrence had very different ideas about the importance of the unconscious and instinctual life. For him, the self-mastery implied by Gurdjieff's 'system' represented stasis. Those like A. R. Orage and Katherine Mansfield took the opposing view. For them, Gurdjieff promised that reconciliation of self and spirit that had acquired such urgency for some of their circle in the post-war period. Such a reconciliation offered the prospect of enlightened self-realization, and augured a longed-for sense of personal peace and fulfilment. As Mansfield wrote to Middleton Murry as she waited to join Gurdjieff at Fontainebleau: 'I feel happy—deep down. *All is well.*'[41]

The version of the self advanced by Gurdjieff, sought by A. R. Orage and members of his psychosynthesis group, and so attractive to someone like Katherine Mansfield, does not necessarily equate with what Max Weber famously referred to as that quintessentially modern Western dilemma—the impossibility of 'living in union with the divine'.[42] Instead, this modern self was characterized by a rejection of the supernatural, particularly as represented by an externalized deity, but a naturalized and often internalized or immanentist understanding of divinity—and ultimate faith in the spiritualized powers of the 'new faculties'

---

[40] See Jon Woodson, *To Make a New Race: Gurdjieff, Toomer, and the Harlem Renaissance* (Jackson, Miss., 1999); Rudolph P. Byrd, *Jean Toomer's Years with Gurdjieff: Portrait of an Artist 1923–1936* (Athens, Ga., 1990).

[41] *Journal of Katherine Mansfield*, 255 [original emphasis]. It is not clear whether this constitutes part of the entry for 10 October 1922 or the superscription appended to it.

[42] See Max Weber, 'Science as a Vocation', in *Max Weber: Essays in Sociology*, trans. and ed. H. H. Gerth and C. Wright Mills (New York, 1958). 'Science as a Vocation' was delivered as a speech at Munich University in 1917, and published in 1919.

of 'the I'. This was a secularized self, then, that was nevertheless fully capable of perceiving, as Middleton Murry put it, 'that the leaven of a religious sense is at work in the world'. The difficulties arose because this 'religious sense' (again, Murry) 'does not know how to express itself'.[43]

More specifically, the problem for the post-war modern age became how to conceive of, and adequately communicate, this 'religious sense', when God, as traditionally understood, was no longer an option. This was precisely Middleton Murry's problem, as characterized by the failure of the *Adelphi* and his own acknowledgement that he was confounded 'by the need of uttering the unutterable'. And it has remained the problem for those who seek and acknowledge the place of spirit in the world but lack or refuse the conceptual vocabularies of systematized world religions, occult cosmologies, or 'systems' of harmonious development. Equally, it explains the appeal of occult rationales or 'systems' of 'psychology' which provide a coded understanding of ourselves and our place in the great order of things (indeed, conceive of a harmonious order within which humankind is placed), while distinctly playing to the naturalized concept of self-realization. It explains, too, the attraction of a community of like-minded seekers dedicated to following a road-map for 'harmonious development'. It is, after all, a difficult and problematic endeavour to spin lone webs of individualized spiritual meaning out of a personal consciousness which is—at a crucial level—*already* secularized.

Whatever the long and complex processes underlying the secularization of Western consciousness—manifesting as the inability to believe in an hypostasized God—the Great War (for all the revisionist history) remains a watershed. 'All who were capable of change,' Middleton Murry wrote in 1916, 'all, that is, who were in whatever degree living—have been changed by the war.' It had, he stated, 'made the dark things clear and the clear things dark . . . The certainties were transposed for us.' Writing in the year of Verdun and the Somme offensive, which saw some of the worst carnage of the war, Middleton Murry was here acknowledging that these cataclysmic events had fundamentally changed those who lived through them—both the self and its cognitive world were forever altered. The war pointed up the inadequacies of orthodox Christianity and the irrelevance of the Church, neither of which proved capable of explaining or dealing with the horror of war on a mass scale; it forced many to rethink what it means to be human and confront their complicity in the sanctioned barbarism of nations; and it

---

[43] John Middleton Murry, 'The Sign-Seekers', in *The Evolution of an Intellectual*, 19. This essay is dated October 1916.

left some yearning for spiritual regeneration and a renewed sense of the richness and wonder of life. Years before the death of his wife and his own 'mystical' experience, and speaking specifically of his own generation (the generation, loosely, of Woolf, Lawrence, and Mansfield), Murry reiterated and expanded: 'We are changed. In us a religious sense has been dimly awakened. The religious sense is not religion, though it may be. But it may take other and equally authentic forms;' adding: 'The hazard of its form is decided by the thousand dispositions which made us what we were before the war.'[44]

The 'religious sense' could take many forms—among them, something conceived as Christian conscience, a particular aesthetic, and a transformative social and political vision. Certainly, John Middleton Murry, A. R. Orage and his circle, Katherine Mansfield, even Virginia Woolf—disparate enough in terms of pre-war 'dispositions', but subsequently part of a loosely connected intellectual world—all acknowledged a kind of 'religious sense' in the post-war years, albeit one very differently experienced and articulated. There is, however, a common theme: having a 'religious sense' involved a spiritualized apprehension of life, and in this vision life itself becomes sanctified. Whatever the metaphysical connotations of Middleton Murry's 'true' self, there is a sense in his formulation that to be a fully explored and understood ('unified') self living in complete harmony—at one—with the unified universe *is* a religious experience. Although Murry consistently distanced himself from Gurdjieff's teachings, this was one of the very attractions of Gurdjieff's Work for Katherine Mansfield. She summed this up in her own distinctive way as she prepared to travel from Paris to Fontainebleau: 'I want to be all that I am capable of becoming so that I may be (and here I have stopped and waited and waited and it's no good—there's only one phrase that will do) *a child of the sun.*'[45]

At the end of August 1922, when Katherine Mansfield returned to London from Europe, she immediately sought out A. R. Orage. They met on 30 August, by which time Orage had made the decision to give up his London life and go to Fontainebleau. 'On that occasion,' she wrote, 'I began by telling him how dissatisfied I was with the idea that Life must be a lesser thing than we were capable of imagining it to be.' Mansfield, aware of a creeping sense that she thought characterized her post-war generation—a sense of "If this is all, then Life is not worth living"—wanted more. She wanted more, she said, because 'I *know* it is not all. How does one know that? Let me take the case of

---

[44] Ibid., 15–16.
[45] 10 Oct. 1922, *Journal of Katherine Mansfield*, 254 [original emphasis].

K. M. . . . through it all, there have been moments, instants, gleams, when she has felt the possibility of something quite other.'[46] Gurdjieff promised the development of 'new faculties' which would open the door to this 'something quite other' as a sustained apprehension of the world. His Institute was presented as the route to a full comprehension and experience of the harmonious self as integral to that world—what Gurdjieff referred to as 'waking up' and Katherine Mansfield movingly imagined as 'becoming . . . a child of the sun'. This was the spirituality that she sought and found with Gurdjieff.

Katherine Mansfield's 'something quite other' was what Virginia Woolf also glimpsed in special 'moments of being' that approached an ecstatic 'revelation of some order . . . of some real thing behind appearances'. She conceived of this as a reality and a meaning lying behind the ordinary, the mundane, and the material obfuscations of daily life. Based on personal moments of illumination, Woolf developed what she called 'a philosophy; at any rate it is a constant idea of mine; that behind the cotton wool [of daily existence] is hidden a pattern; that we—I mean all human beings—are connected with this'. She thought of the 'whole world' as 'a work of art', and humankind as 'parts of the work of art', but insisted that there is no master author, composer, or architect of this wonderful creation—'no Shakespeare . . . no Beethoven . . . no God'. Instead, 'we are the words; we are the music; we are the thing itself'. 'This intuition', she wrote towards the end of her life, 'is so instinctive that it seems given to me, not made by me.' And in a final authoritative statement: 'It proves that one's life is not confined to one's body and what one says and does; one is living all the time in relation to . . . a pattern hid behind the cotton wool. And this conception affects me every day.'[47]

Virginia Woolf, epitomizing the 'Bloomsburies', was shocked by T. S. Eliot's conversion to Anglo-Catholicism ('poor dear Tom Eliot . . . A corpse would seem to me more credible than he is'[48]); and considered that the message expounded by Middleton Murry in the name of 'spiritual regeneration' was third-rate, warmed-up mediocrity. She was emphatic that 'there is no God'. Nevertheless, Woolf experienced privileged 'moments of being' that created for her the conviction that behind the apparent realities of the phenomenal world lie hidden webs of meaning and connectedness. Woolf's 'moments', often experienced as 'sudden shocks', were, she thought, 'a token of some real thing behind appearances'. And the 'rapture' of writing lay in discovering

[46] Undated entry, ibid., 246–7 [original emphasis].
[47] Virginia Woolf, 'A Sketch of the Past', in *Moments of Being*, 72–3.
[48] Virginia Woolf to Vanessa Bell, 11 Feb. 1928, *Letters of Virginia Woolf*, iii. 457–8.

the 'pattern', in putting this 'real thing' 'into words'.[49] For all her denuncia-
tion of 'God', Woolf's convictions accorded with the precepts of the kind of
'mystic religion' upon which she was commenting in March 1923 ('There is a
great deal of mystic religion about'). Her solipsistic notion of 'we are the thing
itself' approximates to the spiritual reading of Gurdjieff's proposed harmonious self, and her intuitive grasp of a 'pattern' comes close to the 'religious
sense' espoused by Middleton Murry—a spiritualized world-view which did
not require God but did hold to a vision of 'the richness and mystery of life'.[50]

Woolf's conception that behind the apparent realities of the phenomenal
world lie hidden webs of meaning and connectedness comes close to
Katherine Mansfield's 'something quite other' and Middleton Murry's 'religious sense'. Unlike Mansfield, however, Woolf was not a spiritual seeker in
any conventional sense, and shied away from spiritualized rationales and
'systems'; and unlike Middleton Murry, she made no attempt to contextual-
ize her ideas in religious terms. Rather, Woolf was emblematic of Middleton
Murry's formulation that the 'religious sense is not religion . . . it may take
other and equally authentic forms'. For Woolf, of course, the form it took
was writing—and more specifically, the novel. In effect, Woolf is symptomatic of the divide between those who sought or elaborated modern forms of
spirituality and those who (however empathetic) kept their intellectual distance. Yet, for all these differences, Woolf, Mansfield, and Middleton Murry,
each in their related ways, acknowledged in themselves a 'religious' sensibility even as they affirmed their conviction that orthodox religion was at best
an irrelevance and at worst an intellectual embarrassment.

The Great War exposed the inability of organized Christianity to speak
with authority and conviction to the dilemmas of modern existence. But
although the decade of the 1920s confirmed the pre-war trend towards an
increasingly secularized personal consciousness, some of the post-war generation of intellectuals and writers became actively involved in an ongoing
search for spiritual meaning in a fragmented, insecure, and seemingly hostile modern world. This search often began with the premiss that there is no
supernatural deity concerning itself with the affairs of humankind, or even
the possibility or desirability of a transcendental experience of divinity.
Instead, it centred on the principle of divine immanence and acceptance of a
holistic or universalized spiritual reality (not unrelated to pre-war British
idealism), combined with the modern idea of the pre-eminent self. This
notion of the self as both creator and arbiter of meaning had been gathering

---

[49] Woolf, 'A Sketch of the Past', in *Moments of Being*, 72.
[50] Murry, *God*, 329.

force since before the turn of the century, but in the context of post-war spirituality it emerged as a self that might still outstrip its boundaries, a self that could acknowledge (along with Virginia Woolf) that life is 'not confined to one's body and what one says and does', a self understood and experienced *as* spirit. It was a self in sympathy with the unbounded and transformed 'I was no longer I' of Middleton Murry's ecstatic episode, an episode understood not in transcendental terms but rather in the context of personal transformation and full self-realization.

This spiritualized personal self, reminiscent of the perfected self of pre-war occultism, represented one way of being religious in a secularized modern age. Before the Great War, those who gathered around A. R. Orage and his periodical the *New Age* had confidently expected the new century to be the harbinger of a new Dispensation. After the devastations of war, Orage was at the centre of a circle who sought a new spiritualized path to the understanding of the human self, and his psychosynthesis group opened the door to Ouspensky and the ideas of Gurdjieff. For some members of the psychosynthesis group and allied personnel, psychoanalysis and 'mysticism' could be reconciled in the reading of the self proposed by Gurdjieff—a secularized self capable of incorporating spirituality into an integrated harmonious and holistic whole: spirit and self as one. For others, represented by the writers Katherine Mansfield and (however differently or implicitly) Virginia Woolf, a modern idea of self might still be reconciled with a kind of spirituality, a 'something quite other' recognized in 'gleams' and 'moments'.

The highly individualistic, often solipsistic, 'religious sense' expressed by these writers and some members of their intellectual worlds played on a secularized understanding of self as pre-eminent, and at the same time embraced the spiritualized concept of an unbounded self existing in relationship with a hidden 'pattern', a 'something quite other', and a unified and animistic universe. Indeed, Virginia Woolf's understanding of a fluid self, of the fluidity of all boundaries, including those of spirit and matter, was consistent with the precepts of pre-war occultism and the kind of 'mysticism' that flourished after the war. But whereas pre-war occultism had held to a highly systematized philosophy and world-view, post-war 'mysticism' tended to focus far more on the spiritual potential and experiential immediacies of the 'I'. This was closely related to an occult view of the self, but it was a spiritualized formulation of self that increasingly jettisoned the arcane apparatus of occultism while resisting the orthodoxies of received religion. Certainly, as Middleton Murry made clear, a post-war 'religious sense' was utterly indifferent to the 'formulated creeds of the Christian Church'.[51]

---

[51] Murry, *To the Unknown God*, 194.

The spiritual impulse that religious systems traditionally seek to encode was increasingly conceived in the 1920s as a 'religious sense' which might be articulated in religious language (for the lack of any other) but distanced itself from organized Christianity. Middleton Murry's assertion that 'it is inconceivable and unimaginable that any human being should believe in the dogmas of the Christian Church' was as emphatic as Virginia Woolf's view of T. S. Eliot's conversion to Anglo-Catholicism: he 'may be called dead to us all from this day forward'.[52] Instead, this post-war religious sensibility claimed that the 'things to be believed are of a totally different order'.[53] This, then, was not about the survival of organized religion, but rather marked a new chapter in the experience of spirituality and its articulation. It was certainly related to the Great War and its cultural aftermath, even perhaps to the art of emotional and spiritual survival in a time of war: Middleton Murry's, 'We are changed. In us a religious sense has been dimly awakened.'[54] Perhaps above all in this post-war moment, the 'religious sense' was characterized by the reaffirmation of life in the face of death, and the assertion that we are all bound one to another (possibly, as Middleton Murry put it, 'for ever') and part of the unified whole. Virginia Woolf recognized some of this almost in spite of herself. As she wryly acknowledged in a letter of condolence written to Gwen (Darwin) Raverat on the death of her husband, a letter in which Woolf, too, spoke of 'eternal' bonds: 'I become mystical as I grow older.'[55]

[52] Ibid.; Virginia Woolf to Vanessa Bell, 11 Feb. 1928, *Letters of Virginia Woolf*, iii. 457.

[53] Murry, *To the Unknown God*, 194.

[54] Murry, 'The Sign-Seekers', in *The Evolution of an Intellectual*, 16.

[55] Virginia Woolf to Gwen Raverat, 11 Mar. 1925, *Letters of Virginia Woolf*, iii. 171.

Olwen Hufton's 'Poor', Richard Cobb's 'People', and the Notions of the *longue durée* in French Revolutionary Historiography

Colin Jones

This will be an essay about the *longue durée*—that is to say, about long periods of time, and about long periods of time as the framework for historical analysis and reflection. The concept of the *longue durée* was originated and popularized by the French historian Fernand Braudel, editor of the historical periodical the *Annales*, and champion of the *Annaliste* cause in contemporary historiography.[1] In this chapter I shall seek to highlight the critical role that the concept plays in the work of two of the most significant and influential historians of the French Revolution practising within British academic life in the last half of the twentieth century, Olwen Hufton and Richard Cobb. What I hope will emerge is a sense of the very varied and flexible uses to which the concept has been—and may be—put.

Autobiographically speaking, I can say at the outset that I have known Olwen Hufton for what seems to have been a *très longue durée* all of its own.[2]

A version of this paper was delivered at the conference in Olwen Hufton's honour in Oxford in July 2004. I am most grateful for the comments offered by participants at the conference. In addition, I record my thanks for help kindly supplied by Ruth Harris, Steve Hindle, Gwynne Lewis, Colin Lucas, Josephine McDonagh, and Lyndal Roper.

[1] For Braudel and the *Annales*, see below, pp. 187–8.

[2] This essay is thus intended to witness to, among other meanings of the term, a *longue durée* of cherished friendship and scholarly gratitude toward both figures—whom I shall henceforth refer to as Cobb and Hufton. I began a DPhil. in Oxford under Cobb's supervision in 1971; Hufton has always been a helpful and supportive influence on my work since I first met her. In terms of footnoting, although I have tried to reference the location of views expressed by both, in some cases I have had to rely on memory of past conversations. I have also drawn on two insightful essays on Cobb's work by other ex-pupils: Martyn Lyons, 'Cobb and the Historians', in G. Lewis and C. Lucas (eds.), *Beyond the Terror: Essays in French Regional and Social History, 1794–1815* (Cambridge, 1983), and Gwynne Lewis, 'Richard Charles Cobb, b. 1917–1996: "A Very English Social Historian of France" ', *Proceedings of the Western Society for French History*, 25 (1998).

I first met her in fact when she gave a paper at Richard Cobb's seminar in his sprawling set of rooms at Balliol College in the late 1960s. I was an undergraduate, a mere child, still in rompers virtually—and Hufton herself was scarcely out of a gymslip. I remember the seminar as an incredibly impressive and cool performance on Hufton's part. She showed great presence of mind, great inner calm. She spoke for more than an hour: the room was totally rapt. She was unruffled by questions of any description from the audience, who hung on her every word. We heard about the vocabulary of poverty, varieties of begging, the family economy. There was a lot about women, too, unsurprisingly for us now—but rather surprisingly for that almost exclusively male audience then. Maybe we even heard for the first time the expression 'economy of makeshifts', for which she has become famous. Cobb—listening intently if abstractedly, as was his wont, then scribbling down in a frenetic fashion some mad note or jotting—was eclipsed. He was just finishing his book, *The Police and the People: French Popular Protest, 1789–1820*, which was published in 1970—the first monograph written in his native language (and he in his fifty-third year!) by a prolific author who became a minor English prose stylist in his own right, though one not as much read these days, I fear.[3] She had recently completed her vivid article 'Women in the French Revolution, 1789–96', which *Past & Present* published in 1971. It was inspired very precisely, she admitted, by a wish to imagine a female equivalent to the male sans-culotte portrayed in the essay on 'The Revolutionary Mentality' which Cobb had published in 1957. At this seminar she was now giving us the first fruits of the researches which would lead to the publication in 1974 of her prize-winning book *The Poor in Eighteenth-Century France*.[4]

For recent work highlighting the enduring significance of Hufton's work on the history of poverty, see S. King and A. Tomkins (eds.), *The Poor in England, 1700–1850: An Economy of Makeshifts* (Manchester, 2003). Biographical information for both historians may be found in K. Boyd (ed.), *Encyclopaedia of Historians and Historical Writing*, 2 vols. (London, 1999), i. 235–6 (Cobb, by Jonathan Beecher) and i. 563–4 (Hufton, by myself). For Cobb, see too Colin Lucas's account in the new on-line *Oxford Dictionary of National Biography*.

[3] Cobb died in 1996. Already, at the time of his death, relatively few of his works were still in print. His influence on Revolutionary studies from the 1960s to the early 1990s was, however, immense. David Gilmour has edited two volumes of essays drawn from across his many publications: *The French and their Revolution* and *Paris and Elsewhere* (both London, 1998).

[4] R. C. Cobb, *The Police and the People: French Popular Protest, 1789–1820* (Oxford, 1970); O. Hufton, *The Poor of Eighteenth-Century France, 1750–89* (Oxford, 1974): Winner of the Wolfson Prize; ead., 'Women in Revolution, 1789–96', *Past & Present*, 53 (1971). For

This seminar—a micro-epiphany, for me at any rate—brought together two of the finest English historians of the late twentieth century who worked on the late Ancien Régime and the French Revolution. Two historians whose names became—alongside those of E. P. Thompson, Eric Hobsbawm, and George Rudé—synonymous with the call for a 'history from below', a history which eschewed high politics in order to try to recapture the texture of past experience for the mass of the population.[5] The names of Cobb and Hufton were often linked in this enterprise. The fact that Hufton contributed to Cobb's Festschrift volume in 1983 made many think she was his pupil. In fact, Alfred Cobban had been her mentor—she contributed to his Festschrift too.[6] Cobb always spoke with unreserved warmth of her work. Her great work on the poor was 'a brilliant and sensitive study of the lost world of the very poor'.[7] Reviewing one of his books in 1971, she praised him for 'a combination of erudition, verve, originality and eminent readability'.[8] This sounds like a description of one of Cobb's books. It also sounds like a description of one of Hufton's.

Cobb, Hufton, and the French Revolution 'from below', then: Cobb and the people; Hufton and the poor. So close, so similar—and yet, for all who have read them both, or known them both, so different too. When one thinks about it if only for a second, the differences between them may even strike one as slightly odd, given that they write, to a very considerable degree, about the same kind of individuals in the past. Cobb's 'people' were not all poor, I suppose, although Hufton's 'poor' must normally have been included amongst 'the people', however one conceived them. If we imagined Hufton's 'poor' and Cobb's 'people' as constituting a Venn diagram, there would be considerable overlap between the two groups.

What I would like to do in this chapter is to explore the intertwined work of these two very major, very different, yet also very closely intellectually related

---

the reference to Cobb's earlier article, see ibid., 90; and O. Hufton, *Women and the Limits of Citizenship in the French Revolution* (Toronto, 1992), 159, n. 21.

[5] Cf. J. Sharpe, 'History from Below', in P. Burke (ed.), *New Perspectives on Historical Writing* (Cambridge, 1991).

[6] O. Hufton, 'The Reconstruction of a Church, 1796–1801', in Lewis and Lucas, *Beyond the Terror*; ead., 'Towards an Understanding of the Poor of Eighteenth-Century France', in J. F. Bosher (ed.), *French Government and Society, 1500–1850: Essays in Memory of Alfred Cobban* (London, 1973).

[7] Cobb, 'The Poor of Eighteenth-Century France', in id., *Tour de France* (London, 1965), 29.

[8] Hufton, review of Cobb, *The Police and the People*, in *English Historical Review* (henceforth *EHR*), 86 (1971), 802–3.

French Revolutionary scholars, one whose work was dedicated to the history of the poor (especially poor women), the other to that of the people. I want to focus less on research findings and results than on their approaches and their styles of argument: less on their incremental additions to knowledge than on where their work is coming from, so to speak, and how it gets there. And how it draws on notions of the *longue durée* to achieve many of its effects. 'History', Hufton remarked, concluding her review of Cobb's book in 1971, 'is or should be literature.'[9] So let us take her—quite belatedly I admit, more than thirty years later—at her word. Let us focus not only on the methodologies of Richard Cobb and Olwen Hufton but also on the poetics and the politics of their writings. My hope would be that the two intellectual histories can serve as a prism to tell us something significant about the character of British historiography in regard to Ancien Régime France and the French Revolution in the late twentieth century—and perhaps more generally too.

Both Cobb and Hufton illuminate the empirical tradition of British historical scholarship. When I first encountered Hufton, there was a widespread feeling that the history from below which she, Cobb, and others practised was populist and indeed inherently democratic, because by assiduous grubbing in neglected achives it amounted to giving the people their own history. Nowadays this may seem to some to represent an expression of sixties naivety—but, if so, it was a good-hearted and well-intentioned one, which, moreover, produced some pretty good history. The archival itch evident in Cobb's work, the love of raw detail, his relish for sexual and social scandals, his taste for recorded speech (he adored police and judicial records in particular) all chimed, too, with a New Left historiography also being practised at that time in Oxford around Raphael Samuel and the Ruskin History Workshop group.[10] History Workshop was open to New Left theory. Theory—new Left, old Left, any Left—was anathema to Cobb. Archive sociability, political hanging-on, and throwaway remarks in his early publications gave him the appearances of a Marxist,[11] but no serious Marxist ever took him for one. Oxford increasingly turned him from an *anarchiste de gauche* into an *anarchiste de droite*—not an unusual maturational trajectory perhaps for

---

[9] Ibid., 804.

[10] The *History Workshop Journal* is testimony to the continuing vitality of this historiographical tradition.

[11] Cf. 'Since 1935 I have walked French popular history, drunk it, seen it, heard it, participated in it, walking hand in hand with fraternity and liberty . . .', *Reactions to the French Revolution*, 'Introduction', p. xix.

someone from a very privileged, upper-middle-class background anyway.[12] He was latterly even known on occasion to praise Mrs Thatcher—though he mainly did it to annoy (and also so as to tease his old friend, Gwynne Lewis, the last of the Welsh sans-culottes).[13]

As Cobb wrote more, it became increasingly apparent that there was no substantive politics in his projects at all. He wanted to know about the popular classes essentially because their lives were interesting. They satisfied the inherent and irreducible curiosity which lay close to his heart (and close to the heart of any card-carrying archival historian). Yet as he moved ever closer into the minutiae of popular life, his approach became more and more solipsistic. Not only was it almost impossible to learn anything much from the past, it was asking too much of the archives to reveal any truth but their own. Certain passages of his work *Death in Paris*, published in 1978, read almost like found poems or else a collage assembled by some wayward, latter-day surrealist.[14] Great chunks from the archives were reproduced verbatim. This sprang less from a fear of mistranslation than from a more insistent hesitancy about the possibility of the signifier ever having a direct, unmediated and unarbitrary relationship with its referent—if I may make Cobb sound proto-Derridean (an adjective not often tossed his way).

The more extensively Cobb wrote, the more apparent it became that his writing served an important existential function. He wrote more and more, and more and more about himself. This was true not only of the straightforwardly autobiographical fragments that he published, but also of his purely historical writings. The overt expression of his own views juxtaposed his referencing novels and biographical writings that he admired, alongside lengthy archival transcriptions. He played up to being that very English, that very Oxford, thing: a character. That character eschewed politics, however, and increasingly practised a kind of individualistic anti-politics, all the more striking for being exercised in regard to one of the most intensely politicized and most collectively driven of historical episodes, the French Revolution. One chapter in his book *Reactions to the French Revolution* was entitled 'The Irrelevance of the French Revolution'. In the same work, he talks of 'the limitless capacity of the individual to live out of the reach of terrible and

---

[12] See Lewis, 'Richard Charles Cobb', 2.

[13] Cf. in particular G. Lewis, *The Second Vendée: The Continuity of Counter-Revolution in the Department of the Gard, 1789–1820* (Oxford, 1966); *The French Revolution: Rethinking the Debate* (London, 1993); and *France 1715–1804: Power and the People* (Basingstoke, 2004).

[14] R. Cobb, *Death in Paris: The Records of the Basse-Geôle de la Seine, October 1795–September 1801* (Oxford, 1978).

dangerous events and to shut the door on the shouting, the screams, the roars, the howls, the ugly surge of collective commitment and of vengeful lust'.[15] One of the points on which he parted company with his erstwhile ally and fellow 'historian from below', George Rudé, was precisely over the character of crowd action: Rudé's 'crowd' was 'altogether too respectable' for Cobb's liking; Rudé, he held, underestimated and sanitized the collective propensity for irrational and vengeful violence on the part of the sans-culotte radicals of the Faubourg Saint-Antoine.[16] Cobb also highlighted a quest for individualism which he claimed to have found among the principal *dramatis personae* of the Revolutionary decade who were increasingly his subject, the small men and women, the marginals, the would-be outsiders who shunned all forms of political rhetoric and just got on with their lives. He was also highlighting the divergence between public and private calendars, even in this most highly politicized period. One of the favourite examples of his quest to prioritize local over general meanings—and a case to which he often returned, and which Hufton too found very striking—was of poor Margueritte Barrois, a country-girl from the east of France, who had come to Paris to find work, but who had been made destitute by being impregnated on 9 Thermidor Year II (27 July 1794), the date of the overthrow of Robespierre.[17] Cobb's intense interest in individualism and privacy was existential as well as archival. One of his memoirs recalled that while he was at school— he was a boarder at Shrewsbury—art classes provided 'an escape from collectivity, a place of my own, an assertion of my own individuality, a mimimum of privacy'.[18] Later, the practice of history was a way of shutting out the century.

If you are going to shut out the century, the twentieth is a good one to start with. Cobb recalled with striking clarity the moment in 1933 when he was introduced to his century's more repellent side: reading the *Illustrated London News* when still a young teenager, he was drawn to a photograph from the Balkans of 'a score of severed heads, laid out in a neat row'—adding, with a sense of the black humour which he later learned to spread over his

---

[15] Id., *Reactions to the French Revolution* (Oxford, 1972), 127.

[16] *The Police and the People*, 89. Cobb was of course referring to Rudé's classic *The Crowd in the French Revolution* (Oxford, 1959).

[17] The first use of the case seems to be in *The Police and the People*, 225 (and see too p. 294). It was then recounted in *Reactions to the French Revolution*, 142. Cf. Hufton, *Women and the Limits of Citizenship*, 87. At the conference at which this chapter originated, Hufton also cited this particular example while paying homage to Cobb's influence on her work.

[18] *A Sense of Place* (London, 1981), 24.

more visceral fears, 'a bit like vegetables, cauliflowers or giant lettuces at a horticultural show'.[19] His later brushes with Fascism, Nazism, more unpleasant aspects of Communism, war, occupation, and all the rest were brushes only for the most part—a beating-up in the police cells of pre-War Vienna, 'the dreadful, naked panic of the summer of 1938' in Paris, service in the army during the Second World War, bitter encounters with the secret police in Communist Bulgaria in the mid-1950s, and so on.[20] Such episodes frightened him, good and proper. One of Cobb's recurrent adjectives in his prose and in conversation in the years that I knew him was 'reassuring'. Its use, it strikes me now, was linked to a strong underlying sense of anxiety. Fear of everything breaking down. Fear of not having enough. Fear of power and violence. Fear of mobs of people (mobs were best experienced as the marginal *flâneur*, observing the crowd, but not part of it). Fear which only regularity, routine, and privacy—and also, very importantly, humour—could exorcize.

It is a coincidence, but at some level also rather psychoanalytically intriguing, that Cobb chose as his doctoral supervisor Georges Lefebvre, author, of course, of *La Grande Peur* (the 'Great Fear'), one of the great classics of collective historical psychology.[21] And it is revealing too that on his return to Paris in 1945 he abandoned his doctoral thesis on the minor Hébertist, Vincent, to concentrate instead on the *armées révolutionnaires* of Year II (1793–4).[22] These paramilitary groups of urban sans-culottes took Revolution out to the countryside, imposing the Maximum, enforcing Terror through intimidation and exemplary punishment, and also ensuring their own subsistence in a context of latent dearth. Their history could thus only be a chronicle riven with fear, violence, passion, hunger, insecurity, and personal threat—all those things which both fascinated and frightened their budding historian. All this, moreover, was a messy transposition of a set of problems

---

[19] *The End of the Line: A Memoir* (London, 1996), 9.

[20] Some of the most helpful autobiographical details of this aspect of his life are covered in *The End of the Line*, which was published posthumously. For the 1938 quotation, see Cobb, *Promenades: An Historian's Appreciation of Modern French Literature* (Oxford, 1980), 24.

[21] G. Lefebvre, *The Great Fear of 1789: Rural Panic in Revolutionary France* (London, 1973; first published in French in 1932). See also R. Cobb, 'Georges Lefebvre', *Past & Present*, 18 (1960), repr. in Cobb, *A Second Identity: Essays on France and French History* (Oxford, 1969).

[22] Cobb, *Les Armées révolutionnaires, instrument de la Terreur dans les départements, avril 1793–floréal an II*, 2 vols. (Paris, 1961–3). Marianne Elliott's excellent translation of this work appeared as *The People's Armies: Instrument of Terror in the Departments, April 1793–Floréal Year II* (London, 1987).

which Cobb himself and all other Parisians were enduring, in the harsh days of hunger, rationing, and political anxiety in the aftermath of the war. Hufton has quite properly chided Cobb for tending to take at face value the view of the sans-culotte in all dealings with the countryside.[23] The roots of this identification lie, I would surmise, in his own very Parisian experiences of the countryside in the late 1930s and 1940s. For Cobb, the rural signified a detestable, probably Vichyite, love of folklore, a greedy wish to profit from urban hunger, and a shifty savagery just below the surface. In his last book, *The End of the Line*, completed as he lay dying, Cobb rarely uses the word 'rural' without adding as qualifier terms such as 'hideously', 'aggressively', and 'irremediably'.[24] 'Folklore, embroidery, ribbons, funny hats, leather shorts are generally', he confidently concluded, 'the outward trappings of some form or other of Green Fascism.'[25] 'The Hottentots, the Sioux, the Iroquois began', he noted on another occasion, 'at the very gates of Paris.' He was actually talking about the views of eighteenth-century Parisians.[26] But it was pretty much his own view of the late 1940s.

Cobb entitled one of his early collection of essays *Terreur et subsistances*.[27] It, as well as much of his other work, underlined the primordial importance which he accorded the question of *subsistances*—food-supply at times of social and political stress, and at moments of Terror in fact—in shaping popular responses and syncopating popular radicalism. *La peur du lendemain*— the fear of going short of sustenance once today's needs had been met—was one of his work's most striking leitmotifs (and one which Hufton imbibed at an early stage of her career). This fear of lack, of shortage, of deficiency, resonated in him at some basic existential level. He didn't have to learn it in the archives. Who can forget, once read, the closing lines of his *The Police and the People* in which he evokes a prescient fear of hunger, a fear which nightmarishly morphs into dread of some terrible apocalyptic pestilence?

> Hunger employs its own outriders. Those who have already experienced it can see it announced, not only in the sky, but in the fields,

---

[23] Cf. *EHR*, Hufton, review of Cobb, *The Police and the People*, 803.

[24] *The End of the Line, passim*.

[25] Ibid., 40.

[26] R. C. Cobb, *Paris and its Provinces, 1792–1802* (Oxford, 1975), 34. For an excellent overview of the atmosphere of post-1945 Paris, see A. Beevor and A. Cooper, *Paris After the Liberation* (London, 1994). See also my *Paris: Biography of a City* (London, 2004), 490–1. Cobb was irredeemably urban. 'The countryside for Richard was somewhere to walk in on the way to a pub', *dixit* Gwynne Lewis (private correspondence).

[27] R. C. Cobb, *Terreur et subsistances, 1793–5* (Paris, 1964).

scrutinized each year with growing anxiety week by week in the hot summer months, by thirty million eyes; in the figures for grain prices on the markets; . . . in the conversation of visiting countrymen or the discreet decrees of government; in the unspectacular efforts of municipalities to extend the limits of their cemeteries; in the number of times two men carrying a covered object emerge from a hospital by night; in unusually massive orders of quicklime; . . . in the anxious faces of women, or in the pallor of those who have eaten dead warhorses; in the sword worn by an imprudent mayor; in the shadow, thrown at a certain hour of the day, seen from a certain angle, of a certain statue, in a certain town. . . . [Hunger] is something that comes by stealth, without fanfare, yet preceded by a thousand imperceptible signs that the eighteenth-century 'marginal' could pick out, just as those who were in the know . . . knew that Gaston, with his broad brown and black back, the size of a large mastiff, displayed behind drawn curtains in his cardboard box, was just one of a race of invaders, a new race of giant rats already in possession of the city and waiting only for the signal to come up from the sewers and take over.[28]

End of book. It is an extraordinary passage. Historians don't finish books like that these days. Cobb footnotes a novel by Marcel Aymé, but the more obvious referent is Albert Camus, La Peste (1947), another post-Liberation offshoot, with its similar metaphorical use of plague infestation and its brilliantly imaginative exploration of collective panic and existential choice.

I am arguing that the things which Cobb 'discovered' in his research on Paris in the 1790s reflect something of what individuals in Paris (including, intermittently, himself) were experiencing in the 1930s, 1940s, and 1950s: the importance of neighbourhood sociability; urban distrust of the countryside; fear and anxiety; sex and drink and bad behaviour.[29] Plus resistance to any form of politics which sought to abstract lessons from the dirty mess of everyday experience. 'More than any other historian,' Hufton notes approvingly, 'he in his works on the Revolution, questioned the gap between language and reality.'[30] Highlighting the gap between rhetoric and what she

---

[28] The Police and the People, 323–4.

[29] Characteristically, when highlighting Hufton's insights into eighteenth-century vagrancy and mobility, Cobb instantly thought to link it with the experience of l'Exode in 1940, with Parisians fleeing Paris pell-mell before the German advance. Tour de France, 24.

[30] O. Hufton, The Prospect Before Her: A History of Women in Western Europe. Vol. 1. 1500–1800 (London, 1995), p. xxv.

called 'the actual experience of real women'[31] became a key part of Hufton's own project too.

Cobb on occasion admitted that his view of Parisian sans-culottes was based on the fact that he had long been living with their twentieth-century descendants. Unless one is a topographical determinist, this is a highly implausible claim, in fact, given the enormous amount of immigration which has over the centuries made up the Parisian population. Scratch any present-day Parisian and one will find a second-generation provincial—or foreigner. The same was true in the 1790s. This certainty in transmission over the centuries in the same site also helps explain Cobb's visceral dislike for the modernization of Paris starting in the mid-1950s, a process which Cobb's friend Louis Chevalier famously dubbed 'the assassination of Paris'.[32] 'I have lived with the *sans-culottes* of our day . . . for a number of years . . .', he wrote in 1970. 'I know that [they] are still with us, though they are fast disappearing in the France of the *Plan* and of the super-technocrats.'[33] In place of the city whose identity could be read not only in the archives but also in boulevard *flânerie*, in bar-room sociability, and in the films of Marcel Carné, technocrats were putting in place 'only a uniform drabness, a common all-enveloping ugliness'.[34] Cobb's anti-politics merged into deep-dyed anti-modernism.

Richard Cobb's highly individual and inimitable take on the people of Paris in the 1790s exemplifies the concept of the *longue durée* which Fernand Braudel and the *Annales* school were developing from the late 1940s through to the 1960s.[35] Braudel thought of the *longue durée* in terms of the barely perceptible changes in the environment which he saw as setting the pace and determining the possibilities of change over time. From the late 1950s, as

---

[31] *Women and the Limits of Citizenship*, p. xix.

[32] L. Chevalier, *The Assassination of Paris* (Chicago, 1994; published in French in 1977). For immigration into Paris from the early nineteenth century onwards, see the same author, *Classes laborieuses et classes dangereuses pendant la première moitié du XIXe siècle* (Paris, 1958). Cf. also Jones, *Paris*, ch. 11.

[33] *The Police and the People*, pp. xix–xx.

[34] *Paris and its Provinces*, 213.

[35] The best general introduction to the *Annales* phenomenon is P. Burke, *The French Historical Revolution: The Annales School* (Cambridge, 1990). For a more astringent view, see F. Dosse, *New History in France: The Triumph of the Annales* (Urbana, Ill., 1994). Characteristically, though denying he was a member of any 'school', Cobb claimed his first book in the English language properly belonged in the 'Histoire des mentalités' series published by Plon and edited by *Annaliste* Robert Mandrou. See *The Police and the People*, p. xv.

Gérard Noiriel has recently highlighted,[36] Braudel extended the concept from geography to psychology, and talked of *mentalités*, the basic mental equipment and frameworks for thinking and feeling, also operating at a similar pace. *Mentalités* were so many 'long-term prisons', or *prisons de longue durée*. Cobb loved cocking a snook at the *Annales*: the journal's infatuation with quantification, the hyperbolic, scholastic, and scientistic language of its adherents, their cliquey fashionableness, their unerring penchant for 'stating a silly idea sillily'.[37] But the concepts of *longue durée* and *mentalité* were at the heart of his project. Indeed, to some degree his work was unthinkable without them.

They were also crucial, I shall argue, to Olwen Hufton—but in rather different ways. After that Balliol encounter cited at the beginning of this chapter, Cobb lurched ever more erratically away from political engagement, and developed an idiosyncratic anti-politics as his forte. Although Hufton provides fewer clues in her writings, her trajectory was very different. Cobb's personality leaps off the page, and he provides a running commentary on his tastes, his loves, his hates, his historical judgements. Hufton writes equally vividly, but her personality and her politics are implied, restrained, and kept in check, not waved about in the reader's face.

Cobb's analysis of Hufton was as follows:

> Olwen Hufton can write with such sympathy of Bayeux because she was partly educated there, of women because she is a woman, of the nuns because she was taught by them, and she can understand what poverty means to the mother of a large family because she is aware from her own experience of the preponderant place occupied by the Catholic Church in the lives of the female poor.[38]

This (somewhat mechanistic, it must be said) attribution of influence to gender, education, and religious affiliation on Hufton's work overlooks the extent to which her views on the poor and the female poor may also have been shaped by her responses to the broader experiences of her whole generation. Whereas Cobb was strongly influenced by the atmosphere of post-war Paris, Hufton's experience of that era was as a child growing up in the straitened circumstances of post-war Britain. This was a world of quotidian

---

[36] G. Noiriel, 'Comment on récrit l'histoire. Les usages du temps dans les *Ecrits sur l'histoire de Fernand Braudel*', ch. 6 of id., *Penser avec, penser contre. Itinéraire d'un historien* (Paris, 2003).

[37] See esp. the wonderfully funny essay, 'Nous des *Annales*', in *A Second Identity*, esp. p. 77.

[38] Ibid., 46–7.

austerity and food rationing, far from the privileged enclaves whence Cobb had originally hailed. In post-war Britain, family, kin, and neighbourhood were deeply entwined, offering means of pulling through for individuals in difficulty. But if this was a period of austerity it also represented an important moment of hope: these years saw the creation of the National Health Service, the establishment of the welfare state, broader access to grammar-schooling and higher education (from both of which Hufton personally benefited), and a wish that poverty should become a thing of the past rather than the present. 'Today destitution has been banished', the Labour party manifesto for the 1950 general election would grandiloquently announce.[39] 'Nine tenths of the poverty which existed in 1936', Labour politician Anthony Crosland would declare in 1956 (at the very moment, in fact, that Hufton herself was going up to university, the first of her family so to do) 'has disappeared.'[40] If Hufton—like many Britons in that era—learnt at first hand about the manifold strategies of an economy of makeshifts, she also, like them, imbibed a Beveridgian sense of the commitment of the state to social amelioration. In 1942 Sir William Beveridge had authored the famous, eponymous Report which laid out the principles and many of the practices of the emergent welfare state. Amidst what was otherwise a highly technical and deliberately colourless account of *Social Insurance and Allied Services*, Beveridge defined the enemies of social progress which he was seeking to overcome as 'five giants' who needed slaying: Want, Disease, Ignorance, Squalor, and Idleness.[41] The phrase was picked up enthusiastically by the British public. For the Beveridgian generation to which Hufton belonged, the assault on poverty was less a political instrument than a moral imperative, almost a mythic crusade for a just society from which destitution had been banished. Super-bureaucrat Beveridge even mixed the language of the radical Left with the everyday experience of an economy of makeshifts, urging his readers to seize the opportunity for social transformation: 'a revolutionary moment in the world's history is a time for revolutions,' he argued, 'not for patching' (*sic*).[42]

Hufton's work, I surmise, offers a reflection of this very distinctive, 'Beveridgian moment' in modern British history at which an economy of makeshifts seemed to be passing into history at the hands of a mythologized

---

[39] Cited in D. Vincent, *Poor Citizens: The State and the Poor in Twentieth-Century Britain* (London, 1991), 133

[40] Crosland, *The Future of Socialism*, cited in ibid.

[41] Sir William Beveridge, *Social Insurance and Allied Services: Report Presented to Parliament* (London, 1942: repr. 1974), 6.

[42] Ibid.

welfare state. Although Hufton's writings on the poor bespeak much greater respect for the traditions of religiously driven charity than many other historians of poverty of her generation (her background doubtless counted for something in this), she, like they, would never think that charity would ever be enough.

If the roots of Hufton's views on poverty were influenced by ideas about and experiences of poverty in the society in which she was brought up, it is also worth noting that the extraordinary impact which her work made as it started to be published from the early 1970s owed something to the context of a 'rediscovery' of poverty as a social issue in Britain at that time. It had by then become abundantly and tragically clear that poverty was a major Third World problem. Even though there was a degree of confidence in high-tech and biomedical solutions achieved by international agencies, Hufton was not alone in making comparisons between the circumstances of Third World countries in the late twentieth century with those of Europe in the early modern period. Poverty was a pre-industrial (or maybe we should say pre-Beveridgian?) problem.[43] Yet since the mid-1960s there had also been an emergent sense that, Beveridge's statements of intent and Labour party optimism notwithstanding, poverty had simply not disappeared from the post-industrial Western world. The groups which researchers such as Peter Townsend and Brian Abel Smith highlighted as particularly at risk in contemporary society—women and young children (the Child Poverty Action Group evolved at precisely this time)—had, moreover, a history in poverty.[44] Hufton's work helped to uncover that history. The thought of giving the poor a sense of their past—and thereby some measure of dignity and social profile—was something which seems intrinsic to her whole project, and it echoed broader political, social, and cultural concerns.

By the early 1970s Hufton was also moving closer towards the cultural politics of feminism. This was a move well-attuned to the *Zeitgeist*, but which also represented a logical follow-on to her work on poverty, since women, she shows, were the linchpins of the family economy whose effective workings were essential to keep a poor family away from destitution. We can be fairly sure that precious few of the twentieth-century poor and the popular

---

[43] See esp. her 'Social Conflict and the Grain Supply in Eighteenth-Century France', in the special issue of the *Journal of Interdisciplinary History*, 14 (1983) devoted to 'Hunger and History: The Impact of Changing Food Production and Consumption Patterns on Society'; and ead., 'Fernand Braudel', *Past & Present*, 112 (1986), 211.

[44] The best way into this literature is B. Abel Smith and P. Townsend, *The Poor and the Poorest: A New Analysis of the Ministry of Labour's Family Expenditure Surveys of 1953–4 and 1960* (London, 1965). See too Vincent, *Poor Citizens*.

classes read the classics of Cobb or Hufton. (If they did they had to have good French, for neither made concessions to monoglottery.) But women did; and feminists did. Hufton also became a key figure in the emergent women's history movement. As is well known, she used her institutional clout—at Harvard, in Florence, and in Oxford—to promote the lives and careers of more than a generation of feminist historians.[45]

Politics and history overlap for Hufton, then—as not for Cobb. Yet the poetics of Hufton's writings do seem to have been influenced by Cobb's style. Cobb's love of quirky character and telling detail is often condensed within particular character typologies. He had an amusing line or two, for example, about finding Robespierre alive and well in a Welsh railway ticket-office. He often tends to romanticize his subjects—something which Hufton invariably avoids. 'They made out under progressively difficult circumstances,' she says of the poor in the late eighteenth century, 'and with progressively less chance of success by their own efforts, devious, ugly, cruel and dishonest as these might be.'[46] Not much romanticism there, then.

Cobb's characterizations often develop into one-offs, micro-historical *pointilliste* displays which highlight the irreducible individualism of his subjects. He loves to linger over his characters, and is always keen to insert them into their local ecology of *quartier* or *cabaret*. Hufton is quite as responsive to the experience and fate of individuals, but she plays down individualism, and indeed she takes her characterizations beyond Cobb's example. She recounts history in terms of a cast-list which comprises a vivid taxonomy of sub-Weberian social types. Thus she tells the story of 'Women in Revolution' in 1971 very deliberately through 'isolating . . . the sort of woman the *sans-culotte* most likely went home to . . . the working woman of the towns; the woman of the bread riots . . . the mother heroine', and so on. And her condensed account of the trajectory of the Revolutionary decade focuses on the moment 'when Citoyenne Defarge [the infamously sanguinary character in Charles Dickens's Revolutionary epic, *A Tale of Two Cities*], ex-*tricoteuse*, put down her (knitting) needles for a set of rosary beads . . .'.[47] She takes as the target of her study 'the experience of real people'. And those 'real people' are viewed as expressive of generalized social phenomena, not of merely personal and idiosyncratic dilemmas.

---

[45] Unsurprisingly, she would be a contributor to the state-of-the-art, five-volumed *History of Women* edited by Michelle Perrot and Georges Duby and published by Harvard University Press: see 'Women, Work and Family' in vol. 3: *Renaissance and Enlightenment Paradoxes* (Cambridge, Mass., 1993).

[46] *The Poor of Eighteenth-Century France*, 367.

[47] 'Women in Revolution', 90, 107.

Then again, in *The Prospect Before Her*, when highlighting what had changed for women by 1800, she writes

> One approach might be to imagine a chronological parade and watch it as it passes, starting around 1500 and ending three centuries later. . . . Who was there when the procession drew to a close and who was not there during the first hundred years and vice versa?

After presenting us with the idea of this pageant of social types, she goes on, strikingly, unforgettably, to speak of the disappearance of:

> the poor old woman transformed into a witch, the infanticidal mother on her way to the gallows because her baby's lungs had floated in a bucket of water, . . . the possessed young girl screaming and writhing and orchestrated by her exorcist, the raving, anorexic 'mystical' nun, those who tortured themselves in the name of religion . . . the child bride, the cruel widowed mother forced to abandon her child . . . [48]

Like Cobb, Hufton knows of course that there is not one statistically 'average' woman—any more than that there is a quintessential sans-culotte. Unlike Cobb, she eschews lingering over individuals. Rather, as the above example suggests, she bombards us with examples of particular social types. She knows, for example, that there is no such thing as *a* poor unmarried mother in Ancien Régime France; things were different in Brittany, for example, in Languedoc, in Alsace, in the Limousin, or wherever. Her work leads us on a whirlwind tour of pre-industrial France (later, Europe). The focus in her work is always on the individual, but the speed of her gait means that she chooses not to imitate Cobb's florid descriptive style for the way material things were. She is however deeply concerned with how material life was locally experience.

Hufton's sensitivity to the diversity, the warp and weft of female experience in the past, is, moreover, also accompanied by a sense of limits—structural limits—which play out over the *longue durée*. I must say that I was quite surprised by the warmth of the accolade which, in 1986, she paid to Fernand Braudel in her obituary of the master-*Annaliste* which appeared in *Past & Present*. After all, Braudel scarcely mentions women in his writings. What she picks up from him, however, is his tripartite division of time into *histoire événementielle* (classically, this represents the much-spat-upon tradition of close political narrative), generational middling time, and the slower

---

[48] *The Prospect Before Her*, 493.

processes of the *longue durée*. Braudel's favourite time period, from the fifteenth to the late eighteenth century, is in fact that which Hufton employs for her *Prospect* book, and in this she largely accepts his idea of the *longue durée* as being composed of 'centuries of common time during which the parameters of human history were unchanged'.[49]

This means that to a considerable extent, to put it starkly, early modern women are viewed as being locked in a box by the constraints of the *longue durée*. 'Everyone who survived the birth process in the 300 years considered here' (1500 to 1800, then), she tells us, 'was a lifelong hostage to the constraints imposed by economic circumstances and belief patterns and was socialised into a set of values, visions, ways of doing things, dependent on class.'[50] Women, like the poor, were confined within a set of circumstances—a Braudelian *prison de longue durée*—from which only economic and social progress, demographic transition, and technological innovation would eventually release them.

One may justly enquire whether this is not too bleak a vision. The eighteenth century is quite a cheery place these days, in fact, chock-full of proto-consumers, precocious shoppers, and enterprising individualists, so that Hufton's economic pessimism seems almost jarring in contrast. When she began her work, she accepted Ernest Labrousse's now rather creaky version of the eighteenth-century economy. Population rose; prices rose, wages dropped; production was outpaced by demand. There were too many mouths to feed. Ineluctable consequence: immiseration. The picture is far more nuanced these days—and partly for reasons which Hufton herself sensed long ago.[51] Labrousse's miserabilist picture was based on wage series in which he assumed that a family of five was dependent on the income of the male head of household. (Intriguingly, the Beveridge Report was eventually criticized for making the same kind of assumption.) Yet as Hufton herself showed, this was a sexist, Third Republic simplification of complex practice. The economy of the poor was a family economy, in which all members sought to contribute. Their 'economy of makeshifts' included migration, begging, dependence on poor relief, and marginal criminality.[52]

---

[49] 'Fernand Braudel', 208.

[50] *The Prospect Before Her*, 488.

[51] For a critique of Labrousse's model see C. Jones and R. Spang, 'Sans culottes, *sans café, sans sucre*? Realms of Necessity and Luxury in Eighteenth-Century France', in M. Berg and H. Clifford (eds.), *Consumers and Luxury: Consumer Culture in Eighteenth-Century Europe, 1650–1850* (Manchester, 1999).

[52] This provides the organizational structure for her *The Poor of Eighteenth-Century France*.

For Hufton, this kind of packaging of family income in the interests of survival was practised on the knife-edge of desperation. Yet for the economic historian Jan de Vries, such behaviour is typical of proto-consumers, maximizing waged labour so as to pool resources and purchase consumer goods in an 'industrious revolution'.[53] De Vries's proto-consumers are not wholly coextensive with Hufton's poor—but there is a good degree of overlap. Post-mortem inventories show a boom in material possessions over the eighteenth century which extended pretty low down the social spectrum. They often include records of debt: but do these demonstrate extensive immiseration, as Hufton assumes—or the deceased individual's access to credit networks, a part of the economy of makeshifts which Hufton arguably underplays, yet which has been the focus of much recent work?[54]

I do not wish to adjudicate here between Hufton's social pessimism about the late eighteenth century and the sunny-side-up economic optimism of certain of the historians of consumer culture. Doubtless the truth lies somewhere in between, and Hufton's work stands four-square in the path of historians who would seek merely to airbrush the problem of poverty out of consideration of any pre-industrial economy. More generally, however, the contrast of views over the issue highlights, I believe, the extent to which Hufton favours a version of early-modern stability and continuity which is both is Braudelian and thus rather deterministic. Whereas for Cobb the *longue durée* covered the period from the 1790s to the 1950s, in which period Parisian *mentalités* were much the same, for Hufton, the period of the *longue durée* was the classic Braudelian time-frame of the fifteenth to the eighteenth century—and would only be broken by processes of modernization. Throughout her period of choice, the economy of makeshifts operated to ensure that the poor—and especially poor women—survived. And Hufton's story is basically all about survival. 'I have always been preoccupied with the business of survival in the past and with . . . *mentalités* which explain why people responded to events the way they did', she states. 'When survival was

---

[53] See J. De Vries, 'Between Purchasing Power and the World of Goods: Understanding the Household Economy in Early Modern Europe', in J. Brewer and R. Porter (eds.), *Consumption and the World of Goods* (London, 1993), esp. 107 and n. 65.

[54] The issue of inventory evidence has of course been opened up particularly by Daniel Roche in his classic *The People of Paris: An Essay in Popular Culture in the Eighteenth Century* (Leamington Spa, 1987): particularly convincing for leaving the middle and upper classes out of the frame of analysis. For credit networks, see C. Muldrew, *The Economy of Obligation: The Culture of Credit and Social Relations in Early Modern England* (Basingstoke, 1998).

the sovereign imperative, a grim determinism prevailed.'[55] The poor used their ready reckoners for survival in all major life-events. Hufton slams down Pierre Chaunu on one occasion for suggesting that the poor over the course of the eighteenth century might have married out of love and affection: for her, 'hard-headed economic considerations' were essentially what counted.[56] Again: 'whatever the changes in the stately home and the urban bourgeois dwelling, the mud cabins and rat-infested hovels of the rural poor remained largely unchanged.'[57]

Cobb the anti-modernist thus contrasts strikingly with Hufton, who is more of a modernist than she sometimes allows, and she eschews nostalgia for a World-We-Have-Lost-(Thank-Heavens!). Women's enemies for Hufton are very much the enemies of social progress as defined by Beveridge, in fact—Want, Disease, Ignorance, Squalor, and Idleness. And she seems to view the way out of the hole in which the European poor and European women have been living since 1500 as being better roads, railways, factory production, full employment, schools, improved health and hygiene, and all the other sundry trappings of modernity—including effective social insurance, Beveridge-style. Tragically, in the interim of the *longue durée*, women would have to wait, and suffer while they waited—and survived.

To a degree, then, Hufton's women are victims. They are, however—and I think this is a highly Huftonian trait - rather perky victims, full of guile and resource. 'The overriding impression given by what might have been expected to be a relentless chronicle of deprivation', Cobb noted of her *The Poor of Eighteenth-Century France*, 'is one of extreme vitality.'[58] Few of the women whose story she recounts throughout her oeuvre indulge in victim culture or self-pity. Even languorous petitions bemoaning distress are instrumental rather than to be taken at face value: women were just trying on the rhetoric as a way of unlocking the purse-strings of rich males.[59] Women might be locked in a determinist box as regards their general position within society over the *longue durée*; but they still had more than enough room for character and commitment to reassert themselves—in keeping the family economy in place and putting bread on the table. Furthermore, if Hufton's women are victims, they suffer more at the hands of nature than of men. Hufton never indulges in androphobia. Rather than

---

[55] *Women and the Limits of Citizenship*, p. xvii; *The Prospect Before Her*, 9.

[56] *The Poor of Eighteenth-Century France*, 342 n.

[57] *The Prospect Before Her*, 14.

[58] *Tour de France*, 23.

[59] *Women and the Limits of Citizenship*, 97.

attack patriarchal values as a source of women's woes, she is more likely to evoke the relative powerlessness of men too when faced with the material constraints of a pre-industrial world. She is forgiving even towards those males who seek to right the wrongs of the world on the basis of a lack of material experience. She acknowledges, for example, that the free-trade policies in grain espoused by Turgot and the Physiocrats in the 1770s caused untold hardships to the economy of the poor; yet is charitable enough to regard Turgot's views as well-intentioned and 'not inhumane'.[60] Women's problems lie less in Culture (male or otherwise) than in Nature. And this includes women's biological nature: 'no one could plough a five-inch furrow', she wryly notes, 'in a condition of advanced or even early pregnancy.'[61]

Given such an interpretation of the early modern period and of the late eighteenth century in particular, it is hardly surprising that Hufton has little time or patience for the French Revolution. Cobb hated the rhetoric of regeneration covering machinations of violence and power: the Declaration of the Rights of Man was a bore, and a mischievous bore at that. Hufton's view is more nuanced (it would be difficult to be less). She admits that 1789 brought more women, especially literate women, into the public sphere. Yet the literate few, she points out, 'didn't have to worry about the contents of the bread-bin'.[62] In contrast, the mass of women—poor women—did have that concern, and for them the Revolution would prove to be what Hufton calls a 'Bad Time'.[63] Revolutionary and feminist ideas largely passed women by. Even those women who did take up the Revolutionary cause were motivated essentially by a wish for survival: 'The mass of women involved themselves in the Revolution not to change the status of women but to protect their own [and their families'] interests.'[64] Women's biggest achievement throughout the Revolutionary decade, in fact, would be the informal restoration of the Catholic Church, which had been severely beaten up by the Revolutionaries. In the absence of an effective system of social insurance, religious charity was as good as women were going to get. Women had to endure the Revolution—and then had to clear up the mess the men had made. The determinist box was too hard to break out of—yet.

Hufton looked forward to social progress, economic growth, and technological modernization to break down the determinist material structures

---

[60] O. Hufton, *Europe: Privilege and Protest, 1730–89* (London, 1980), 335. Contrast Cobb: the Physiocrats were 'absolute shits' (private conversation).

[61] *The Prospect Before Her*, 5.

[62] *Women and the Limits of Citizenship*, 5.

[63] *The Prospect Before Her*, 488.

[64] Ibid., 459.

within which the poor, and poor women, lived their lives. So now, she saw the feminist movement of the later nineteenth century as providing the yardstick against which earlier efforts for women's emancipation fell short. Modern feminism would be a largely secular phenomenon. Yet it is a very distinguishing feature of Hufton's work that she sees the Church in the early modern period as hughly supportive of women, notably in regard to their survival. Jobs for poor girls in teaching and poor relief, charity for hard-pressed mothers and widows, care for the aged and the very young—she views the Church almost as a primitive (perhaps we could even say proto-Beveridgian?) version of modern welfare.

For a writer who has much to say about the Church, however, Hufton has less to say about spirituality. Her lecture on the history of nuns—which she gave as the Hayes Robinson Lecture at Royal Holloway College in 2000—explored spirituality as well as religious and charitable activities[65]—without separating it from material realities. It would seem sometimes for this through-and-through non-Marxist that the struggle for biological survival shaped ideas and infused religious vocations, and it is in this context that religious cultures must be understood. Survival is all about scrimping and saving, deploying family strategies, keeping bread on the family table. It is as though spirituality and even ideas *tout court* were luxuries for the bulk of the population.

Despite her underplaying the role of ideas (as, of course, did Cobb), the picture Hufton paints is strikingly vivid and persuasive, and has proved massively influential. Even though the modernization framework which she deploys would seem to place pre-industrial women in a quite different mental and emotional register from our own, this proves not to be the case. For it is part of Hufton's achievement as a writer that she allows us, her readers, by a generous effort of her imagination, to enter into the disparate worlds of her largely illiterate subjects—worlds notoriously difficult for the historian to access. 'She has taken . . . infinite trouble to penetrate places where no contemporary other than a few *curés* had ever gone,' Cobb rightly noted of her *Poor of Eighteenth-Century France*, 'and to explore the semi-secret world of the desperate with the help of a code understandable only to them.'[66] This archival truffle-hound, as she would seemingly account herself,[67] is important, then, for what she roots out from the archives—but also, and even

---

[65] O. Hufton, *Whatever Happened to the History of the Nun?* Hayes Robinson Lecture, Royal Holloway College, University of London (2000).

[66] *Tour de France*, 29.

[67] 'Fernand Braudel', 213. Here she is following a playful categorization of historians, devised by Emmanuel Le Roy Ladurie, as either 'truffle-hunters' or 'parachutists'.

more so, for how she contrives to render her findings dramatically and with considerable literary skill. Few historians have evoked the life dilemmas of individuals in the past with as much emotional force. She allows us to weigh up public events, political rhetoric, and life dilemmas not so much like the man on the top of the Clapham omnibus, but rather as the good mother at the empty bread-bin. We might not all be mothers—but we have all had one, and thus at some level every one of her readers has a means of relating to this powerful, virtually trans-historical angle of vision.

Like Cobb, Hufton practices a verbal alchemy which allows her to transcend the historicist structures which she erects, almost as a distancing device, around her subjects. Once she has performed her historical truffling, she writes her conclusions in a way which imaginatively conveys to her readers the pathos of the very humblest individuals in the past of whose existence we have evidence. The pre-industrial box into which she has sought to locate the experiences of eighteenth-century women and paupers proves insufficient to keep them confined within.

Both Hufton and Cobb are rare amongst their peers, I would ague, in having the eerie power of which Jules Michelet, still one of the greatest—and certainly the most extraordinary—of historians of the French Revolution, spoke: namely, the capacity to reach across the generations and, by scrutiny of the traces which even the humblest in the past have left, to make the dead live again. For Michelet, history was indeed '*Resurrection*', an ability 'to make the silences of history speak'.[68] The archives established a duty incumbent on the historian, he held, to act as the poor's legally appointed executor, to represent to future generations the fates of even such *miserabiles personae*, whose existences, however lowly, contributed to the making of *le peuple*. For Michelet, these *damnés de la terre* require the services 'of an Oedipus who will explain to them the riddle of their existence which they have not understood, and who will tell them the meaning of their words and actions which they have not understood'.[69] The historian's work in the archives was almost a form of necromancy: 'the more I breathed over their dust,' Michelet recorded of his time in the national archives, 'the more I saw [the dead] rise up . . .'[70] Then again:

---

[68] His italics and capitalization: 'j'ai défini l'histoire *Resurrection*'. J. Michelet, *Histoire de France*, 'Préface à l'édition de 1869', in id., *Oeuvres. Vol. IV*, 22.

[69] Ibid., 614; and a passage from 1842 cited by Roland Barthes, *Michelet* (Paris, 1954), 79.

[70] I thank Carolyn Steedman for reminding me of the extraordinary demiurgic power of these lines of Michelet. In her *Dust: The Archive and Cultural History* (Manchester, 2001), esp. 164–7 and nn., Steedman follows in a distinguished line of analysts of historical creation (Edmund Wilson, Hayden White, Roland Barthes, Benedict Anderson) who have pondered these extracts.

I have given succour to many of the dead and the too-forgotten . . . I have exhumed them for a second time. . . . History welcomes and renews disinherited glories. It gives new life to the dead, resuscitates them. . . . They now live amongst us and we feel we are their friends or relatives. Thus is made a family, a commonwealth (*cité*) between the dead and the living.[71]

Cobb and Hufton may thus have very different political agendas, but to study the hauntingly resonant poetics of their oeuvre is to reveal a striking rapprochement in their style of writing. Both are 'historian-resurrectionists' in the Michelet mode, whose words allow us to grasp with immediacy a sense of the experiences and the dilemmas of people in the past from the poorest origins. Yet where they part company with their fellow-resurrectionist Michelet, it seems to me, is just as instructive in regard to what is distinctive about their work. For whereas Michelet was committed to a collectivist view of the past, both Cobb and Hufton focus their empathy on individuals rather than groups. Where Michelet mythologized *le peuple* as a transcendent political force of historical destiny, Cobb and Hufton shy away from such perspectives and reject outright ideologies of any jib. Cobb's work, I have suggested, underlines the primordial importance of the value of fear— supplemented at will by a colourful array of the cardinal vices—in explaining individual motivation. Hufton's work is largely structured around the problems of individual or family survival—and this is conceived of in very grim, materialistic, quotidian terms which nonetheless leave room for subtle emotional transactions, such as those she describes between rich widows and priests in the early years of the Jesuit movement.

Given their approaches, it is hardly surprising that, taken together, the two respond so unenthusiastically to the notion of the French Revolution as a moment of collective and world-historical self-transformation. Michelet had emplotted the Revolution as the Romance of *le peuple*, Cobb and Hufton see it rather as tragedy.[72] Both writers plumb the gap between the the words and the acts of Revolutionary politicians in the 1790s, and find these men massively

---

[71] *Oeuvres. Vol. 21*, 628. On several occasions in her work—e.g. *Women and the Limits of Citizenship*, pp. xviii–xx—Hufton considers Michelet's writings on women in the French Revolution. Her main source of criticism is Michelet's wish to fashion what Hufton calls a 'generic woman', thus underplaying variability and individualism, and she does not consider Michelet's poetics, as here.

[72] H. White, *Metahistory: The Historical Imagination in Nineteenth-Century Europe* (London, 1973), 135 ff. I write 'tragedy' rather than 'Tragedy' quite deliberately: Cobb had a whole ironic number about the pretensiousness of the *majuscule*.

wanting. Despite their fine words and world-historic pronouncements, the Revolutionaries are shown to be either pathetically out of touch with everyday material realities (Hufton) or else (as in Cobb) as quite as riven by the baser emotions as those who opposed them (and they were hypocritical, to boot). What emerges from the writings of both historians on the Revolutionary era are the futility and malevolent fatuousness of public rhetoric; power as a cloak for base self-interest; the world-historic registered at individual level through an array of passions; nagging anxiety, latent fear; a dramaturgy of vice, envy, hatred—but also of self-sacrifice and commitment; and the exigencies of biological survival. For both writers, the Revolution was indeed 'the best of times', but most of all it was 'the worst of times'—as the opening lines of Charles Dickens's *A Tale of Two Cities* (1859) have long informed every British schoolchild.

I bring Dickens into my analysis quite deliberately at this point. In this chapter I have focused on the *longue durée* in a variety of forms: the *longue durée* of early modern material conditions; the *longue durée* of the economy of makeshifts of the poor; the *longue durée* of women's struggle in the face of material hardship; the *longue durée* of pre-modern Parisian popular sociability. Perhaps it is not out of place also to evoke the *longue durée* of the collective imaginary as regards our understanding of the French Revolution—a *longue durée* in which, I shall argue, Charles Dickens has an honoured place.

In his account of historical writing in the nineteenth century, Hayden White has highlighted the notion of enduring forms of historical consciousness which bridged professional history-writing and the imaginative domain of fiction over the course of the century.[73] White makes no mention of Dickens. Yet there can be little doubt that—with the exception of Carlyle (who was, of course, one of Dickens's principal sources and inspirations)— none of the rather pallid and tame British historians of the French Revolution in the nineteenth century provided much with which to compel our attention, and none left a lasting dent on the national psyche. As Cobb noted, moreover, in a review of a solid monograph on this subject, most such historians preferred studying from their Oxbridgian studies than in the dust of the archives.[74] There would be no resurrectionism for them. In contrast, Dickens provides, I would argue, one of the most enduring of metanarratives

---

[73] Ibid. White focuses on historians rather than poets and novelists—though Michelet is considered (pp. 152 ff.). I am aware that what I am proposing here does not fit with the schematic model which White offers.

[74] Review of K. Ben-Israel, *English Historians on the French Revolution* (Cambridge, 1968), in *Tour de France*. Interestingly, there is no mention of Dickens in Ben-Israel's book.

in British culture as regards collective and ideologically driven political action, a metanarrative which is evident not only among British historians but also more extensively within the national culture across the *longue durée*.[75] In particular, what more telling proof of the power of the Dickensian paradigm could there be than the fact that Sir William Beveridge's 'five giants'—Want, Disease, Ignorance, Squalor, and Idleness—on whose destruction enduring social progress and the triumph of the Welfare State in the twentieth century were predicated are—rather precisely, in fact—a scarcely veiled updating of Dicken's identification of the prevalent traits of the Faubourg Saint-Antoine in which the French Revolution was incubated: 'cold, dirt, sickness, ignorance and want.'[76] Sir William was doubtless still haunted by his childhood reading. His Report, as we have seen,[77] both called for and mythologized a 'revolution'. But it was to be an English-, not a French-style revolution: a transformation in social insurance, not an exercise in sanguinary collective violence as chronicled by Dickens.

Remarkably, then, the long shadow of *A Tale of Two Cities* can thus be detected at the very heart of the project of the post-Second World War Welfare State—a project which, I have argued, strongly influenced the attitudes of Hufton and her generation towards the problem of poverty. Beveridge had renewed and updated the Dickensian vision of social progress for late twentieth-century Britain. Others of Hufton's 'Beveridge generation'—such as William Doyle, Norman Hampson, and Simon Schama, who rank amongst the most widely read and authoritative scholars on the French Revolution in the late twentieth century—are equally in thrall to the Dickensian paradigm, all honoured cellmates in the *prison de longue durée* for the historical profession constructed by Charles Dickens in 1859. All emplot the Revolutionary decade as tragedy as much in terms of societal immaturity as human wickedness; all draw heavily (Schama not least) on a Dickensian the-

---

[75] Cf., for example, popular film in which Dickens's influence is only rivalled by that of Baroness Orczy's Scarlet Pimpernel. For an approach to the question, cf. R. Maniquis, 'La Révolution française dans le cinéma américain et anglais', in J. C. Bonnet and P. Roger (eds.), *La Légende de la Révolution au XXe siècle. De Gance à Renoir et de Romain Rolland à Claude Simon* (Paris, 1988). I have used the Penguin Classics edition of *A Tale of Two Cities*, ed. R. Maxwell (London, 2000), along with A. Sanders, *The Companion to A Tale of Two Cities* (Mountfield, new edn., 2002). *Dickens Study Annual: Essays on Victorian Fiction*, 12 (1983) is devoted to Dickens, Carlyle, and the *Tale of Two Cities*. More generally, see too C. Crossley and I. Small (eds.), *The French Revolution and British Culture* (Oxford 1989).

[76] Dickens, *A Tale of Two Cities*, ch. 5, 'The Wine-Shop', p. 32.

[77] See above, p. 189.

matic of individual freedom in the face of violent state oppression; all underline the difficulties of achieving personal happiness in the face of collective violence.[78] Cobb and Hufton fit comfortably within the Dickensian paradigm too, of course. Dickens's hero, Sydney Carton, would have heartily concurred with Cobb's condemnation of the sanguinary hypocrisy of the Revolutionaries (though he might have diverted his gaze over some of the gleefully recounted gory details). He would have warmed to Hufton's marvellously resilient women, stubbornly reconstructing the Church in the 1790s, and seen them as blood sisters of Miss Pross (who, we may remember, gave *tricoteuse* Madame Defarge more than a good run for her money).

The exceptional writerly gifts of Cobb and Hufton echo *A Tale of Two Cities* in another way too. For one of the great themes of Dickens's novel—rescue from confinement, obscurity, and vengeance—echoes the Micheletian 'resurrectionism' to which I have drawn attention in the approach of both historians. As a young man, Dickens in fact joked that his profession could be that of a 'Resurrectionist'.[79] 'Recalled to Life'—the title of 'Book the First' of *A Tale of Two Cities*—might stand not only as an emblem of Dickens's writing practice but also as an inspirational epigraph to Cobb's and Hufton's oeuvre. In Dickens's narrative, moreover, the dead and living are brought into contact not through the Revolutionary making of *le peuple* in the Michelet manner, but under the much more solidly English prism of family ties, links of friendship, and generational continuity.[80] For Dickens,

---

[78] I take these as the best-selling authors in the field, and exclude American scholars, who seem less affected by the Dickensian paradigm. For Doyle, *The Oxford History of the French Revolution* (Oxford, 1989), '[the Revolution was] in every sense a tragedy' (the last words of the book). Hampson's more measured view, expressed in *The Social History of the French Revolution* (London, 1964), still highlights the Revolution's 'tragic stature'. Schama's *Citizens: A Chronicle of the French Revolution* (London 1989) is even more Dickensian, and furthermore reinstated Dickensian melodrama at the heart of his account. As I noted in my review of *Citizens* in 1989, Simon Schama is in some senses the Sidney Carton of modern French Revolutionary historiography: see 'The Return of the Banished Bourgeoisie', *Times Literary Supplement*, 21–7 July 1989, pp. 791–2.

[79] See the account of the anecdote in the excellent A. D. Hutter, 'The Novelist as Resurrectionist', in the cited volume of *Dickens Study Annual*. Hutter discusses not only the more general themes of imaginative links between the dead and living, but also the issue of body-snatching by 'resurrection-men' such as Jerry Cruncher in the novel. It was the latter sense, incidentally, that the Dickens anecdote exploits. It does not seem that Dickens had read Michelet.

[80] These themes, present throughout *A Tale of Two Cities* in a variety of forms, are crystallized exceptionally powerfully in Sidney Carton's vision of the future in the very last paragraphs of the novel: see the Maxwell ed., 389–90.

the Revolution was a ghastly sideshow to individual destinies and private pains and joys. So too for Cobb and Hufton. Their depiction of collective radical action in the Revolutionary decade is closer to Dickens's bloodthirsty mob than Michelet's sanctified *peuple*.[81]

If we respond so warmly to the writings of Richard Cobb and Olwen Hufton, it is not only, I would contend, as a result of their considerable gifts as archival historians, but also a testimony to the powerful poetics of their work. They play—and we find it difficult not to respond, whatever the colour of our overt politics—within a Dickensian paradigm operating in the *très longue durée* within British culture. Their writings work within an emotional and aesthetic register which *A Tale of Two Cities* has imprinted on the national imaginary, and from which it is extraordinarily difficult to shake our British selves free.[82]

---

[81] Cf. comments on Cobb and Rudé, above, p. 199.

[82] The difficulty for twentieth- and twenty-first century British historians of working outside the Dickensian paradigm is a major issue which it would be useful to consider.

Index